COMING OF AGE

COMING OF AGE

Teachers in Iowa
1954 to 1993

Fred R. Comer

Iowa State Education Association
Des Moines, Iowa

The Iowa State Education Association
4025 Tonawanda Drive, Des Moines, IA 50312

© 1993 by the Iowa State Education Association.
All rights reserved. Published in 1993.
Printed in the United States of America.

Library of Congress Catalog Card Number: 93-78742

ISBN 0-9637413-0-6

Book design by Sheri Michaels
Photographs provided by the Iowa State Education Association

To Jim Knott and Doris Mauer,

two dedicated, professional teachers

who lived this history.

ACKNOWLEDGEMENTS

My gratitude is extended to the members of the ISEA Executive Board for allowing me the opportunity to write this book. Special thanks go to the members of the personnel committee who supported my request; Stanley Van Hauen (chair) and members Doug Harrold, Karen Howard, Lana Morgan, and John Mesicek.

It is not possible to appropriately thank Sally Comer. We celebrated our 27th wedding anniversary on December 18. For 23 of those 27 years I have worked for the Association. She has never once complained about my job. Never once!

We have often wondered if perhaps the success of our marriage was related to the fact that we are often apart. We have speculated that perhaps in retirement our close proximity to one another for extended periods of time would be its death knell. We have been together around the clock for three months and have passed the test.

I am grateful to John Vint for acting as executive director in my absence, and to the other associate executive directors, Bill Pritchard and Jim Smith, to president Angie King, to my administrative assistant Janet Wilson, and to all of the other officers and staff whose work load increased because I was gone.

I am also grateful to my editors — the ISEA communications staff of Lana Oppenheim and Bill Sherman — and to my book designer Sheri Michaels. Be assured the book you are reading is in much better form than it was when they received it from me many months ago.

Thanks also, to the contributors: George Brown, George Duvall, Walter Galvin, Freida Griffin, Gerry Ott, Bill Pritchard, and Bill Sherman. Each contributed to this book by sharing information with me. Some shared aging files. Others shared aging recollections. Each made a special contribution in his or her own way.

And a final thank you to Jim Glenn and the staff at Maxie's in West Des Moines who have been our gracious hosts when most of the important management and staff decisions have been made over the last decade.

CONTENTS

	Introduction	xi
1 /	The Times	1
2 /	The Schoolmen	6
3 /	The Teachers	11
4 /	The Battle	17
5 /	The Aftermath	26
6 /	Sideshows—The Union	28
7 /	Sideshows—Unification	34
8 /	Leadership	40
9 /	The Executive Director	46
10 /	The President	49
11 /	Politics	57
12 /	LACs, CACs, DACs and a SAC	60
13 /	The Herschel C. Loveless Affair	63
14 /	IPACE and ISEA-PAC	67
15 /	The PAC and the Members	73
16 /	The Terry E. Branstad Affair	75
17 /	Collective Bargaining	80
18 /	Inside the ISEA . . .	84
19 /	The Trouble in Keokuk	87
20 /	Finally . . .	92
21 /	An Interesting Story	96
22 /	The Next Day	99
23 /	Crackpots, Weirdos, and Perverts	102
24 /	The Awakening	109
25 /	The Law	113
26 /	The New Days	117
27 /	The Emerging Profession	120

28 /	The Standards Board	122
29 /	The Reports	125
30 /	The Projects	129
31 /	The Reunion	135
32 /	Salisbury House	139
33 /	Heather Manor	158
34 /	A Personal Reflection	167
	Epilogue	180
	ISEA Presidents Since 1954	181
	ISEA Executive Directors Since 1954	184
	Vice Presidents of the ISEA Since 1954	185
	Treasurers of the ISEA Since 1954	186
	NEA Directors from Iowa Since 1954	187
	ISEA Friend of Education Award Winners	188
	Charles F. Martin Award Recipients	189
	ISEA TEAM Award Honorees	190
	At a Glance	191
	Index	206

INTRODUCTION

Five years ago Joan Wainwright, a longtime and faithful employee of the Iowa State Education Association, found a box full of copies of *Milestones*, the history of the first 100 years of the ISEA.

President Ken Tilp and I inscribed them, wrapped them in Christmas paper, and presented them to the Executive Board members at the December meeting.

This gift stimulated an interest on the part of the Board in writing the sequel to *Milestones*. One hundred years had not passed, but it was believed that more had transpired since 1954 than had transpired prior to that time. The Board decided that it should be written now.

The project was assigned to a staff person. After two years, given his other interests and responsibilities, little progress had been made.

I decided that I was interested in undertaking the task. I had completed 11 years as executive director. I had also decided, Executive Board willing, that this would be my last regular, full-time job.

With 11 years down and five or more years to go, I requested that the personnel committee permit me to experience a "change of pace" for a short period of time. The agreement was that I would spend the months of September, October, and November, 1992, at our vacation home in Glen Arbor, Michigan, and that I would return to Des Moines on December 1 with a book.

It was risky business for all of us. I regularly write columns and speeches, but I had never written anything longer than my master's thesis, some 100 pages or so. I did not know if I could do it. Nor did I know, if I could do it, how long it would take me.

I will leave it to the reader to determine if I could do it or not. In terms of time, I am writing this introduction on January 7. When it is finished, the book is done. I returned to Des Moines on December 1 as planned, with most of the work complete. I retreated to Glen Arbor on December 29 to tie up loose ends.

Most of the information comes from four sources: minutes of Executive Board meetings, minutes of Delegate Assemblies, *Midland Schools*, and *The Communique*. Other information was provided by very special people who are noted in the acknowledgements.

I intended for the book to be readable, fun, and historically accurate. There are no footnotes or bibliography. It would not meet a graduate school's standards as a thesis or dissertation. Yet I assure you, all of the quotations are accurate, at least to the degree that they were accurate when printed in their original source.

I made no attempt to cleanse the language of racist or sexist terminology—to make it politically correct by contemporary standards. Administrators were men and teachers were women in the vernacular of the 1950s and 1960s.

Early in my research it became apparent that the "story" was the emergence of teachers—the coming of age. That is the story that I tell. There are dozens of other stories that are intriguing or amusing that are not included because they are not directly related to the central theme.

There is little here about the changes in the structure of staff and governance over the years—the elimination of county councils, the emergence of UniServ, or the internal battles between the proponents of state units versus the proponents of autonomous units.

There are chapters on collective bargaining, advocacy, and political action because the creation of these programs was an integral part of the coming of age. There were other programmatic changes, some of them traumatic, which are not covered. The elimination of the state convention and the magazine, *Midland Schools*, are two of them.

Prior to commencing my research I assumed the book would include chapters on Student ISEA, retired teachers, education support personnel, and higher education. It does not. Those members are an integral part of the fabric of the Association and their individual stories are part of the larger one.

Two chapters of the book do not fit with the others. I was compelled to include chapters on Salisbury House and Heather Manor because they have dominated the business affairs of the Association since 1954. I readily admit that these real estate ventures have nothing to do with the coming of age of the profession except as distractions.

I have enjoyed my time as a researcher and writer immensely. I hope the same is true of your time as a reader.

Fred R. Comer
ISEA Executive Director

CHAPTER 1

The Times

Irving H. Hart wrote *Milestones* to celebrate the first 100 years of the ISEA. It is a history of the Association from the day it was born in the Muscatine County Court House on May 10, 1854, until the day exactly 100 years later when the leaders of the Association returned to Muscatine to dedicate a plaque commemorating the centennial. It is appropriate that the celebration took place in the county school superintendent's office.

This is the second volume of history of the ISEA. Its purpose is to chronicle the significant events in the life of the Association that have transpired since all of the leaders last met in Muscatine. According to the calendar, nearly 40 years have gone by. In that relatively short period of time, the Association has changed so dramatically that virtually the only thing that remains the same as it was in 1954 is the name.

Much has already been written about the evolution of the National Education Association (NEA). Most see its evolution as a process through which a professional association of teachers became a public employee labor union. Those who believe that over the past 40 years the ISEA has evolved from a professional association of teachers into a public employee labor union are wrong on all counts.

The ISEA was never a "professional" association. Professional associations control their professions in much the same way that professionals control their own working lives. Professional associations set enforceable standards for professional preparation. They control entry into the profession by establishing the criteria for licensure. They set and enforce standards of professional practice. None of these professional prerogatives were ever enjoyed by the ISEA.

Beyond that, the ISEA was not even an "association of teachers" in 1954, let alone a "professional" association. Back then the Association was controlled by the school superintendents; "schoolmen" they were called. Most of the teachers were members of the ISEA because the schoolmen told them it was expected. The teachers paid their dues, but the schoolmen ran the Association.

Furthermore, the ISEA never became a public employee labor union, at least not in the traditional sense. The long-standing objective of the teachers in Iowa has been to create a truly professional association. One of the great ironies of the past 40 years is that the teachers were forced to take on some of the trappings of a labor union in their effort to achieve professional status. Collective bargaining has never been an end in itself for the members of the ISEA. It is a weapon in the fight to achieve legitimacy as a profession.

Nor is what has transpired been an evolution. The changes did not result from a gradual process of growth and development that took place over a long period of time. What happened is that an old organization ceased to exist and a new organization with the same name was created to take its place. It all happened in a short period of time.

Had Arthur Deamer, the former superintendent of schools from Cedar Rapids, visited the ISEA in 1965, he would have found it much as he remembered it to be when he was president in 1942. Had he visited again in 1975, almost nothing except the name would have seemed familiar to him.

There is no specific date on which the old Association ceased to exist and the new one was born. But, if one were forced to choose a date, it would be July 22, 1969.

On that afternoon Wayne Begg of Ankeny handed the president's gavel to Jack Hudson of Davenport. Begg was a high school principal and Hudson was a classroom teacher. Prior to July 22, 1969, 114 different people had served as the president of the ISEA. Of the 114 presidents, 52 of them had been school superintendents, 29 had been higher education faculty or administrators, 22 had been principals, and only nine had been classroom teachers. The other two presidents were not educators. One was a clerk of court and the other was a minister. Since July 22, 1969, 13 people have served as ISEA president, and all of them were classroom teachers.

On that same afternoon the newly elected members of the Executive Board were seated. As a result of the spring elections, the composition of the Board for 1969-70 was eight classroom teachers and seven administrators. For the first time since the ISEA was created in 1854, a majority of the members of the governing board were classroom teachers. It would always be the case from that day on.

The changes that occurred in the presidency and the Executive Board on July 22, 1969, were symbolic of the changes that had been under way in the ISEA for several years before and would continue for several years to come. The process began when the Iowa Association of Classroom Teachers demanded that teachers be represented on boards and committees of the Association. The process ended when the Iowa Association of Elementary Principals withdrew from the Association in 1973. The superintendents and secondary principals had left two years earlier.

The demise of the old Association and the ascendance of the new one were inevitable. Teachers were different than they had been before. A few leaders saw the change coming, but most did not.

John Harold, who served as ISEA executive secretary from 1961 until 1964, was one of the first leaders to observe that things were different than they used to be. "There is some natural conflict," he said, "between the well-being of the administration of the local school district and the goals of a professional association."

Harold's comments were part of his formal remarks to the Executive Board, during which he announced his resignation as executive secretary. "Only by leaving the organization," he concluded, "can I teach that I came only to serve."

Harold was a professional schoolman. He had been superintendent in several Iowa districts throughout his career. Cedar Falls was the most recent. He had much in common with the other schoolmen who sat on the Executive Board. Yet they were unresponsive to his admonitions that teachers had different goals and aspirations than they had had in years past.

His most direct comments came after his resignation was effective. Harold's "Pedagogical Pete" column was a regular feature in the ISEA magazine, *Midland Schools*, before, during, and after his stint as executive secretary. In one of his last contributions he wrote, "Teachers too often feel that administration has become the master rather than the servant of the teaching process. No successful teacher ever makes it appear that he gives and students receive, or no administrator should perceive his role as God's gift to the teacher."

Teachers had different goals and aspirations than they used to have because teachers were different than they used to be. Profound and permanent change was under way in the nation and world. The change was scientific, technological, political, economic, and demographic. It affected every aspect of human lives. Teachers were not exceptions.

The population of the United States exploded in the years immediately following World War II. The full impact of the "baby boom" was felt by the schools during the decades of the 1950s and 1960s. The nation's school-age population nearly doubled in a decade.

The need for teachers increased in proportion to the increase in the number of students. The immediate result was a shortage of teachers. Veterans were encouraged to go to college on the GI Bill and become teachers. Some states created their own programs to give scholarships and loans to college students who promised to become teachers.

In 1957, the Soviet Union launched Sputnik, the first satellite made by human hands to orbit Earth. The space race was on and the United States was behind. As a reaction the federal government established the National Defense Education Act (NDEA). The NDEA made low-interest loans available to college students. A graduate who taught science or mathematics for five years would have half the loan forgiven. Soon foreign languages were added to the list. Eventually the loan-forgiveness program was extended to all who taught.

The various state and federal government programs were successful. By 1970 the teacher shortage was over. By 1970 the teaching force was much different from what it had been in 1950. It was much larger and it was much younger.

It was different in other ways as well. Teaching had always been perceived as a polite vocation for unmarried ladies. Early in the 20th century, many school districts formally barred married women from teaching in their schools. By 1950 that practice had disappeared, but most of the districts still forced pregnant women to resign from their teaching jobs, whether they were married or not. Prior to 1950, maiden ladies were the backbone of the teaching force.

Among the few men who were teachers, most viewed it as a stepping-stone to becoming a schoolman. Those who remained in teaching for life were suspect. They were thought to lack self-confidence, ambition, competence, or perhaps something else entirely.

By 1970, the teacher shortage, together with the success of the various state and federal programs, had changed all that. School districts were unable to be as selective as they once had been. The maiden ladies were joined by married women, pregnant women, and mothers with children. Veterans from World War II and the Korean Conflict took advantage of the GI Bill, and many of them became teachers. The government's incentive programs made teaching as a career attractive to thousands and thousands of young people from poor and working-class families for whom a college education would otherwise have been difficult. By 1970 the teaching force was not only much larger and much younger, but it was also more representative of the general population in terms of economic status, social class, and sex—even though women still outnumbered men and always would.

This was also the first generation of teachers for whom a college degree was required. It is incredible, but true, that during this period of great scarcity the requirements for entry into the practice of teaching were enhanced.

Early in the 20th century, teaching certificates were issued by county school superintendents. Their standards varied and their practices varied greatly. Generally, though, 12 weeks of normal school preparation and regular participation in teacher institutes were enough to get and keep a certificate to teach. Over time the standards increased. Finally, in 1961, it was established that one must possess a bachelor's degree and have completed a professional curriculum in order to receive a provisional certificate to teach. This larger, younger, and more diverse teaching force was better educated than any generation of teachers that preceded it.

Those who received their college educations in the late 1950s or in the 1960s learned new lessons outside of their classrooms as well as inside of them. The United States was experiencing great social and political turmoil. McCarthyism, civil rights, Vietnam, and women's rights were a few of the issues that colored the nation's reality during the period. The colleges and universities were centers of organized dissent and protest. By the time this larger, younger, and more diverse teaching force received their college degrees and teaching certificates, some of them had burned their draft cards and others of them had burned their bras. Virtually all of them had a different sense of fairness and justice than that of the previous generation of teachers.

That is why it was inevitable that the old Association would disappear and that a new Association would take its place. It was not possible to educate a generation of teachers and then deny them professional prerogatives either in their classrooms or in their Association.

The older, undereducated maiden ladies submitted to the authority of the schoolmen. This new generation of teachers clearly would not do that. Their finely honed sense of fairness and justice led first to their cry for equity and then to their demand for power.

Most schoolmen did not understand what was happening. Their roots were in a different time and place. Some may have understood the significance of the events that rumbled and roared by them in the world at large, but few saw the impact those events would have on themselves personally or on the Association they led.

CHAPTER 2

The Schoolmen

The ISEA was run by the schoolmen in 1954, the same as it had been run from the beginning.

Most of them were decent and honorable fellows. They believed that they had the best interests of their teachers and principals at heart. They worried about the school systems they had been hired to administer. Throughout the entire history of the Association, the documents are replete with evidence that they cared deeply about young people and that they were committed to strong public schools.

The ISEA accomplished a great deal while under the control of the schoolmen. State financial aid for local school districts was enacted, and by 1954 the total amount had risen to $19 million. A continuing contract law was enacted. It did not protect teachers or administrators from unfair termination, but it did establish a deadline past which the school board was prohibited from acting arbitrarily. A fiscally sound retirement plan was approved. Certification standards were upgraded. And salaries were increased each year.

The schoolmen had something in common with Charles Wilson, the former president of General Motors and secretary of defense for President Eisenhower. Wilson said, "If it is good for General Motors, then it is good for the country." The schoolmen believed that if it was good for them, then it was good for everybody else connected with the schools.

Often they were right. State aid, continuing contracts, a secure retirement, and higher salaries were all good things for school superintendents and everybody else connected with the schools. Superintendents and teachers have much in common. But, in 1954, whenever the interests of the administrators and teachers diverged, the administrators prevailed.

The schoolmen believed they were the professional leaders. As such, they accepted their responsibilities and exercised their privileges.

The most powerful individual in the ISEA was Charles F. Martin, the executive secretary. Charlie Martin was a consummate schoolman. He was appointed school superintendent for Jackson County in 1927 and he served there for 19 years. While superintendent he served on the ISEA Executive Board and as ISEA president in 1944-45. He was hired to be Executive Secretary in 1946. He was 57 years of age at the time of his employment. He served until 1961 when, at the age of 72, he decided to slow down a bit. He created the position of deputy executive secretary and appointed himself to it. He resigned from that position in 1964 at the age of 75, reluctantly agreeing to the retirement terms set out for him by the Executive Board.

While Martin was the most powerful individual in the Association, he did not run it alone. The Executive Board ran the ISEA with the help of Charlie's good advice and powerful counsel. The Board made all of the critical decisions about budget, finance, personnel, and program.

Much of the Board's time was occupied by issues unrelated to schools or teachers. In many ways the ISEA was like an investment club. Members sent in money and the Executive Board members invested it. They bought a 42-room Tudor mansion, acres of prime Des Moines real estate, and an extensive collection of art. They built an apartment house and a nursing home. They invested heavily in the Horace Mann Insurance Company. And they created a statewide credit union.

The Executive Board was dominated by school superintendents. There was always a classroom teacher on the Board. There usually was a principal or two and a college of education faculty member or administrator. There were even years when the superintendents were outnumbered by all of the others combined. Even then, the schoolmen still dominated the Board.

The president of the ISEA was a figurehead. He, or in rare instances she, served a single one-year term. The president continued to be a full-time employee of his school district during his term of office. The amount of time the president could devote to the affairs of the Association was largely determined by the position he held back home. Superintendents and college professors were able to spend more time on their presidential duties than were principals and teachers. As the time demands increased over the years, the Executive Board began to worry that perhaps the time had come when a principal or teacher could no longer be the ISEA president.

Most often the president was simply the presiding officer. He presided at the meetings of the Executive Board and at the Delegate Assembly. He was front and center at the annual ISEA Convention. There were some very powerful presidents, but they brought their own power with them to the office, and they took it with them when they left. There was no inherent power in the office of president of the ISEA.

The president was a figurehead and the Delegate Assembly was a rubber stamp. Its composition varied from year to year, but commonly about one-half of the delegates were classroom teachers. There were years when the delegates were angry about decisions that the Executive Board had made, as when the Board bought Salisbury House, but rarely, if ever, did they do anything about it.

That would change as the years went by. The schoolmen lost control of the Delegate Assembly before they lost control of the Executive Board. In the end it would be decisions made by the Delegate Assembly that caused the administrators to be so upset that they decided to leave the Association.

At the same time that the superintendents were dominating things at the state level, they were absolutely in control of things at the local level. The system was designed to work that way.

All ISEA mailings to local associations throughout the state were sent to the office of the local superintendent of schools. He would distribute the information to the people he felt should receive it. It was not until 1967 that the Delegate Assembly stopped the practice by directing that mail be sent instead to "local-education-association-designated individuals."

As a matter of professional courtesy, Association staff members would advise the local superintendent of all requests received for information or help from members in his district.

The ISEA membership forms were shipped each year to the local superintendent. That is why, in most districts, ISEA membership was either implicitly or explicitly a condition of employment for teachers and principals.

There were six local school superintendents in Iowa who were not members of the ISEA in 1956. Those six were the cause of a great deal of consternation on the part of the members of the Executive Board because the whole scheme of things revolved around them. There was rarely a local association at all in a school district where the superintendent was not a member.

One of the non-member schoolmen was particularly offensive to Verl Crow, a high school dean of students and Executive Board member from Sioux City. "We ran across that one superintendent from Westfield," she reported; "I thought his attitude was dreadful. They had one ISEA member there last year and he fired that one. Trying to get him interested was just like batting your head against a stone wall."

"I do not think it is wrong to remind these superintendents rather forcefully that they are the professional leaders in their schools, or should be," added Louis L. Pickett, the Board member from Ruthven. "If they are not promoting the Association then they are just falling short of their jobs," he said.

The ISEA expected local school superintendents to apply pressure on the few principals and teachers who did not have enough sense to join on their own. Individual letters were mailed midyear to all of those who were eligible for membership but had not as yet transmitted their dues. At the same time, a list of their names was supplied to each local superintendent, along with the request that he do what he could in the way of encouraging them to join.

By 1958 Verl Crow was serving as the NEA Board of Directors member from Iowa. At the conclusion of her report to the Delegate Assembly that year, she was asked by a delegate whether or not it was ethical for a superintendent to put pressure on teachers to join the Association when they applied for a position. She answered: "Membership is one of the obligations of the teacher under the Code of Ethics of the profession; thus, it is the privilege and responsibility of the superintendent to make the prospective teacher aware of this fact."

That is the way things were and always had been. The superintendents were the "professional leaders." It was their "privilege and responsibility" to run the ISEA.

The ISEA never acted as an advocate on behalf of a teacher who had been fired unless the action taken by the school board was contrary to the recommendation of the superintendent.

The ISEA never involved itself in the discussions between the local association salary committee and the school board unless invited to do so by the superintendent.

In fact, the first gutsy stand ever taken by the ISEA on behalf of members came at the behest of the local school superintendent. In the spring of 1964, in response to school board meddling, Superintendent Fred Nus of Pleasantville and 19 of the teachers resigned. The ISEA imposed sanctions against the school board and urged prospective teachers to look elsewhere for jobs.

Just because that was the way it was and the way it always had been did not mean it was the way things would always be. This new group of teachers was qualified, they believed, to educate young people without undue interference from school boards and administrators. They were brash, cocky, and irreverent. They had learned how to challenge authority and get away with it. They asked why and they expected a good answer. If teachers were going to pay dues to an Association, then they expected teachers to have a say in how it was to be run. If a majority of the members of the Association were teachers, then they expected teachers to run it.

CHAPTER 3

The Teachers

The ISEA enjoyed a large and diverse membership. While the superintendents ran the show, all of the professional educators were welcome to join: teachers, principals, superintendents, college faculty, college administrators, and the professional staff at the Department of Public Instruction.

In order to try to meet the needs of such a diverse group of members, a number of departments were created within the Association. Superintendents and the other central office administrators joined the Iowa Association of School Administrators. Secondary school principals and assistant principals joined the Iowa Association of Secondary School Principals. Elementary principals and assistant principals joined the Iowa Association of Elementary School Principals. Teachers joined the Iowa Association of Classroom Teachers (IACT). Other departments were created from time to time: for higher education members, for special education teachers, for any identifiable special group with 250 members or more.

The departments were not intended to be either governance subdivisions or special interest caucuses within the Association, though they served the latter purpose. Each department had its own officers, but they were not afforded any official standing within the governance framework of the ISEA. The purpose of the departments was to develop and administer programs designed to meet the professional needs of their particular membership. For example, they offered workshops and drive-in conferences, and each had its own special interest sessions during the annual ISEA Convention.

The IACT represented the interests of their members with increasing vigor as the years went by. They advocated released time for teachers so that they could serve along with superintendents on the ISEA committees. They demanded that at least 75 percent of the members of all committees, commissions, and task forces be classroom teachers. They flooded the Delegate Assembly with resolutions and new business items calling for things like collective bargaining and tenure. They endorsed candidates for internal Association offices.

It was never the intent of the IACT to drive the administrators out of the ISEA, though some of the IACT leaders believed it should be. It was not until after the administrators had left the Association that Delegate Assemblies considered action items that would deny membership to administrators. Even then, the items were defeated.

The objective of IACT was for teachers to have authority and control inside the Association equal to their numbers. If 90 percent of the members of the ISEA were classroom teachers, then most of the Assembly delegates, Executive Board members, and ISEA presidents should be classroom teachers, too. Once teachers were fairly represented, when the interests of the superintendents and teachers diverged, it would be the interests of the teachers that would prevail.

The first attempts by the IACT to bring about change inside the ISEA were modest and they all failed one way or another.

The 1959 Delegate Assembly actually adopted a motion which directed that a study be initiated by the Professional Relations Division to determine ways and means of encouraging classroom teachers to participate more fully in the Association as delegates and officers. The motion directed that particular consideration be given to how it was that teachers might be released from school without forfeiture of salary.

Charlie Martin was annoyed by the motion. "We are always making this kind of study," he grumbled, "but we will do it again as directed."

Four months later Martin reported that he had surveyed the states. "Fourteen states said they have it. Twenty-one said they do not, and five said they did so partially. Two said there was no limit. If the Board wishes further study, it will be made," he said. The Executive Board was satisfied.

A motion was made at the 1962 Delegate Assembly that said, "Because of the apparent lack of proportional representation of classroom teachers on the Executive Board of the ISEA, we recommend the adoption of much-needed studies and procedures as will eliminate or greatly ameliorate such misrepresentation." The motion was tabled.

A motion was made at the 1964 Delegate Assembly that said, "In the future at least one of the two Iowa NEA Directors shall be a classroom teacher." The motion was defeated.

Motions like these came from the IACT Delegate Assembly after Delegate Assembly. They were always tabled or defeated. As the years passed by, the margins by which the motions were tabled or defeated grew smaller and smaller. By the mid-1960s it was becoming apparent that sooner or later something would carry.

During these years the relationship between the IACT and the leadership of the ISEA, particularly the Executive Board, became increasingly tense. The parties were not able to address the big issue: a fair share of power for the teachers in the governance of the Association. Rather, they sparred over little issues.

Robert Hamilton from Ames, who was public relations chairman for the IACT, asked for a "center spread" in *Midland Schools* sometime during the 1962-63 school year.

The four center pages of the journal were routinely printed on colored paper and were devoted to a current "hot topic." During the 1961-62 school year, for example, the center spreads were devoted to such topics as "Low-Cost Life Insurance Is Now Available Exclusively To You," "IPERS and You," and "Membership In All 3 Organizations: Local, State, National."

Executive Secretary John Harold, who was more open than many to expanding roles for classroom teachers in the Association, was troubled by the request. "There is no question that space should be provided to the teachers," he told the Executive Board, "but my own recommendation is that the center spread should be reserved for items that affect every member."

Even Executive Board member George Fischer, a classroom teacher from Des Moines who later, as president of the NEA, would make his mark by attacking school administrators, among others, did not support the IACT's request. Instead, he moved "that the matter be referred to a special committee for study and to develop an explicit policy for the use of the center spread of the *Midland Schools*." The motion carried.

"To deny this now," Fischer argued, "could cause some difficulty that we could sidestep if we take some time to develop a clearer policy and to explain to the classroom teachers why we took such action."

The parties moved on to another minor issue. Each of the larger departments within the Association was served by a consultant, usually a retired member, who was employed by the ISEA on a part-time basis. In the summer of 1965 the IACT requested that the Executive Board authorize payment of their consultant's travel expenses from ISEA funds rather than from IACT funds.

George Fischer, supporting the request, argued, "We would be making a mistake to deny this. They appear to feel that the ISEA is run by administrators and there are so many more of them than there are members of the other departments."

But Executive Board member Wayne Begg, the high school principal from Ankeny, offered a more popular opinion: "If we give on this they will come back with a new request. They are going to be unhappy until they get what they want."

As the problem with the classroom teachers persisted, the Executive Board members became more and more frustrated. On August 20, 1965, they decided it was time to take the IACT leadership to the woodshed. They decided to invite the teachers to the next Board meeting in order to clear the air.

Some Executive Board members thought it would be courteous to tell the teachers about the purpose of the meeting in advance. The majority, however, decided it would be better to let them find out when they arrived.

On September 18, 1965, the officers of the IACT dutifully appeared before the Executive Board: Helen Brown, president; Dick VanderWoude, president-elect; Lowell Cook, vice president; Bob Flick, past president; Evelyn Schauland, secretary; and Helen McCracken, treasurer.

What transpired may have had little or no effect on the overall relationship between the ISEA and the IACT or on the history of the ISEA, for that matter. But, in fairly short order the classroom teachers were patronized, demeaned, ridiculed, and threatened by the members of the Executive Board.

That was how teachers were often treated by administrators back in their own districts and that is how they were treated by administrators in their own Association. It is not surprising that the battle was engaged. What is surprising is that it had taken so long.

The chief villain that day was Roger O. Blake, president of the ISEA and superintendent of schools of the West Sioux district in Hawarden.

"We have invited you," Blake welcomed, "for the purpose of an exchange of ideas and to get some of your thinking as to how we can do a better job of helping the teaching profession."

"We are aware," he continued, "that on the national scene, and from there it drifts down, the classroom teachers feel at times that they are not properly represented in Association affairs. We have heard rumors that there might be some dissatisfaction among classroom teachers in Iowa. But, we sincerely believe that any actions we have taken have been in the best interests of classroom teachers."

Helen Brown responded, "There are many who say that classroom teachers should have more voice. In the past it has been that superintendents were better qualified because they had more education on the whole, more experience, but that is changing."

"I believe there should be a classroom teacher on the ISEA Board, several of them," Blake answered, "I do not believe once they are on here they will always vote as a classroom teacher, though. Certainly there are classroom teachers who do not agree with all of the sentiments of the IACT."

As the meeting progressed, Roger O. Blake dug his hole deeper and deeper.

"We hire our principals and superintendents as professional people. We expect them to go to professional meetings and then hold meetings back home to bring the teachers up-to-date," he said. He continued, "I compare the administrators and the classroom teachers in my own district. The administrators are 100 percent members and 95 percent of the time they attend meetings. I try to encourage the teachers but they are only 30 percent members."

Executive Board member M. M. Rogers from Sumner got into the act. "I know you people back home think the superintendent or principal or whoever serves on this Board leaves home Friday and what a heyday we have in Des Moines," he said defensively. "But, we meet once a month, Friday, starting at noon, run until midnight, start at nine Saturday morning and run straight through, hoping to get out at three. All we see of Des Moines is that hotel. We run out here, go back and get our clothes. I would like to know how long your IACT board meetings last."

Finally, after lengthy discussion, Blake laid his cards on the table. "If I were a classroom teacher again," he said, "I would not want to alienate the people who determine what my salary and working conditions are."

Nearly three hours after the meeting started, Blake wrapped things up. "I think we have a general feeling for what you people are thinking and I am sure the Board will consider it seriously."

The minutes of the meeting note that "the members of the IACT executive committee thanked the board for the invitation and the informative day. The classroom teachers then left at 1 p.m."

After they left a Board member concluded, "They do not really even know what they want." Another Board member answered, "But then, remember, they did not know the purpose of the meeting, either."

It was inevitable that the old ISEA would disappear and that a new ISEA would take its place. It is not possible to educate a generation of teachers and then deny them professional prerogatives either inside their classrooms or inside their Association. These brash, cocky, and irreverent newcomers would not be patronized, demeaned, ridiculed, or threatened for long.

CHAPTER 4

The Battle

The schoolmen maintained control of the officers' positions and the Executive Board as long as they could. As time went by some were willing to share power; one-third, one-third, one-third or maybe even fifty-fifty. Had those who were willing to share power prevailed, the administrators would have remained a part of the Association for a while longer. Ultimately, though, the administrators still would have left. The classroom teachers would not be satisfied with one-third or one-half of the power when they had ninety percent of the members. The administrators, on the other hand, would not pay dues to an Association that was run by the teachers. That would not be right. It was supposed to be the other way around.

Poor John Harold tried his best. As early as 1961 he warned the Executive Board, "We are beginning, more and more, to feel this gap between administrator and teacher. We need to bridge it."

Harold had a pretty good suggestion. "We need to talk about it," he said. He proposed that the Association sponsor a seminar for 18 teachers, 18 principals, and 18 superintendents. There would be general sessions with presentations. There would be small discussion groups. Sometimes the composition of the groups would be homogeneous and sometimes heterogeneous.

"Our Association could well afford," Harold said, "to have an interaction of ideas between teachers, principals, and superintendents." Nothing happened to his suggestion.

A year later William Anderson expressed a similar concern in his first remarks to the Executive Board as ISEA president. The Cedar Falls superintendent said, "The problem we face is division in our group. The worst thing that could happen would be for us to lose the feeling of unity, that feeling that all of us can be helped in the same way."

Elmer C. Gast of Keokuk was the last superintendent, though not the last administrator, to be president of the ISEA. His term ran from July of 1967 until July of 1968. The end was approaching.

"One of the most important issues of our professional Association," Gast said upon taking office, "is to correct the impression some people have that the classroom teacher, the administrator, and the school board are all going their own ways."

"There is a changing relationship," he went on, "but this does not mean these groups necessarily have to be less closely allied for the common cause."

Midway through his term, when talking about "professional negotiations" and teacher and administrator relationships, Gast said, "It is apparent that the school boards want the administrators on their side and that is where the teachers are putting them. I still believe that the administrators should be part of the professional organization."

At the end of his term, while discussing the collective bargaining proposal advanced by the Iowa Association of School Boards, Gast commented, "If their proposal becomes law it will only be a matter of time before the ISEA loses most, if not all, of its members except for the classroom teachers. Then it will no longer be an Association of the profession. It will merely be a classroom teachers' association. It will be a much weaker Association."

Harold, Anderson, and Gast were among the more enlightened schoolmen. They sincerely believed that the professional Association should include all professional educators, and all three were willing to share power. None of the three would deliberately speak in a fashion that was demeaning to teachers. Roger O. Blake of Hawarden would, but Elmer C. Gast would not.

Yet Elmer Gast's comment that what would be left would be "merely a classroom teachers association" and "a much weaker association" is demeaning, even though he did not intend it to be. It is demeaning because it unmasks the truth. The schoolmen, even the enlightened schoolmen, really believed that classroom teachers could not accomplish very much without their help and guidance.

Teachers needed schoolmen to help them teach, to protect them from unruly students, to rescue them from irate parents. Teachers needed schoolmen to represent their interests to the local school board. Teachers needed schoolmen to run their Association, invest their dues, and propose their laws.

Schoolmen still viewed teachers the way teachers had been viewed in the past. That was demeaning to teachers and a serious mistake for superintendents.

While the schoolmen whined about the schism as it grew wider, the classroom teachers drew a bead on the Delegate Assembly.

"It has been my experience that the classroom teachers hold their meetings and adopt a lot of resolutions and hand them in to Delegate Assembly," Roger Blake complained. "I think we should just consider at Delegate Assembly those things that are pertinent for the entire organization."

A lot of the resolutions that the classroom teachers handed in to Delegate Assembly had to do with the internal Association governance. Many had to do with guaranteed representation.

Those who opposed guaranteed representation for classroom teachers argued that the best person for the job should be elected without regard for the position that person held in the school district. "What a shame it would be," they argued, "if the best man for the job could not even run for it, because it had already been guaranteed to somebody else."

The opponents of guarantees also argued that there was no need for them. "This is a democratic organization," they would remind the proponents. "Every member gets to vote. Teachers are in the majority in every district. They can elect anyone they want. Those superintendents were all elected by the teachers."

The real problem was that classroom teachers did not run for the seats on the Executive Board very often. Their local superintendents would not let them. Serving on boards and committees of professional organizations was part of the job of school administrators. It was professional for them to be absent from the district. Teaching children in the classroom every day was the job of teachers. It was not professional for them to be absent from the district.

The Executive Board met once each month. Meetings started at noon on Friday and ended by late afternoon on Saturday. That meant that a classroom teacher who served on the Board would have to miss nine full days of school each year. In addition, there would be days for the Delegate Assembly and who knows what else. It was simply out of the question in most districts for a teacher to miss that much school.

It was suggested that perhaps the Executive Board could start its meetings on Friday evening rather than Friday noon, making it more convenient for teachers to serve. That was out of the question because of the large amount of business that the Board needed to transact each month.

It was suggested that perhaps it would be possible for the Board to meet into the evening on Saturdays as a substitute for Friday afternoons. That, too, was out of the question. It would require that most Board members spend an additional night in Des Moines, which would increase the costs. Also, most Board members wished to be home on Sunday morning in order to attend church with their families. It would be unseemly for the Association to interfere with the members' family and religious obligations.

No, there was nothing that could be done.

Nevertheless, the IACT brought motions to Delegate Assembly year after year. It was especially difficult because effecting guarantees for elected bodies required amendments to the Articles of Incorporation and Bylaws which required the consent of two-thirds of the delegates present and voting.

It was not until the 1971 Delegate Assembly that something finally passed. When it did, it applied only to committees. The motion read, "The ISEA shall be represented by at least a 75 percent majority of classroom teachers on all its appointive boards, committees, and commissions that are intended to be generally representative of the interests of members. In selecting persons to serve, the ISEA president and/or Executive Board shall, as terms expire, raise classroom teacher representation to at least a 75 percent majority."

The administrators, themselves, made implementation of the directive easy. Within six months from the date it passed, most of them were gone from the Association.

A lot of the resolutions the classroom teachers turned in had to do with collective bargaining. The schoolmen did not understand the teachers' fascination with collective bargaining. It was something that labor unions did. It was antithetical to their concept of professionalism.

Besides, the ISEA had always advocated higher salaries for teachers. That was true. The ISEA always had. And, over the years, teachers had gotten some pretty good raises. That was also true. Teachers had gotten some pretty good raises. Was not one of the ISEA's big events every year the "salary school?" And did not hundreds and hundreds of members attend it? Almost every local association had a salary committee that met with the school board and that worked well. That was not really true. It did not work well.

So what was the problem? The schoolmen thought that collective bargaining might be a fad. Fads come and go in education. Wisconsin had it and Michigan had it. Some Iowa teachers thought they should have collective bargaining, too.

The schoolmen were partially correct. The ISEA had consistently, over the years, been an advocate for higher salaries for teachers. And, also over the years, the average raise paid to teachers in Iowa had pretty much allowed the state to maintain its position in relation to other states as far as average salaries were concerned.

But there was a problem. The problem was not so much the average salary paid to teachers in Iowa. The problem was the great disparity in the individual salaries, which were all added together and divided by the number of teachers in order to determine the average salary. That was the problem.

And the problem with the disparity was not so much the fact that the average salary in one district was a lot higher than the average salary in another district, that the teachers in Davenport were paid more money than the teachers in Sibley. No, the problem was the great disparity in salaries paid to teachers inside the same district and the reasons that they were paid disparately.

Men teachers were paid more than women teachers. Most other disparities flowed from that fact. High school teachers were paid more than junior high school teachers. Junior high school teachers were paid more than elementary teachers. Heads of households were paid more than those who were not. Teachers in high-visibility positions, such as coaches and band directors, were paid more than those in low-visibility positions, such as English teachers and foreign language teachers.

The problem was not one of discrimination against women, per se. The problem was one of the exploitation of teachers who were unable to relocate, the vast majority of whom were women. Teachers were scarce in the 1950s and 1960s. School boards and superintendents would pay as much as they had to pay to get a teacher they needed, or as little as they had to pay to keep one.

Men teachers benefited because they were more mobile than women. There was no compelling reason to give many of the women teachers raises at all. They were not likely to relocate without their husbands and their husbands were not likely to sell their farms or shops to go with their wives.

Classroom teachers were angry about the unfairness of the amount of money they were paid compared to what other teachers in the same district were paid. College degrees, teaching experience, even merit did not count for much where teachers' salaries were concerned.

Virtually everything else in most of the school districts was disparate, too. Some teachers had preparation periods and some teachers did not. Some teachers could leave school during their preparation periods and some teachers could not. Some teachers got days off for personal business and some teachers did not. Some teachers came to school late and left school early. Other teachers did, too, and got into trouble for it.

The superintendents thought collective bargaining was about money. It was not. It was about fairness and equity and the fact that teachers did not trust the superintendents very much. The principals apparently did not trust the superintendents very much, either. The ISEA surveyed its members in the fall of 1967. A majority of the teachers and a majority of the principals were in favor of collective bargaining. Only the superintendents were opposed.

On this issue, too, the IACT came back to the Delegate Assembly year after year.

The first motion to pass the Assembly came in 1966. It was "professional" in tone, but the message was there. The ISEA was in favor of some form of professional negotiations or collective bargaining.

The resolution said, "The ISEA believes that local professional associations have the professional right and should have the mandatory legal right, through appropriate professional channels and democratically selected representatives, including classroom teachers, to negotiate with boards of education in determination of policies affecting professional services of teachers, including improvement of instruction, curriculum planning, salaries, and other conditions of work."

The IACT struck gold in 1968. They followed up on the statement of philosophy approved two years earlier with a call to action.

It was moved "that the ISEA shall make the achievement of professional negotiations legislation the primary goal of the Association's 1969 legislative program." The motion carried.

That motion was followed by one from the IACT's Dick VanderWoude from Spencer. He moved, "The Executive Board shall take the necessary steps to employ an additional staff member in the Professional Relations Division to work in the area of professional negotiations." That motion carried, also.

It would be years before the Iowa General Assembly would adopt a collective bargaining statute. But from the 1968 Delegate Assembly on, both the IACT and the ISEA were in favor of collective bargaining with the boss. The boss became increasingly uncomfortable with the ISEA.

Other things made the boss uncomfortable, too — things such as tenure, for instance.

The ISEA had been in favor of strengthening the continuing contract law since early in the 1960s. In 1963 the Delegate Assembly approved a resolution that put the Association on record as being in favor of a provision that would require school boards to give written reasons for terminating a teacher. The Association also favored the creation of a state authority, like a tenure commission, to which a teacher might appeal a dismissal.

The powers and duties of this "state authority" were never defined by the Delegate Assembly or by the Executive Board. Then, in 1971, the Delegate Assembly decided that the statutorally mandated standard for the termination of a teacher should be "just cause." The administrators were certain that they knew what "just cause" meant. It meant that teachers cannot be fired. That made them very uncomfortable.

Politics also made them uncomfortable. Personal one-on-one politics did not make school superintendents uncomfortable. They had practiced that kind of politics for years and some of them were very good at it. The schoolmen knew their legislators well and they did not hesitate to apply some pressure when the circumstances demanded it. It was deliberate and it was often effective.

But the 1970 Delegate Assembly authorized the creation of a political action committee. That was a different matter entirely. The Association was on its way to becoming overtly political in partisan elections. Most schoolmen did not think much good could come from that.

The Delegate Assembly was not the only battleground. Unpleasant things were beginning to happen in local associations, too.

It was discovered that some local associations had rewritten their constitutions in a fashion that denied local memberships to the administrators. The Executive Board directed that the Field Service Division ferret out the offenders and see to it that the situation was corrected.

In DeWitt, the administrators were allowed to join the local association, but the teachers would not let them come to local association meetings, at least when salaries or other work related problems were being discussed. A local administrator complained to the ISEA and again, the Field Service Division was dispatched to see to it that the wrong was righted.

And finally, the membership in the ISEA among school administrators began to slip. The percentage of administrators and teachers who "voluntarily" joined the Association each year had always been high, 90 percent or more; but the percentage had always been higher among the administrators than among the teachers. In 1969 the rankings were reversed. Administrators had become sufficiently uncomfortable inside the ISEA that they had started to leave one by one. Soon they would start to leave department by department.

Not surprisingly, the first movement came from the superintendents. In January, 1969, the Iowa Association of School Administrators (IASA) appointed a committee to consider the relationship between the IASA and the ISEA. The committee report was adopted by the IASA on April 3. The report recognized "that the professional goals of the ISEA and the IASA are more compatible at present than different, but concluded "that some change in the relationship needs to be initiated." The report recommended that another study be undertaken to determine how different that relationship should be.

One year later, at the annual meeting of the IASA on April 2, 1970, a motion was made that the IASA withdraw from the ISEA. The motion was defeated, with 57 members voting yes and 232 members voting no.

Another year later, at the annual meeting of the IASA, this time on April 1, a motion was made that the IASA withdraw from the ISEA. This time 89 percent of those present and voting said yes. On July 1, 1971, the schoolmen became part of the history of the ISEA.

Obviously the administrators had been talking to one another, for both the Iowa Association of Secondary School Principals and the Iowa Association of Elementary School Principals (IAESP) scheduled votes on similar motions for dates shortly following April 1.

The vote by the secondary principals was scheduled for April 24. Unfortunately for them, not enough members showed up at the meeting to constitute a quorum, so the vote was delayed. They tried again in May. This time a quorum was present and so were enough votes to withdraw from the ISEA. The motion passed, and on July 1, 1971, the secondary school principals joined the superintendents as part of the history of the ISEA.

The outcome of the elementary school principals' meeting was different. The move to withdraw was defeated and the IAESP would remain as a department of the ISEA for another two years.

They were not happy years for either the elementary school principals or for the ISEA. The elementary principals were under considerable pressure from the superintendents and secondary principals to withdraw from the ISEA. At least in part because of the pressure, the number of elementary principals who joined the ISEA declined substantially.

On September 16, 1972, Roy Karlson, the ISEA president, told the Executive Board that he had been advised by the president of the IAESP that another vote was scheduled. This time the IAESP Executive Board was supporting withdrawal unanimously. Their district presidents and their committee chairmen were also supporting the withdrawal unanimously.

President Karlson had been told that the problems were unified dues, a declining IAESP membership, the role of the principals in negotiations, and events taking place at the national level. It was pretty obvious that the skids were greased this time, and they were.

On June 30, 1973, the IAESP withdrew from the ISEA and all school administrators became part of the history of the ISEA.

There was one large department left in the ISEA: the IACT. On July 31, 1973, it, too, left the Association. "With the administrators gone, ISEA is the teachers' organization now," said Jim Knott of Carroll, president of the IACT. "We led the fight within the ISEA to get the organization into a position of power and teacher advocacy. IACT led the way for negotiations, defense of teacher rights, more involvement for members in decision making, and instructional improvement activities. We battled the administrators all of the way on these."

"These things are all an integral part of the Association program now," Knott continued, "so the administrators might as well leave. Now, IACT is no longer needed."

CHAPTER 5

The Aftermath

The immediate cry of the school administrators was that they were "kicked out" of the ISEA. To this day, decades later, an occasional administrator whose mind is no doubt dimmed by time and chalk dust will remember back to the early '70s when he personally was kicked out of the ISEA.

As early as November of 1971, less than six months after the superintendents and secondary principals withdrew, Executive Secretary Kenneth P. Wells was responding to this allegation. "The ruling bodies of both the IASA and the IASSP voted to disaffiliate their department status with the ISEA on July 31, 1971. Please note," he wrote in *The Communique*, "that it was the decision of these groups to disaffiliate. They were not 'kicked out' in any sense."

In fact, at the very next Delegate Assembly following the action of the superintendents and secondary principals to withdraw, those who were left behind passed a motion which said, "The ISEA shall take every measure possible to ensure cooperation among superintendents, principals, and classroom teachers. All must be welcomed into the Association. Although diversified, we must be of one body and one voice."

Three years later, in 1975, there was a proposal to amend the Articles of Incorporation to deny membership to "management persons such as superintendents, assistant superintendents, principals, and assistant principals." The proposed amendment was defeated.

The only limitation on administrator membership in the ISEA was established by the Executive Board in 1976 as an amendment to the Bylaws. It denies membership to "any individual who negotiates on behalf of a school board or board of trustees of a higher education institution in opposition to a local affiliate of the ISEA."

With that one exception, school administrators are and always have been eligible for full active membership in the ISEA.

As time went by, the administrator organizations allied themselves more closely with the Iowa Association of School Boards (IASB). It is fair to say that, together, the four organizations became the enemy of the ISEA.

Most often the battles were fought in the Legislature. The ISEA supported collective bargaining for teachers. The school board and administrator organizations opposed it. The ISEA supported improvements in the continuing contract law. The school board and administrator organizations opposed them. The ISEA supported establishing an autonomous professional standards board. The school board and administrator organizations opposed it. That is the way it was for more than a decade. Much of the rest of this history is about those battles.

The ISEA won most of them. The role of the other organizations became that of the spoiler. Their first mission was to hold out for as long as possible. They perceived that one more year without collective bargaining was a victory for their side. Their second mission was to make certain that the ISEA victory was not total and complete. Therefore, when the Legislature required that school boards bargain with teachers off a "laundry list" of topics, rather than on everything, as the National Labor Relations Act requires in the private sector, they considered it a victory for their side.

It took less than five years to prove that Elmer Gast was wrong. This "mere classroom teachers association" was much more powerful than it had ever been when the administrators were part of it. Gast believed that the administrators were the strength of the ISEA, but came to find out the administrators sapped the strength of the ISEA. The "teachers association" became more confident, more self-assured, and more powerful as each year went by. The Association and the teachers both became legitimate at the same time.

CHAPTER 6

Sideshows — The Union

The struggle between the administrators and the teachers for control of the Association was not unique to Iowa. The same dynamics were at work in virtually every other state in the nation. It happened in some places earlier than in others, but eventually it happened everywhere.

Most teachers sought to reform the Association from within. Others believed that reform was out of the question and they sought to replace the Association with another organization. The American Federation of Teachers (AFT) was a ready alternative.

The AFT had existed for years. Its members were mostly teachers in the nation's largest cities. Union members were an odd lot, as far as most of Iowa's teachers were able to tell. The union leaders lurked about on the outer fringes of acceptable political thought and behavior. "They were probably Communists and the rest of their members were dupes, or maybe they were anarchists, or maybe . . ."

There was nothing about the AFT that would appeal to the old-fashioned teachers in Iowa. That was for sure. The maiden ladies did not feel comfortable around union types. But the younger teachers were another matter entirely.

The Colleges of Education at the universities hosted debates for their students. A representative from the Association and a representative from the Federation were given equal time. Invariably, the representative of the Association was a quiet fellow. Often he was a school superintendent. He appeared timid in comparison to the Federation representative. The Association representative talked about professional responsibility, professional standards, and the Code of Ethics.

The Federation representative was loud. He talked about fairness and justice. He talked about teacher power and strikes. He said "damn" and "hell," which was very unprofessional of him. The Federation representative accused the Association of being a "tea and crumpets" club. He said the only thing that the Association does is make flower arrangements for the annual retirement tea.

William Anderson, the president of the ISEA, observed such a debate at the State College of Iowa in 1962. This time the debate was between the president of the AFT and a member of the NEA research staff. Anderson was upset by what he observed. He was still upset when he reported to the Executive Board sometime later.

"It would be better for the NEA to decline to participate in these things," Anderson said, "if they cannot send someone who knows how to debate. There was nothing wrong with his material; he just did not know how to dramatize his message."

"We came out a poor second in this debate," Anderson decided, "and these debates have a tremendous influence on those who are being prepared for a teaching career."

George Fischer agreed with him, saying, "In the Des Moines schools, at least, it is the new or beginning teacher who is not joining the profession."

There was nothing special about the Iowa Federation of Teachers (IFT) except that it was not the ISEA. The IFT was a ragtag operation without any authority or responsibility. Therefore, it was free to make unreasonable demands and outrageous promises. Those demands and promises struck a note with some of Iowa's younger teachers.

The leaders of the ISEA pondered the impact that this emerging union would have on their professional association.

Executive Secretary John Harold waxed philosophical on the issue more than once. "If the professional educator does not remain objectively classless," he asked, "would he not forfeit his right to speak professionally for the children of all the people?"

"Both professionalism and unionism have a firm place in our society," Harold offered on another occasion, "but intelligent citizens will distinguish clearly between the two. In a profession, if the welfare of the teacher and the child are in conflict, child welfare will always be given the priority."

The NEA Board of Directors member, J. E. Smith of Emmetsburg, agreed with Harold. "Teacher unions are teacher welfare organizations. In the Association the students always come first."

William Anderson blamed the IACT for the increased interest in the

IFT. "Some groups within the ISEA are unwittingly helping the union cause," he said, "by stressing the teacher-administration relationship wherein the teacher feels that the administration is dominating not only the school but the professional organization."

In the end, John Harold made the most astute observations. He said, "Either teachers will find a strong collective voice in the professional Association or they will seek it through other alliances such as the AFT."

"This is the revolution of rising expectations among teachers," Harold said. "It is urgent that the professional organization work to meet the needs of the teachers."

The revolution of rising expectations among teachers manifested itself in several ways: in the increasing militancy of the IACT; in the increasing number of teachers who, despite what their superintendent and principal suggested, refused to join the ISEA; and finally it manifested itself in the increasing membership of the IFT.

Actually, over the years, the IFT received more attention from the ISEA than it probably deserved. Membership in the IFT peaked in 1962 with only 854 members.

During its "heyday," the 20-year period from 1958 until 1978, the IFT had at one time or another only 11 locals: Burlington, Cedar Rapids, Council Bluffs, Davenport, Des Moines, Maquoketa, Ottumwa, Sioux City, the Council Bluffs principals, a faculty unit at the University of Northern Iowa, and staff at the Osteopathic College of Medicine in Des Moines.

Its largest local membership was in Cedar Rapids in 1961 with 265 members. Its local with the highest percentage of potential members was most likely Ottumwa in 1959 with 151 members, though it may have been the principals' local in Council Bluffs that peaked in 1963 with 22 members.

In some states the AFT threatened the very existence of the state education association. Today, it has by far the larger membership of the two organizations in the State of New York. By virtue of representing teachers in the larger cities, the Federation has a significant percentage of the teachers as members in states like Florida, Illinois, Massachusetts, Michigan, Minnesota, and Pennsylvania.

That was never the case in Iowa. With the possible exception of Ottumwa, the Federation never really posed a serious threat of becoming the majority organization in any school district.

The ISEA's first concerted effort to beat back a Federation initiative came in Des Moines in 1958, long before collective bargaining. As a result of what W. Henry Galbreth, the ISEA associate executive secretary, called "a series of misunderstandings between the administration and the DMEA," some disgruntled Des Moines teachers organized a Federation local.

They held a general meeting for all who were interested in a union. A second meeting was held for those who had signed commitment cards at the first meeting. The ISEA and the NEA responded with a meeting of their own on May 5. Dr. McCaskill, the executive director of the National Association of Secretaries of State Teacher Associations came, as did Roy Wilson, the director of press and radio relations for the NEA, and Eric Rhodes, who was described by Galbreth as "the NEA's top salary consultant."

The outcome of all of the meetings was the creation of the Des Moines Federation of Teachers, an affiliate of the IFT and the AFT. Federation membership figures indicate that the DMFT's membership over the next decade fluctuated from a low of 99 members in 1959 to a high of 162 members in 1961.

The first teacher bargaining election in Iowa occurred in Des Moines in the fall of 1967, which was also long before collective bargaining was mandatory.

The Des Moines Board of Education voluntarily agreed to bargain with the teachers. At the same time, it established its own procedures for determining who would represent the teachers in the process. It was decided by the school board that the teachers would be represented by a team of five and that the five seats would be divided between the Des Moines Education Association and the Des Moines Federation of Teachers in proportion to the number of votes each would get in an election.

The question was, could the Des Moines Federation of Teachers get at least 10 percent of the vote? If it could, then it would be allotted one of the five chairs at the bargaining table, according to the rules established by the Des Moines Board of Education.

It was touch and go for the Association. Fewer than 10 percent of the Des Moines teachers were members of the Federation. It was closer to eight percent. But it was believed that some Association members would vote for the Federation to represent them in bargaining. There were teachers who would not personally choose to be a member of a union but who would vote for one to represent them in collective bargaining, especially if it was a secret ballot.

The DMEA argued that all of the members of the two organizations should be allowed to vote in the election, not just the teachers. The Board of

Education decided that since the bargaining would be only for the teachers, only teachers could vote. That was a setback for the DMEA, since it was believed that the vast majority of the administrators who were members would vote for the Association if they had the opportunity.

The ISEA perceived that the election was critical. Over the course of the three-week campaign, virtually every staff member spent some time in Des Moines. Once totaled, it was determined that the ISEA spent over $2,500 of its own money on the effort.

When the votes were counted, the Des Moines Education Association had captured only four of the five seats. The Federation got the votes it needed from DMEA members in order to secure the fifth seat.

Other Federation locals came and went over the years.

The Burlington Federation of Teachers was organized in 1962 because the teachers were "disturbed with the present practice of basing salaries on factors not clearly known to all of the professional staff and in which the staff did not have ample opportunity to participate."

William Robinson of the ISEA Professional Relations Division met with the Burlington teachers on two different occasions. "It is my opinion that the majority of the teachers in Burlington do not want to organize a union," Robinson reported to the Executive Board. "However, they will insist upon receiving more recognition than the superintendent and the school board have given them during the past few years."

Executive Secretary John Harold and NEA staff member John Starie visited Burlington. At a meeting with all of the Association members present, including the superintendent, Harold told them, "A teacher should have a guarantee that no policy affecting all of the teachers in the system would be changed unless a majority of the teachers accepted it."

"The Burlington teachers," Harold reported back to the Executive Board, "feel that there is no one who will stick up for their rights."

The Burlington Federation of Teachers was organized. There were 43 teachers who joined, which was the highest number of members the local ever enjoyed.

The Maquoketa Federation of Teachers, with a membership of only 10 or so, prevailed upon the Maquoketa Education Association to put the ISEA on probation.

In September of 1973, the president of the Maquoketa Education Association wrote to ISEA Executive Secretary Ken Wells to advise him that in the opinion of many of the MEA members, as well as the MFT members, the ISEA had not been doing too good a job lately. Therefore, the MEA was placing the ISEA on probation for a period of one year. They would consider, at the end of the probationary period, whether or not they wished to remain a part of the ISEA.

The suspense ended early for Wells and the ISEA. The MEA president wrote back in May to say that because the ISEA had been so successful in lobbying the Legislature during the winter months the probation was being lifted early.

Most of the battles with the IFT were won before the Iowa General Assembly ever enacted collective bargaining. Once the administrators withdrew from membership and the Association began to advocate on behalf of teachers in earnest, the Federation threat, such as it was, disappeared member by member and local by local.

The only serious bargaining election challenge in a K-12 school district came in Ottumwa. The ISEA and the NEA pulled out all of the stops. Walter Galvin, the ISEA president, and James Harris, an Iowa teacher who was serving as the NEA president at the time, were part of the Ottumwa campaign. It was the first time in Iowa that the IFT and the ISEA opposed one another for bargaining rights in an election supervised by the new Public Employment Relations Board. The Association won that election on May 13, 1975, and the AFT was never again a serious threat in any Iowa school district.

They did mount a vigorous campaign at the University of Northern Iowa 18 months later. The Federation at UNI opposed the United Faculty, which was affiliated with both the ISEA and the American Association of University Professors. The election was held on November 18 and 19, 1976, and those voting chose the United Faculty as the bargaining agent by a margin of 288 to 133. After that, the AFT was never again a serious threat anywhere in Iowa.

The spoils from the victory over the IFT really belong more to the IACT than to the ISEA.

The existence of a department inside the Association that vigorously advocated on behalf of the interests of the classroom teachers served as a safety valve. Had the IACT not been so loud nor so effective, more teachers would have looked outside of the ISEA for help.

No doubt the ISEA would still have prevailed over the IFT in the long run, but the victory would have been much longer in coming and would have been achieved at a much higher price.

CHAPTER 7

Sideshows—Unification

First there was the ISEA. Then the ISEA, with the help of nine other state education associations, created the NEA. Sometime later, local associations were created and one by one they affiliated themselves with the ISEA.

It used to be, superintendents notwithstanding, that an individual teacher or administrator had the right to choose which one or ones, if any, of the three associations he or she wished to join. Most joined their local association. Almost as many joined the ISEA. A lot fewer joined the NEA.

The relatively low NEA membership in most states was a cause for concern, so the NEA proposed a deal to the state affiliates. The NEA promised that it would not accept into national membership any person who was not a member of the state association if the state association would agree not to accept into state membership any person who was not a member of the national association. And for good measure, both of them would agree to require that their members join the local association. The NEA called this "unification."

The first state association to "unify" was Oregon in 1944. Twenty-five years later only one-half of the state associations were unified. The NEA first offered incentives to the state associations, then bribes, and finally mandates. By the early 1970s it was unify, or else. In 1975, Texas became the last state association to fall into line. That, of course, does not count Missouri, which refused to unify one time too many and got the "or else." The Missouri State Teachers Association was booted out of the NEA and was replaced by a new association called the "Missouri-NEA."

The ISEA was trying to decide whether or not it should be unified at the same time it was trying to decide whether teachers or administrators should run the Association.

Members' support for unification, or their opposition to it, had little or nothing to do with what their jobs were back in the school district. Some teachers were for unification and some were against it. The same thing was true for administrators.

Unification did, however, speed up the exodus of administrators from the ISEA. Once the decision was made to unify, many of the administrators who had wished to remain a part of the Association but who were opposed to unification headed for the exits along with their colleagues who wanted to leave, period.

Most of the arguments that were advanced on behalf of unification were predictable.

"In unity there is strength!"

"The local association cannot be strong if the state and national associations are weak. The state association cannot be strong if the local and national associations are weak. The national association cannot be strong if the local and state associations are weak."

"Every member benefits from the good work of the Association at all three levels. Therefore, it is only fair that every member should support the work of the Association at all three levels."

Most of the arguments advanced in opposition to unification were predictable, also.

"It is un-American!"

"It is an unwarranted interference by the NEA into the affairs of the state and local associations."

"I am pleased to pay my local dues, but I disagree with some of the positions taken by the state and national associations." Or, "I am pleased to pay my local dues and my state dues, but I disagree with some of the positions taken by the national association." No one ever said, "I am pleased to pay my national dues, but I disagree . . ."

"The state and local associations will lose members because if teachers have to join all three associations some will not join any."

Eventually, the NEA agreed to hold the state associations harmless. The NEA guaranteed that for a period of three years following unification, it would make up whatever dues revenue the state association lost as a result of declining membership.

An opponent of unification could still argue that the state and local associations would lose members, but it was no longer legitimate to argue that the state association would lose dues revenue as a result of unification, at least for three years.

As time went by, the arguments from the proponents of unification became less ideological and more pragmatic, reflecting the fact that every year the NEA upped the ante. When unification was finally approved by the ISEA Delegate Assembly, it was believed that NEA funding for the new field staff program was contingent upon the state being unified. It was also widely rumored that any financial reimbursement from NEA to help defray the legal costs incurred by the ISEA was also contingent upon unification.

The first official discussion of unification in Iowa occurred at the Executive Board meeting on October 17, 1962. The two members of the NEA Board of Directors from Iowa, J. E. Smith from Emmetsburg and Leland J. Gritzner from Osage, were under pressure from their colleagues on the NEA Board to advance the unification agenda in Iowa. The two NEA Board members shared information with their Iowa colleagues, and the Board agreed informally that a target date for unification would be set sometime in the future.

That sometime was January 31, 1963. On that date the Executive Board determined that the ISEA would unify with the NEA when 90 percent of the ISEA members were also members of the NEA. In 1963 about two-thirds of the ISEA members were also NEA members so it was likely to be a while before the ISEA and the NEA were unified.

The NEA commenced to offer attractive incentives to state associations in order to entice them to unify. At the same time, the pressure continued to escalate. For the most part it was peer pressure: pressure by NEA Board members from unified states applied to NEA Board members from states that were not, pressure by state presidents and executive secretaries from unified states applied to presidents and executive secretaries from states that were not. By the mid-to-late 1960s it was no longer popular or politically expedient for those state leaders who were active at the national level to be from a state that was not unified.

The unification timetable was accelerated. On November 13, 1965, the Executive Board voted unanimously to place the issue before the 1966 Delegate Assembly. The Executive Board would recommend that, effective September 1, 1966, the ISEA would be unified with the NEA.

The Executive Board members then returned to their districts and reported what they had done. At the very next meeting on December 10, 1965, the Executive Board voted, this time eight to seven, to place the issue before the 1967 Delegate Assembly. It was now the recommendation of the Executive Board that, effective September 1, 1967, the ISEA would be unified with the NEA.

Having received such a negative reaction to their bold move on unification, the Executive Board members decided that perhaps the members should be surveyed on the issue. A questionnaire was mailed to all members in October, 1966. Of those who responded, 4,106 said that they were in favor of unification and 8,833 said that they were opposed to it.

The 1967 Delegate Assembly came and went without an up or down vote on the issue of unification. There were three motions related to the issue, though. Two of them were passed and one of them was tabled.

One motion that was passed said, "The ISEA believes that every teacher should be a participating member in the local, state, and national education associations by continuous membership through annual renewals. A profession thus united will be recognized as the official voice of the teachers. The ISEA supports the principle of unified membership."

The other motion that was passed said, "The ISEA shall continue to study unified membership."

The tabled motion, made by John Vint of Algona, was more significant. It said, "Unified membership shall not be adopted in Iowa unless a majority of the ISEA members approve it in a statewide referendum."

The Delegate Assembly directive to continue the study of unification was referred to the Membership Committee. The Membership Committee studied the issue and recommended in their report to the 1968 Delegate Assembly that the ISEA unify with the NEA effective on September 1, 1968. The Delegate Assembly refused to accept the committee's report.

The Executive Board decided to take a different approach. It was decided that when 51 percent of the members of the ISEA were from local associations that required unified membership, the ISEA would unify with the NEA.

It had been permissible for some time for local associations to unify on their own. A local association could require state and national memberships as a condition of local membership. During the 1968-69 school year 55 local associations in Iowa were unified. That represented only about 12 percent of the total. But many of the larger local associations were among the 55. As a result, over 25 percent of the members of the ISEA were already unified.

The Executive Board made it official by amending the Bylaws to specifically prohibit the ISEA from accepting into state membership any person from a unified local who was not a member there.

By the time the 1970 Delegate Assembly rolled around, nearly one-third of the ISEA members were from unified local associations and nearly 80 percent of the total ISEA membership were also members of the NEA.

In addition, the NEA Representative Assembly, scheduled for San Francisco, California, in July, was set to vote on a massive staffing proposal which would become known as "UniServ." Should the proposal be adopted, and it appeared that it would be, state associations that increased the size of their field staffs would be eligible for large amounts of money from the NEA to help offset their expenses. The way the proposal was written, only those locals or states that were unified would receive the assistance from the NEA.

The time appeared to be right. A special evening session of the Delegate Assembly was called for the purpose of "discussing" unification. A motion came during the special session. It stated, "The ISEA shall start immediate negotiations with the NEA to become unified by September 1, 1970, and the Bylaws shall be amended to provide for unified membership starting with the 1970-71 school year."

Had the motion been to actually amend the Bylaws it would have required a two-thirds vote in order to be adopted. But it was not. Rather, it was a resolution directing the Executive Board, who also had the power to amend the Bylaws, to do so. Therefore, it required only the support of a simple majority of those voting in order to be adopted.

A total of 352 delegates voted on the motion. Of those, 233 voted yes and 119 voted no. The motion had received the support of 66.19 percent of those delegates present and voting.

On July 20, 1970, the Executive Board voted to amend the Bylaws to provide, "Commencing with the 1970-71 membership year, any active member must also be and remain a member of the NEA and of a local association affiliated with the ISEA where memberships in these organizations are available."

Within weeks thereafter, the ISEA president and executive secretary traveled to Washington, D. C., where they signed the necessary papers making Iowa the 27th state association to unify with the NEA.

The matter was not resolved, not quite yet. Eugene Johnson, president of the Decorah Education Association, challenged the action of the Executive Board. His argument was that since the Delegate Assembly action had the effect of amending the Bylaws, it should have received a two-thirds majority vote in order to pass. Because it had not, Johnson reasoned, the Executive Board acted without proper authority when it amended the Bylaws.

Marvin Adams, the ISEA legal counsel, was consulted. It was Adams' opinion that since the Executive Board had the authority to amend the Bylaws without any direction from the Delegate Assembly, there was most certainly nothing improper about its doing so at the behest of 66.19 percent of the delegates.

Motions came to the 1971 and 1972 Delegate Assemblies to rescind the action taken by the Executive Board. The motions were defeated. At the 1973 Delegate Assembly a motion was made to "remove the unified membership requirement for membership in the national, state, and local education associations. Support for and membership in national, state, and local associations should be encouraged but not required for teachers." That motion was defeated, also.

After that, the issue of unification was never debated again.

CHAPTER 8

Leadership

The NEA elects a president and employs an executive director. The NEA president is elected by the Representative Assembly, and the executive director is employed by the Executive Committee. Each of the 50 state associations does the same. In Iowa, the president is elected by the Delegate Assembly and the executive director is employed by the Executive Board. In a few of the state associations the executive director is still called the executive secretary, and in one, the chief of staff, but they all use the same model.

It is a model built on the premise that two heads are better than one, especially when one head is elected and tends to matters of program and policy development and the other is employed and tends to the implementation of program and policy and the management of staff.

On paper it may appear that the twain never meet, but where the model works well, the twain meet all of the time. When contemplating new programs and policies, it is wise to consult with the person who will implement them. When implementing programs and policies, it is wise to consult with the people who created them. It is a simple and good system.

Both the ISEA president and the ISEA executive director have job descriptions. The president presides at meetings, appoints committees, keeps in close contact with members and leaders, and serves as the spokesperson for the Association, among other things. The executive director hires and manages the staff, approves purchases and expenditures, keeps track of the assets of the corporation, and makes sure the grounds are free of litter, among other things. But most important of all, the president and the executive director help each other do their jobs. It is a simple and good system.

Throughout the history of the ISEA it has not always been so simple nor so good. There have been presidents and other elected officials who coveted the responsibilities of the executive director and the other management staff. There have been executive directors and other management staff who coveted the responsibilities of the president and the other elected officials. There were times when both things happened at once.

Most often it happened because the people involved did not know better. They did not know better because the system had not been defined.

The local school district served as the management model for the ISEA. The school district was run by a school board. A school board consisted of five or seven people who volunteered their time to run things. Some school board members had noble motives. They wanted to help run a good school. Other school board members had motives that were not so noble. They had axes to grind. Noble motives or axes to grind, school board members tended to meddle in the administration of their school districts.

School superintendents were the primary victims of the school board members who meddled. Principals and teachers were their secondary victims. The superintendent was hired to manage the school system but it was often difficult to do because school board members wanted to manage the school system, too.

School board members would interview prospective teachers, hire them, and fire them, sometimes over the objections of the superintendent. There was no detail too small to escape the attention of the school board. At one time or another, somewhere, a school board has dealt with every issue, even issues like how short the grass should be mowed and how often green beans should be served in the school cafeteria.

It was tough to be a superintendent. It was so tough that superintendents developed survival techniques that sometimes did them in. Often there was a "good" faction and a "bad" faction on a school board. The superintendent provided the good faction with a lot of "inside" information while the bad faction got no information at all. Sometimes, when there was an especially bad board member, the superintendent would work behind the scenes to help someone else get elected when that board member ran again.

Early on, the ISEA Executive Board was like a school board made up of school superintendents and the executive secretary was like a school board member serving as the superintendent.

Later on, when the teachers took control of the Association, there was a different set of problems. Many of the teachers who served on the Executive Board brought with them a hefty anti-management bias. To them, the executive secretary was not much different from a school superintendent. The executive secretary was not to be given too much authority or too much responsibility.

The problem was that no one else had much authority or responsibility, either. The ISEA president still served a single one-year term of office and was not even released to do that on a full-time basis until the 1971-72 school year. The standing committees did pretty much what they wanted to do and so did the staff. At times the situation approached anarchy. During this period, some bad habits developed that took years to break.

It took a long time for the jobs of president and executive secretary to grow up and, after that, it took a while longer for them to grow together.

Back in the old days the schoolmen were in control. They ran things. And things have not been run that way since.

For example, the Executive Board members approved every single expenditure. No item was too small or too insignificant to be unworthy of their attention.

Each month a different board member would visit the business office to personally review each transaction that had taken place. Often there were concerns that would be shared with the other members during the Board's monthly meetings. Sometimes lengthy discussions would ensue.

M. M. Rogers of Sumner determined that the telephone bill was too high. He directed the executive secretary to meet with each staff member in order to decide if all of the calls that had been made were necessary.

Wayne Begg of Ankeny noticed that a staff member had been eating with leaders from some of the larger local associations and that the ISEA had been paying for one-half of the total bill. He wanted to make certain that when staff members ate with leaders from smaller associations, the ISEA paid for one-half of the total bill then, also.

Over the years the Executive Board resolved that all bills received from vendors should be added again in the business office in order to make certain that the total was correct, that it cost too much to mow the lawn, and that there should be more detail on hotel bills.

The Executive Board members took their responsibilities just as seriously as the school board members took theirs back home.

On December 19, 1964, Wayne Begg shared a discovery with the other members of the Executive Board. It was, perhaps, the kind of discovery that made the Executive Board members' attention to detail worthwhile. He had discovered that the ISEA had paid $120 to Rent-Alls, Inc. for a Lawn Boy mower. He thought that was a pretty high price to pay for the rental of a lawn mower, and he was certain that the other members of the Executive Board would also. Executive Secretary Ken Wells explained that the ISEA had actually purchased the lawn mower from Rent-Alls and that they had thrown in a leaf pulverizing attachment for good measure.

Two years later Begg was to suggest that perhaps the Executive Board really did not need to go to all of this trouble. Roger Blake disagreed. "No," Blake said, "this shows the membership that the Executive Board is in charge."

The Executive Board paid every bit as much attention to the employment and management of staff as they did to the payment of bills.

In 1965 the Delegate Assembly determined to create three new positions called "field representatives." No such position had existed before. Ray Stephens had been the field services staffer operating from the ISEA headquarters. Now he had been assigned as the manager for the three new employees who would be hired.

He and Executive Secretary Wells proceeded to implement a hiring process. By March 13 they were ready to make their first recommendation. It was Marvin Larson, the high school principal from Hampton. A motion was made to grant Wells the permission to hire Larson. A secret ballot was called for and the motion was defeated.

The Executive Board meeting was then recessed while the Board's Personnel Committee met with Ken Wells and Ray Stephens. At the conclusion of the committee meeting, the committee chairman, M. M. Rogers, reported that the next two positions would be filled by "men who are vigorous, strong, courageous, and firm in their convictions."

That was assured because the Executive Board members would provide Wells with names of men who fit that criteria. Wells and Stephens would sift through the names that were provided and would arrange for the Personnel Committee to interview a number of them. The Personnel Committee would then bring a recommendation to the next Executive Board meeting.

After the Personnel Committee's report, a motion was again forthcoming to grant Wells the permission to hire Larson. This time the motion was passed, eight to six.

While the Executive Board was busy paying the bills, hiring the staff, and generally managing the affairs of the Association, the executive secretary and the other managers had time to do other things.

The executive secretary spoke for the organization. He represented the interests of the members to the public. The executive secretary was the alternate member of the NEA Board of Directors from Iowa. When one of the regularly elected directors could not attend a meeting, the executive secretary attended instead. The executive secretary and other staff members, too, were actively involved in all of the campaigns for NEA office by George Fischer and James Harris.

The system, or lack of one, did not work very well. That is one of the reasons that John Harold resigned as executive secretary. "There is growing conflict between the role of the executive secretary and the role of the president," he told the Executive Board on the day he quit. "The executive secretary and the staff, which must be completely under his direction if the organization is to be effective, carry out the program designed by the elected officials."

"The elected officers should decide what should be done at staff headquarters and leave the 'how' to the executive secretary and staff," Harold went on. "Far too much time of the staff is now spent negotiating conflict instead of promoting positive programs."

That was the old system. The administrators were not even officially out of the door when the new regime commenced its reign of terror against the management staff.

On March 20, 1971, the Executive Board declared that all of the management positions were vacant. Executive Secretary Wells, who had been in that position for nearly seven years, was directed to post notices that his job, and the other management jobs as well, were open and all staff were welcome to apply.

Wells applied to be executive secretary again and he was rehired. The next year the Executive Board froze his salary. The next year Dorothy Helmick, the longtime administrative assistant to the executive secretary, retired and the Executive Board determined not to replace her. Then Mike Fleming, one of the three associate executive secretaries, resigned to become executive secretary of the South Carolina Education Association. The Executive Board determined not to replace him, either. The new leadership was clearly in favor of downsizing ISEA management.

In the spring of 1974, Ken Wells announced his retirement. He admonished the Executive Board, "The ISEA is in more danger of being torn apart than at any time in its history."

"The bickering and struggling that have gone on among various groups seeking more and more power and autonomy has fragmented and destroyed this Association as leaders in almost every field," Wells said. "I believe that you (the Executive Board) must attack this problem head on, objectively, dispassionately, and intelligently."

The time was approaching when the ISEA would need to get its internal house in order if it was going to be able to deliver on all of its promises to the teachers of Iowa.

CHAPTER 9

The Executive Director

The ISEA was founded in 1854. For the first 64 years of its history there were no staff members. The Association functioned as a club. The president arranged for the meetings. The secretary recorded the minutes and wrote the correspondence. The treasurer received and disbursed the funds.

By 1915 the club had grown in membership, reputation, authority, and responsibility. It was apparent that the old internal structures would not meet the new external demands. Therefore, a committee was appointed to draft a new constitution. It was approved and became effective in 1917.

The new constitution provided for the position of executive secretary. It was the first ISEA staff position. Over the years the number of staff positions would increase to 100. All of them are extensions of the first one, the position of executive secretary.

It was the job of the executive secretary to do those things that the officers did not have the time to do, could not do so easily, or could not do at all. The first executive secretary assumed almost all of the major responsibilities of the elected officers. He made the arrangements for the meetings. He recorded the minutes of the meetings. He wrote the official correspondence for the Association. He received and disbursed the funds and made an accounting of the transactions. The only major responsibility left for the officers to do was for the president to preside at the meetings.

The only other task that was assigned to the executive secretary at the outset was to create a journal for the purpose of publishing the official proceedings of the Association. *Midland Schools* was created and the executive secretary was its editor.

While the position of executive secretary was created for the purpose of providing aid and assistance to the elected officers of the Association, it soon became more than that.

The Executive Board and the Delegate Assembly created new programs. They were assigned to the executive secretary for the purpose of implementation. Soon there were so many programs that the executive secretary could not implement all of them by himself. Staff were hired. Soon the executive secretary spent more time managing the staff than he did providing aid and assistance to the elected officers.

Another dynamic was also at work. The elected officers were full-time school employees who were geographically dispersed throughout the far reaches of the state. Communications and transportation were still relatively primitive in 1918. It was not easy for the officers to meet together or to communicate with one another or with anyone else, for that matter. The executive secretary filled the void. He communicated on behalf of the officers. Soon the executive secretary became the personification of the ISEA to the members and to the public.

While the role and responsibilities of the executive secretary grew in scope and stature, the role and responsibilities of the elected officers and the Executive Board members remained stagnant.

The executive secretary was the recognized leader both inside and outside the Association. The executive secretary had great influence over the program, the budget, and the policies of the Association.

Like the local school board members back home, some Association officers and board members had noble motives. They wanted to help build a good Association. Others had motives that were not so noble. They had axes to grind. Also, like the local school board members back home, whether their motives were noble or not, the Association officers and Board members meddled in things that would have been better left for the executive secretary to handle.

The more frustrated the leaders became with the increasing power and influence of the executive secretary, which they believed came at their expense, and the more frustrated they became with their seeming inability to deal with the situation, the more petty and meddlesome they became.

Two things needed to change. The position of executive secretary was one and the position of the president was the other.

The executive secretary position was created to be an extension of the Association governance. The earliest responsibilities assigned to the position were all ones that had previously been assigned to the various elected officers.

The Executive Board had, over the years, reinforced the perception that the essence of the position was governance. They did it by hiring executive secretaries from the ranks of governance. Between 1918, when Charles F. Pye was hired to be the first executive secretary, and 1975, when Kenneth Wells retired from the position, six executive secretaries had come and gone. All six of them had held important elected positions in the ISEA. Two, Charles Martin and Ken Wells, had been president. Not a single one of the six had ever held a management position in an association, or even a staff position, prior to becoming executive secretary.

It is not surprising that executive secretaries who were hired directly from the top echelon of elected leaders to serve in a position that had evolved as an extension of governance would act more like leaders than managers.

The position was renamed and redefined in 1978. It became the "executive director" rather than the "executive secretary." When Beverly Wolkow was named executive director in 1978, she became the first person to hold the position who had any previous association management experience at all.

The officers and Executive Board members made a serious effort to exert themselves as the policy-makers of the Association. At the same time, they made a serious effort to allow the executive director to manage the affairs of the Association without undue interference from them. It took a few years to work the bugs out of the new system.

For a long time some of the leaders had tried to strengthen the office of the president. They perceived, and correctly so, that as long as the president was a full-time school district employee and a part-time president and as long as the president served a single one-year term, the office would be only ceremonial. It would be necessary for the president to serve full time and to serve longer than a single year before he or she would be able to exert any real power or influence over ISEA programs and policies.

CHAPTER 10

The President

As long as the presidency of the ISEA was, for the most part, a ceremonial position, it probably did not make much difference how the person who held the position was elected. It probably did not matter too much who was elected to the position, either.

The process established by the Articles of Incorporation and Bylaws for the nomination and election of the president and vice president of the ISEA was simple and straightforward. Each year at the Delegate Assembly nominations were opened for each office, candidates were nominated, and the delegates voted. The candidate for president who received the largest number of votes was elected. The candidate for vice president who received the largest number of votes was elected also.

However, informal traditions had evolved over the years, all of them quite consistent with the provisions of the ISEA Articles and Bylaws. The traditions required that there be only one single candidate for the presidency each year and that most often there be only one single candidate for the vice presidency, too.

Tradition required that the only nominee for the office of president be the vice president who had been elected by the previous Delegate Assembly. The vice president was, in effect, the president-elect, even though the governance documents did not provide for that. Another candidate, other than the vice president, could have been nominated from the floor at the Delegate Assembly. No one ever was. It was a powerful tradition.

The informal process for determining who the nominee for vice president would be was somewhat more complicated. There was no obvious candidate, as was the case with the office of president. But by 1950 a process had evolved.

According to tradition, the process required that a county superintendent of schools be the nominee for the office of vice president. Who that was to be would be determined by the county superintendents of schools. The next year the nominee would be a secondary school principal who would be selected by the Iowa Association of Secondary School Principals. The secondary school principal was followed by a city superintendent, who was followed by a higher education faculty member or administrator, who was followed by a classroom teacher. The nominee or nominees were selected by the department within the ISEA to which they belonged. At the end of five years the cycle began again.

The earliest concerns about the traditional system came from the elementary teachers and principals. They were not part of the cycle. Elementary teachers and principals never got to be the vice president or president of the ISEA.

President Frank Hildreth, a classroom teacher from Des Moines, first raised the issue in 1954. He appointed a committee to study the matter and offer recommendations to the Executive Board. The committee was chaired by Edith Kuhl, an elementary classroom teacher.

The committee determined that there was nothing that could be done to help the elementary classroom teachers. Their problem was not with the ISEA. Rather, it was with the IACT. There was nothing to prohibit the IACT from selecting an elementary teacher to be its candidate for vice president if they wanted. It was just that they preferred secondary teachers, or at least it appeared so up until then.

The elementary principals, however, had a legitimate concern, according to the committee. They did not have access to the cycle. The committee recommended that the Executive Board approach the Iowa Association of Elementary School Principals and request that it nominate a candidate or two for consideration by the Delegate Assembly in 1956.

According to the minutes from the meeting of July 16, 1955, "the Executive Board lacked enthusiasm and the proposal was withdrawn." It was the sentiment that since the cycle was informal, it would not be proper for the Executive Board to inject itself into it.

There was a long debate on the issue at the 1956 Delegate Assembly, and according to the delegates, there was more wrong with the informal system than just the fact that elementary classroom teachers and principals were not included in the election cycle, though the delegates believed that was a problem, too.

Some argued that the system was very undemocratic. "In four years out of five, groups varying in size from four-tenths of one percent of the membership to four percent of the membership select the nominee," the classroom teachers argued. "Only once in five years do 90 percent of the members have any real voice in the selection of the candidate."

"The system requires that a president be nominated from a particular group, even though other groups may have better candidates that year," others argued.

And finally, almost everyone agreed that the system was so cut and dried that there was practically no interest on the part of the membership in the election of the president.

It was directed that the Executive Board return to the 1957 Delegate Assembly with a proposal to change the way the officers of the ISEA were elected.

The Executive Board did as it was directed to do. What the Board proposed not only required amendments to the Articles of Incorporation and the Bylaws, but it also dismantled the traditional process that had been in place for years.

First of all, the Executive Board proposed that the title of vice president be changed to president-elect and that the traditional practice of that person automatically succeeding to the presidency be memorialized in the governance documents.

Next the Executive Board proposed an open process of nominations and elections, both primary and general. Any member who wished to be a candidate for the position of president-elect could be one. All that member needed to do was submit a petition to the executive secretary, prior to June 1 of any given year, bearing the signatures of 600 other members.

If more than two candidates submitted petitions, a primary election would be held at the first county meetings in the fall. Every member was eligible to vote. The results would be forwarded to the state headquarters. The votes would be counted and the two top vote-getters in the primary election would oppose one another for president-elect in the general election held during the Delegate Assembly in February.

If only two candidates were nominated by petition, there would be no primary election. If only one candidate was nominated by petition, the Executive Board would nominate a second one. If no candidates were nominated by petition, the Executive Board would nominate two candidates.

The Delegate Assembly accepted the new procedure as recommended by the Executive Board.

There was considerable excitement generated among both the leaders of the Association and the members about the new process for electing the officers. Three candidates submitted nominating petitions bearing at least 600 signatures. They were Ray Bryan, a member of the faculty at Iowa State College; Fern Wilson, a junior high school counselor; and Edith Kuhl, the elementary classroom teacher who had chaired the committee on elections procedures two years earlier.

The first and only every-member primary election was held that fall. Participation was heavy. The two top vote-getters were Bryan with 9,156 votes and Wilson with 7,729. Edith Kuhl finished third with 6,883 votes. Ray Bryan was the winner of the general election at the Delegate Assembly in February.

There was one other occasion when three members submitted petitions bearing the required number of signatures in order to qualify as candidates for the office of president-elect. However, one of the three candidates withdrew shortly after the petitions were filed, thus eliminating the need for another primary election. Shortly thereafter, the governance documents were amended again, this time eliminating the every-member primary and substituting a primary election at the Delegate Assembly instead.

By the early 1960s it had become obvious to some that the presidency of the ISEA was changing. The Executive Board discussed the issue for the first time on July 19, 1961. Board member Jeanette Williams of Cedar Rapids raised the issue. "Over the last several presidential administrations, haven't we somewhat changed the image of the ISEA president?" she asked.

Most of the Executive Board members seemed to agree that the more recent presidents had spent more time traveling around the state than had been the case before.

"It seems that the presidents have become better acquainted with the membership and the membership with them," Williams observed.

Ray Nyhan, a principal from Marshalltown, was the president of the ISEA at the time. He wondered if the demands on the office were mounting to the point where it might no longer be possible for a classroom teacher to serve in the position. "Perhaps we should see," Nyhan suggested, "if some arrangement might be made to grant the president released time or perhaps even arrange for a leave of absence with pay."

Nothing happened until the 1964 Delegate Assembly, when a motion was adopted which provided, "The ISEA Executive Board shall appoint a committee to study the feasibility of providing the president of the ISEA with a salary and encouraging the school board of the president's employing district to grant a one year's leave of absence during his tenure as the ISEA president."

The committee that studied the issue was comprised of Etta Cosner, the incumbent president; Roger Blake, the president-elect; and two former presidents, Ray Nyhan and Joe Gettys. Cosner was the coordinator of elementary education for the Davenport school system, Nyhan was a junior high school principal, and Blake and Gettys were both school superintendents.

The committee recommended against a year's leave of absence for the ISEA president. They had two primary reasons for their recommendation. The committee did not believe it would be a good idea to have both a president and an executive secretary at Salisbury House all year long, and they believed it would eliminate the possibility of a classroom teacher serving as the ISEA president. Regarding the second reason, the committee thought it unlikely that a school district would ever be willing to release a classroom teacher for a whole year.

The committee made its report to the Executive Board on November 14, 1964. The minutes of the meeting indicate that "the Board appeared to be in agreement with the recommendations of no leave of absence and no salary for the president."

The issue next came to the attention of the Delegate Assembly in 1967. This time the motion provided that "the ISEA shall include an item in each budget so that the president, at his option, may be employed by the ISEA as a full or part-time employee during the school year of his presidency, providing the approval of the president's school board has been secured and that he can return to the same position." The motion was tabled.

The Delegate Assembly dealt with the issue again in 1968. This time the motion directed that the Executive Board develop a plan for a full-time presidency and submit it to the 1969 Assembly for its consideration. This time the motion was carried.

Those who opposed the motion argued that a full-time president might well overstep his bounds and become involved in the administration of the Association. Its proponents pointed out that the motion simply asked that a plan be developed. There would be ample time at the 1969 Delegate Assembly to debate the merits.

The 1969 Delegate Assembly directed that amendments to the Articles of Incorporation be drafted and submitted to the 1970 Assembly that would specifically provide for a full-time ISEA president.

The following amendment to the Articles of Incorporation was presented to the 1970 Delegate Assembly: "The president may at his discretion serve the Association on a full-time or part-time basis during the term of his office, for which he shall be compensated at a rate whereby he would receive the same compensation as he would have received in his employment as an educator but on a twelve-month basis."

The motion that was adopted by the Delegate Assembly in 1969 calling for the consideration of an amendment to the Articles one year later required only a simple majority vote for passage. The amendment itself, which was considered in 1970, required a two-thirds majority vote for passage. It appeared that a majority of the delegates favored the amendment, but clearly two-thirds did not. The amendment was defeated.

It would take only one more Delegate Assembly. Virtually the same amendment was submitted again in 1971. The only change from the one that was defeated the year before related to the president's salary. The 1970 amendment provided that the president would receive the same salary that would have been forthcoming from the employing school district, prorated for twelve months. The 1971 amendment provided that the president would be paid twice the average Iowa public school instructional staff salary for the preceding school year. In 1971 the amendment was carried.

The February 1971 issue of *The Communique* reported, "For the first time in history the ISEA will have a president working as a full-time staff member. ISEA President-Elect Walter L. Galvin has indicated he will ask for a leave of absence from his teaching duties at Des Moines Technical High School in order to devote full time to ISEA affairs."

Having resolved the issue of whether or not the president of the Association should be a full-time position, the proponents of a stronger presidency turned their attention, almost immediately, to the questions of how long the president's term should be and how many terms one person should be allowed to serve.

It was argued that in order for the president to have any significant impact on the direction of ISEA programs and policies, it was necessary for that person to serve more than one year. All a person could do in one year as president was get acquainted.

The 1975 Delegate Assembly considered a new business item which directed that "appropriate amendments to the Articles of Incorporation and

Bylaws be prepared and submitted to the 1977 Delegate Assembly which provide that the ISEA president shall be elected to a term of two years and that the president shall be eligible for re-election to succeed himself/herself after each term." The motion was defeated.

The opponents expressed a number of objections during the course of the debate. They argued that there are a large number of leaders in Iowa who are qualified to be president of the Association who would be shut out if one president could serve forever. They worried about what would happen to the president-elect and the past president. The opponents argued that only teachers from large school districts could be president because small districts would never agree to extend leaves of absence for an indefinite period of time.

Sensing that the "unlimited terms" provision of the 1975 proposal was perhaps a bigger issue to the opponents than the "two-year term" provision, the proponents came back to the Delegate Assembly in 1977.

This time the proposal provided that "the president shall be nominated as provided in the Bylaws and shall be elected at the annual meeting of the Delegate Assembly for a two-year term. The president shall not be eligible for re-election as president to a second consecutive term." This motion was defeated also.

Two separate motions came to the 1978 Delegate Assembly. The first motion was to amend the Articles of Incorporation to provide for a two-year term of office for the president. A two-thirds majority vote was required for approval. The voice vote was inconclusive and a card count was called for. Nearly 72 percent of the delegates had voted in favor of the motion and the president's term of office was lengthened from one year to two.

The second motion was to amend the Bylaws to provide that a person would not be eligible to serve more than two consecutive two-year terms as president. The second motion passed overwhelmingly.

George Duvall of Ames, who had served a one-year term as president in 1978-79, was elected again at the 1980 Delegate Assembly. Thus, he became the first person to be elected president of the ISEA for a term of two years.

Several presidents had served more than one term. The first was D. F. Hill in 1857-58 and 1860-61. The second was C. C. Nestlerode in 1858-59 and 1862-63. Then, over a century later, Walter L. Galvin did it again. His terms were in 1971-72 and 1974-75. Duvall, though, became the first president who was eligible to be elected to two consecutive terms. Since he chose not to run for re-election as president in 1982, it was his successor, Phoebe Tupper of Davenport, who became the first person to serve two consecutive terms as president of the ISEA.

There have been two attempts to increase from two to three the number of consecutive terms that a president may serve. The first came in 1989. Again, a two-thirds majority vote by the Delegate Assembly was required for passage. Fewer than 50 percent of the delegates supported the proposal. Another effort was made the next year. It, too, was defeated.

The two presidents who have completed two two-year terms have made a significant impact on ISEA programs and policies, just as the proponents of longer terms said they would.

Phoebe Tupper, the first of the two, led the Association through an extensive and complicated process of long-range planning. She also took the first steps toward establishing a new and different relationship with the school administrators and school board members.

Ken Tilp of West Des Moines, the second of the two, positioned the ISEA as an advocate for school reform and transformation at a time when most of the state associations and the NEA were popularly viewed as opponents of the two.

The result of all of these changes is that it now matters who serves as the president of the ISEA. It matters because the presidency has become an important and powerful position.

CHAPTER 11

Politics

There have been many disagreements about politics among ISEA leaders over the years, but there have been very few disagreements about how important politics is to education.

The slogan, "Every decision that affects education is a political decision," goes back a long time in the history of the ISEA.

In May of 1956, Executive Secretary Charles F. Martin devoted his *Midland Schools* column, "Editorially Speaking," to the subject. "Political activity is a fundamental responsibility of any citizen," he wrote. "Because it is so important to our democratic form of government, the responsibility is even greater for teachers than it is for many others."

"The fact that education depends so heavily on favorable political action is, in itself, a very important reason for teachers to be interested," Martin continued. "Certainly no other group is better informed or better qualified to speak on the importance of maintaining a strong educational program."

Charlie Martin used the words "political action" in his column in *Midland Schools*: "Education depends so heavily on favorable political action," he said. Martin may have coined the phrase in that column, for the term was not yet in use in 1956. And it would not be in use for another decade or more. The efforts by the ISEA to affect politics and to influence legislation were referred to as "public relations" back then.

Some leaders worried that politics might be dangerous for teachers. J. C. Hoglan, an Executive Board member and the school superintendent from Marshalltown, was one. "A teacher, in most instances, doesn't dare do it," he said.

Other leaders worried that the teachers were afraid of politics or perhaps that they did not understand how important it was to their workaday world. According to Raymond Jones, an Executive Board member and the curriculum coordinator from Council Bluffs, "I talk politics to a teacher and I get the idea that they think it is something for the boys in the front office to worry about."

It is clear that the boys in the front office did worry about politics. So did the ISEA officers and members of the Executive Board.

There were two critical legislative issues as far as the ISEA was concerned in the mid-1950s: state aid for schools and property tax relief. It was the position of the Association that the State of Iowa should provide at least 25 percent of all of the funds available to operate the local school districts. It was also the position of the Association that the local districts should rely less on the property tax as the source of revenue for schools.

The property tax position was especially important, for as J. C. Wright, the state superintendent of public instruction, said, "Any program that has any chance of success in a legislature that is dominated by the Farm Bureau should receive their endorsement beforehand." Property tax relief was important to the Farm Bureau and the Farm Bureau was the most powerful lobby in Iowa in the mid-1950s.

There were a few individual Association members who were active in partisan politics back then, but not too many. The ISEA did not involve itself in partisan politics, either. Association representatives would meet with political party officials from time to time in an effort to influence the content of the party platforms, but that was about as "partisan" as the Association became.

As a lobbyist, however, the ISEA was at least modestly successful. In the mid-1950s the Association was represented on the Hill by Roy E. Jennings, whose title was director of public relations. Jennings was supported by the school superintendents who served as a network of lobbyists back home.

Some of the schoolmen were very effective at pressuring the legislators and some were not. Those who had served for a number of years in the same community had established themselves, were generally well-respected, and were known by the legislators, could have an impact on votes.

That was the "public relations" system in 1955. The ISEA steered clear of partisan politics, for the most part. The leaders developed a legislative program which they set about to have enacted. The ISEA hired a lobbyist who worked closely with the school superintendents back home and with the Farm Bureau in Des Moines.

It was not a bad system, but the leaders of the ISEA grew impatient. "I know that it has been the tendency of public employees to keep out of politics," observed Ruth Melcher, an Executive Board member and classroom teacher from Charles City, "but it is very definitely the case that we are not getting anywhere with this Legislature." Her sentiments were shared by every member of the Executive Board.

J. Leonard Davies, an associate professor of education at the State University of Iowa and the immediate past president of the ISEA, made a stunning motion on May 7, 1955. His motion was supported by L. L. Woodruff, the county superintendent of schools from Burlington. All of the members of the Executive Board voted for it.

Davies' motion provided "that the Executive Board go on record in favor of developing a more aggressive program of activity in politics and that a planned program of operation be recommended at the local, county, and state levels."

The leaders toyed with implementing their motion for many months without moving forward. It was as if they were shocked by their own audacity. Finally the issue became, "Are we going to implement our motion or are we not?" They decided to do it.

CHAPTER 12

LACs, CACs, DACs and a SAC

The ISEA called a conference of local leaders to be held on the campus of the Iowa State Teachers College in Cedar Falls on the dates of August 4 through August 7, 1957. It was the first summer leadership conference. The charge to the conference participants was to develop a "public relations structure and strategy."

The participants recommended the creation of LACs, CACs, DACs, and a SAC—Local Action Committees, County Action Committees, District Action Committees, and a State Action Committee.

The CAC was intended to be the critical committee in the organizational structure. It was the job of the County Action Committee to collect as much information as possible from and about candidates for the state Legislature. "This was to be done," according to Harold Weber, the Clinton High School principal and ISEA past president, "through conferences with the candidates, their answers to questionnaires, their discussion on legislative points, how they have responded or not responded to questions, their voting records, etc."

It was then the responsibility of the CAC to compare the positions of the candidates for office with the official ISEA positions. Having done that, the CAC was to share its findings with the LACs who would, in turn, share the findings with the members.

The State Action Committee would use the same process with the candidates for statewide office. It was envisioned that the SAC would also publicly air its findings. It was believed that some public-spirited citizens would value having access to information that compared the candidates' positions on education issues to those of the ISEA. The ISEA would also divide $10,000 among the various District Action Committees which, in turn, would make money available to the various LACs and CACs for voter education projects.

The recommendations from the participants at the first summer leadership conference were forwarded to the Executive Board's Public Relations Committee, where they were perfected. They were then adopted by the Executive Board. It was a new day for the ISEA.

The November 1957 issue of *Midland Schools* published a major story entitled, "Greater Political Activity for ISEA Members." It reported, "A plan for active participation in Iowa politics has been outlined for ISEA members by the Public Relations Committee. It calls for a newly organized action program at the state, district, county, and local levels."

Harold Weber, who was also chairman of the Public Relations Committee, was quoted: "The importance of school legislation is becoming more clearly apparent every day to the members of the profession and the lay public. Much can be accomplished . . . if ISEA members will become politically wise and politically active during the months ahead."

Because of the ISEA's tax status, it would not be possible for the SAC or the CACs to actually endorse candidates for office or "name names" as it was referenced in 1957. But that was not a problem, according to Weber. "Why should our teachers be told who to vote for?" he asked.

"I feel it is our obligation to gather as much information about candidates as possible and to make it as readily available to each of our members and to anyone who wants to look at the record, read, or listen to the information, as we possibly can. Then," Weber questioned, "what is wrong with a person making up his own mind?"

There was a flurry of activity at all levels, LAC to SAC, from early in February through election day on November 4, 1958. Not everything went smoothly. Some County Action Committees had spats with other County Action Committees over the money that was available from the District Action Committees. Some County Action Committees "named names." That was offensive to some members and worrisome to the ISEA. But, generally speaking, for a first-time effort, it was a smashing success.

The Executive Board paused after the June primary elections to take stock of how matters had progressed so far. According to Harold Weber and Charles Martin, things had gone very nicely.

Weber reported, "Candidates for major offices and many candidates for the Senate and House were very much aware of the fact that we were concerned about what happened and the quality and outlook of the candidates."

According to Martin, "This has given the Association considerable political stature in the minds of the public and the politicians. We should move ahead on that assumption with reasonable optimism."

While the DACs, CACs, and LACs went after the little fish in the General Assembly, the State Action Committee went after the big fish "with reasonable optimism."

CHAPTER 13

The Herschel C. Loveless Affair

The Republican candidate for governor in 1958 was Iowa State University professor Dr. William G. Murray of Ames. The Democratic candidate for governor was the incumbent, Herschel C. Loveless of Ottumwa.

Professor Murray supported an increase in the sales tax from 2 percent to 3 percent, a $30 million state aid package for schools, and property tax relief. According to Murray, "Whether or not the boys and girls of Iowa have adequate schools depends on whether we provide adequate state aid."

Governor Loveless opposed an increase in the state sales tax. He described Murray's state aid proposal as "a $30 million tax grab that is ill-considered and unjustified." According to Loveless, "I believe our schools should continue under LOCAL CONTROL—not state and federal control."

Exactly how the State Action Committee and the ISEA responded to the two candidates is a matter for debate.

The ISEA contended that it published the positions of the two candidates so that the members and the general public could make an enlightened choice. As Joe Gettys, the school superintendent from Oskaloosa, said, "It is just that nobody who heard Loveless talk could say that he had a constructive education program."

Governor Herschel C. Loveless contended that the ISEA had endorsed the candidacy of his opponent, Dr. William G. Murray, and he did not like it one bit.

Who knows for sure what happened? *The Des Moines Register* reported that "Murray campaigned on a program of using the additional one cent of sales tax for the benefit of local school tax relief. He received actual and tacit support from forces within the ISEA."

The ISEA bought a series of large newspaper advertisements. The ads read, in bold letters, "Support Good Schools. Increase State Aid. Relieve Property Tax." The copy, in smaller print, went on to say, "The only answer is increased state aid as has long been proposed by the ISEA. For better schools, vote November 4 in support of this program."

Perhaps, because "this program" bore such a striking resemblance to Bill Murray's program, that is why both *The Des Moines Register* and Governor Herschel C. Loveless concluded that the ISEA had made an endorsement, or at least a tacit endorsement, in the governor's race.

The campaign between Murray and Loveless was not a friendly one. When Loveless ran for governor the first time, in 1956, he had accepted money from the Teamsters Union. Now, according to Murray, Loveless was Jimmy Hoffa's candidate. By the time the campaign ended, Loveless would neither shake hands with Murray nor appear in pictures with him.

Two days before the election Governor Loveless came after the ISEA. He attacked the ISEA in a long and rambling letter that was printed in *The Des Moines Register*.

The letter began: "What are the radical Republicans hiding with their smog campaign? Why have they virtually abandoned the legitimate issues? Why are they trying to confuse the voters? The answer is plain. Behind the smear and smog is a thirty million dollar tax grab that they know will be rejected by the voters unless they can hide the facts behind a smoke screen of personal vilification."

"This administration has never opposed any reasonable and justifiable increases in state aid to public schools," Loveless continued, "But we do oppose an enormous thirty million dollar tax grab that the king-makers are attempting to sell the people of Iowa on the basis of false statistics. Such a pork-barrel promotion is definitely not in the long-range interests of our educational system."

Then, using uppercase letters once more, the Governor wrote: "THE DISTORTED FACTS DO NOT COME FROM THE SINCERE, CONSCIENTIOUS TEACHERS WE ALL RESPECT. They come from a paid professional lobby whose job is to get all the money they can get."

The letter from Loveless and, especially, the particular lines about "distorted facts" and "paid lobby," hit the ISEA like a powerful right cross. Worse yet, the leaders did not see it coming. The ISEA had ventured into the real world of partisan politics for the first time. The Association had taken the first punch. The leaders were shocked when someone punched back.

On Tuesday, November 4, the ISEA got hit with the left hand, too. Governor Herschel Loveless was re-elected to office with 54.6 percent of the vote.

Poor ISEA had the darndest luck. The Association became involved in partisan politics for the first time. It became involved on behalf of a Republican candidate for governor who was running against a Democratic incumbent. The Association's timing was awful, for the 1958 elections turned out to be a Democratic landslide, nationwide. It was the first time in history that one political party gained more than 50 seats in Congress in a single election.

The ISEA was battered and bruised and it had not even heard from the membership yet. But it would. The "sincere, conscientious teachers we all respect" had a thing or two to say to the "paid professional lobby."

Three months after the election, the Delegate Assembly convened. There were two questions on the minds of the delegates. Who created the State Action Committee? And who made the decision to endorse Bill Murray?

The first question was easier to answer than the second one. The Executive Board had determined that the ISEA should become more involved in politics. In an unusually open and democratic gesture for the times, the Board convened a conference and consulted with a large number of local leaders about how best to proceed. The conference offered recommendations which were considered by the Executive Board's Public Relations Committee. Then the Executive Board approved the action committee structure as recommended to it by the Public Relations Committee.

Furthermore, the action committee issue had actually been before the Delegate Assembly twice the previous year. It was the major portion of the report by the Public Relations Committee which was accepted by the Assembly. Also, the proposed budget, which was approved by the Assembly, included a whopping $50,000 line item earmarked for the action committee program. No, no one could reasonably argue that the State Action Committee had been hatched in secret by the agents of the paid professional lobby.

"Who made the decision to endorse Bill Murray?" was a far more difficult question to answer. It was especially difficult to answer because it was widely believed that someone had. Superintendents told the teachers that the ISEA had endorsed Bill Murray. Teachers told their friends that the ISEA had endorsed Bill Murray. Newspapers reported that the ISEA had endorsed Bill Murray. The fact of the matter is that nobody at the ISEA ever formally endorsed Bill Murray.

Perhaps it is better stated that Bill Murray endorsed the ISEA. Joe Gettys, the former ISEA president and superintendent from Oskaloosa, tried to explain to the delegates. "We cannot control what any political candidate decides to adopt as his program," Gettys said. "The fact that Dr. Murray did, in his platform, include the things that we have stood for for years is not our fault."

"If a candidate comes out and supports the things that we stand for, we are going to favor that candidate," Gettys continued. "It would be silly for an organization that has deeply held convictions to be silent when a candidate agrees."

Other questions came. "How come we only supported the Republican Party?" a delegate asked.

"We did not support the Republican Party," Gettys responded. "We attempted to determine the attitude of the man. No one will ever deny us the right to support candidates from both parties when they are willing to support the things we stand for."

"How come no one responded to the Governor Loveless letter?"

"We did not have time. The letter appeared in the paper on November 2 and the election was November 4."

When the tide subsided, a strangely worded motion was made, seconded, and approved by the delegates, which said, "The Delegate Assembly gives a standing vote of confidence to the groups implementing the political action program of the ISEA." Shortly thereafter, the action committee died.

CHAPTER 14

IPACE and ISEA-PAC

One can speculate about what might have happened had William Murray defeated Herschel Loveless: an increase in the sales tax, perhaps; a $30 million increase in state aid to schools, perhaps. No doubt "the groups implementing the political action program of the ISEA" would have received a standing ovation from the Delegate Assembly rather than a "standing vote of confidence."

But this was big-time partisan politics and big-time partisan politics involves taking big-time risks. Taking risks involves winning and losing. The psyche of the ISEA was too fragile to sustain a loss of such a magnitude. Other things needed to happen first. Then the ISEA could try again.

At the August 22, 1959, meeting of the Executive Board a motion was made and approved that eliminated the State Action Committee and provided that its responsibilities would be transferred to the Public Relations Committee. After that it was politics as it had been at the ISEA before J. Leonard Davies made his motion directing that the ISEA develop "a more aggressive program of activity in politics."

Eight years would pass before the issue of a political organization or structure was mentioned again during a meeting of the ISEA Executive Board. Eleven years would pass before the first (or second) ISEA political action committee was created. In the meantime, other things were happening.

Young people were entering the teaching ranks in record numbers. Many of them were political activists. President John F. Kennedy had energized an entire generation with a stirring challenge in his inaugural address, "Ask not what your country can do for you. Ask what you can do for your country." Hundreds of thousands of young people had, they believed, done things for their country. And many of those had done things through politics.

When both Senator Eugene J. McCarthy of Minnesota and Senator Robert F. Kennedy of New York entered the contest for the Democratic presidential nomination in 1968 in opposition to a sitting president, Lyndon B. Johnson, it caused quite a stir. When President Johnson withdrew from the race a few months later, it was the thousands of college students who had traveled from state to state working for their candidates who took the credit.

Many, in this generation of young people, had walked, marched, struck, sat-in, and sat-down on behalf of a hundred different causes. They had registered others to vote before they were old enough to register themselves. They had worked the polls before they were old enough to vote there. They were changing the world, or so they thought, and they were doing it through politics. Many of these newer teachers liked politics.

The teachers were changing and so were the issues. Taxes, school finance, and retirement had always been the most important issues to the ISEA. These were issues upon which most educators agreed. Therefore, there was no problem with the superintendents representing the interests of the teachers on these issues in their face-to-face lobbying sessions with legislators.

The superintendents, however, could not be trusted to represent the interests of the teachers on the emerging issues—issues such as collective bargaining and tenure. More and more of the younger teachers were interested in creating a structure or system through which they could participate directly in the political and lobbying programs of the ISEA.

Some were doing it without a structure or system. Groups of Association leaders, some whose names were very familiar, were endorsing candidates for office and publicizing the fact to members across the state. On campaign letters, their names would be followed by their ISEA positions.

During the fall campaign in 1968 it was necessary for the ISEA to write to every local president and building representative to advise them that the ISEA did not endorse candidates for office. "The use of one's official title in no way implies official ISEA sanction," the letter said. "The ISEA endorses principles rather than candidates."

Other changes were under way as well. The NEA had eschewed partisan politics from the beginning. Now the NEA was in its earliest stages of organizing for political activity and was encouraging its state affiliates to join in.

Also, on January 1, 1969, George Brown joined the ISEA staff. He would become the "father" of the ISEA-PAC. Brown was a native of Detroit,

Michigan. He had taught school for a very short period of time before joining a news wire service as a reporter. Most recently he had worked for the Iowa Republican Party and for Governor Robert Ray.

George Brown brought a different perspective to the ISEA staff in 1969. Brown said things such as, "I don't get mad. I get even," and "Fair is a sissy word."

One of Brown's jobs was to lobby, but as he said, "We cannot be persuasive without being in the political field." So Brown and others set about building a political action committee.

The 1969 Delegate Assembly approved a motion which said, "The ISEA shall make an investigation and, if feasible, organize a political action arm which should be set up in accordance with NEA recommendations and report back to the Delegate Assembly in 1970 with recommendations."

A committee was formed to investigate the possibilities. James Freeman of Cedar Rapids was named the chair. The other members of the committee were George P. Alton, Fort Madison; Robert Arnold, Cedar Rapids; Wayne Begg, Ankeny; Dr. Robert Benton, Council Bluffs; Patrick F. Ferrone, Des Moines; Richard Lee Grove, Barnum; Larry Homes, Montezuma; Ray Nyhan, Marshalltown; Rey Satory, LeMars; and Dr. Louis A. Sullivan, Oskaloosa. Politics was obviously men's work in 1969.

The committee recommended the creation of a political action committee. The recommendation was included in a report which was never officially shared with the delegates to the 1970 Assembly.

After the delegates became knowledgeable about the existence of the report and the nature of the recommendations through unofficial channels, they passed a silly motion. It said, "The Delegate Assembly recognizes that such an organization as this could exist and that this expression is advisory only."

By this motion, the ISEA-PAC was born. It was called the Iowa Political Action Committee for Education (IPACE). Those involved believed it would be dangerous for the words "Education Association" to appear in the name of the PAC. They believed it would be dangerous for the same reason that they passed a motion at Delegate Assembly authorizing the establishment of a PAC while pretending that they did not know what they were doing. "It was the law," they were told.

At the time it was created in 1970, both federal and state law required that a political action committee be established separate and apart from the parent association. There could be no formal, legal linkage between the two.

There was, however, nothing in either the federal or state law that required the ISEA to pretend it did not know that a political action committee was being organized by a group of its own members. There is no legal reason to explain the secrecy and stealth that enfogged the creation of the PAC.

Perhaps it had to do with the fact that the administrators were still a part of the ISEA in 1970. Their control had waned at all levels, but they remained influential at the Executive Board level. If the younger teachers were the driving force in the new PAC, and their primary objective was to help elect legislators to office who would vote in favor of collective bargaining and tenure, then perhaps it was preferable to have the PAC as free and independent of the Executive Board as possible.

A motion came to the Executive Board meeting in October of 1971, relating to George Brown's job responsibilities. It said, "Whenever the legislative and political action specialist is acting in the area of legislative activity, he is accountable to the Executive Board. Whenever he serves as a political action specialist, he is accountable to the IPACE Executive Board. The exact amount of time spent on political action activity will be decided by the legislative and political action specialist and/or the ISEA cabinet."

The PAC advocates had already created IPACE as an entity separate from the ISEA. Now they were staffing it. By this motion, when it came to politics, Brown would work for IPACE and not the ISEA. Not only would the ISEA Executive Board be unable to control IPACE, neither would the management of the ISEA be able to control the IPACE staff if ever the need should arise. That is the way it had to be, the people were told.

Given this beginning, it is not surprising that IPACE—later the ISEA-PAC—grew apart from the ISEA. It was an entity unto itself. While the membership and the general public perceived that the decisions made by the PAC were ISEA decisions, the Association had no control over them. While much of what the ISEA was or was not able to accomplish was impacted greatly by the decisions made by the PAC, the Association had no control over them.

The degree to which the ISEA and the ISEA-PAC were able to cooperate over the years was determined in a large part by who the officers of the two organizations happened to be at the time. A PAC "crowd" emerged. If the officers of the ISEA were part of the PAC crowd or at least friendly toward it, there was ample communication and cooperation between the two. However, if that was not the case, then the relationship between the Association and the PAC was strained.

People believed that it was a legal requirement for the two organizations to maintain their distance from one another long after it no longer was. There was nothing in the law that prohibited the political action committee from operating inside the Association. There was nothing in the law that prohibited the Association from endorsing candidates for office. There was nothing in the law that prohibited the president of the ISEA from also being the chair of the PAC.

The only things that the law required, in addition to regular reporting to government agencies, were that all of the contributions to the PAC be absolutely voluntary and that no dues money be used in public campaigns.

Not only was it legal for the PAC to be part of the Association, but there was also much to recommend it. The NEA was organized that way and so were most of the other state associations.

George Duvall was the first ISEA president to raise the issue. In 1981, he appointed a committee to study the matter. It was not until five years later, however, that the Delegate Assembly, as part of the long-range planning process, directed that the ISEA-PAC be abolished as a separate entity and that it be reconstituted as a committee of the ISEA. It was done shortly thereafter.

In the meantime, IPACE hit the ground running. Its first endorsements were made on May 6, 1972, following an old-time political rally in Monticello. The endorsements were for Robert D. Ray for renomination as governor and Arthur Neu for nomination as lieutenant governor. Both Ray and Neu were Republicans. IPACE also endorsed John Tapscott for nomination as governor in the Democratic primary.

Ray and Neu were successful in their primary elections and both were then endorsed by IPACE for election to office in the fall. IPACE also endorsed Democratic candidate Dick Clark for election to the United States Senate over the Republican incumbent Jack Miller. All three were successful in November. It was an auspicious beginning.

In short order, IPACE became a fixture in Iowa politics. Candidates enthusiastically sought the support of the "ISEA." An IPACE endorsement did not mean much in terms of money for the candidate. Often, there was no money at all. Until very recently the ISEA-PAC did not have much money. But the ISEA had members everywhere, in virtually every precinct in the state. A fair number of those members were enthusiastic about politics and were willing to work for candidates who had been endorsed by the Association. The volunteers were more valuable to candidates than money.

Also, the ISEA was well respected throughout the state. A good education platform had always been good politics is Iowa. Therefore, the candidates viewed the ISEA endorsement as a seal of approval. It said to the voters that the candidates were good for education and it helped them to get votes.

That period, from the day early in May of 1972 when the PAC made its first endorsements through the remainder of the decade of the 1970s, would be the most productive legislative period in the history of the ISEA. In addition to collective bargaining and job security, major gains were made in school finance, retirement, and a number of other important areas.

The success was the result of the confluence of a number of different factors. Of those, it was the establishment of the PAC that was most significant. Aeschylus wrote, "I cannot weep for you lest you grieve." Teachers finally demanded fairness and equity from the politicians who were ultimately responsible for their fate. They backed their demands with promises and threats, some of them direct and some of them implied. The politicians responded. That is the way the system works and always has. The teachers had never been a part of the system before. It was as simple as that.

CHAPTER 15

The PAC and the Members

While the ISEA-PAC has been extremely successful, it has never been universally popular with the members. Some members dislike politics. Other members object to political action committees. Nearly everyone has been offended by a particular PAC recommendation or two over the years. But by far the most common complaint has been, "I resent being told for whom to vote!"

It has never been the intention of the ISEA to tell its members for whom to vote. From the earliest days of the SAC, DAC, CAC, and LAC, through IPACE and ISEA-PAC, it has been the intent of the ISEA to share information. What the news of an endorsement is intended to convey is that a group of teachers has considered the candidates and their positions on the issues and has determined that one of the candidates has positions that are more closely aligned with the positions of the ISEA than have the others. There is nothing more intended, and nothing less.

Leaders of the Association understand that a candidate's position on education issues is only one of the factors that will influence how a member votes. When all of the factors are weighed, some members will vote for the other candidate.

The ISEA retained a West Des Moines firm, Quester, to do attitudinal research among the members. Quester reported that the term "endorsement" was offensive to members. The term "recommendation" was not, however. Therefore, since the research was completed, the ISEA-PAC has "recommended" candidates rather than "endorsed" them.

The second most common complaint has been that the ISEA-PAC always endorses the Democratic candidates. That statement is not true. A statement to the effect that the ISEA-PAC always endorses a lot more Democratic candidates than Republican candidates would be true. There are two reasons.

First, there is a Democratic bias inside the Association. While the membership of the Association is divided almost equally among Democrats, Republicans, and Independents, with a modest advantage to the Democrats, the staff and leadership of the Association are heavily Democratic. Almost all of the professional and management staff are Democrats. Almost all of the officers have been Democrats. And, since the late 1970s, the larger percentage of the members of the Executive Board have been Democrats, too.

While the ISEA-PAC Central Committee, which is responsible for making recommendations for candidates for statewide office, is comprised of an equal number of Democrats and Republicans according to the guidelines, there never are an equal number of the two at the meetings. There are always more Democrats than Republicans in attendance. As a result, there have been occasions when a Democrat has been recommended when a Republican probably should have been, but not too often.

More often, more Democrats are recommended for office than Republicans because there are more Democrats than Republicans who support ISEA positions.

As an Association that represents the interests of public school employees, the ISEA has always pushed for a steady and plentiful source of funding for schools. Some have said, "The ISEA never met a tax that it did not like." Also, the ISEA supports legislation that would strengthen collective bargaining and job security — union issues, to some. In these areas, the ISEA is more often at odds with Republicans than it is with Democrats. As a result, fewer of them are recommended.

Over the years, the close relationship between the ISEA and the Democratic Party lost some of its luster. The Republican Party came to disregard the Association fairly early. Shortly thereafter, the Democratic Party began to take the Association for granted. Democratic legislators said things such as, "If you think you can get a better deal from the Republicans, why don't you try?"

By the early 1980s the ISEA was popularly viewed as an adjunct of the Iowa Democratic Party. As a result, the ISEA had little or no leverage with the Republicans and a diminishing amount of leverage with the Democrats.

CHAPTER 16

The Terry E. Branstad Affair

The relationship between the ISEA and the two political parties was a special concern for Ken Tilp when he became president of ISEA in 1986.

Tilp was one of the PAC "crowd." Involvement in ISEA-PAC had been his entrée to statewide Association activities. He was also a Democrat—a doctrinaire, straight-ticket, party-line, Dubuque Democrat. Tilp was also a wily political strategist. He understood that being perceived as an adjunct of the Democratic Party was not serving the best interests of the ISEA. It became one of his objectives to help the ISEA become more bipartisan in its politics.

Tilp got help from an unexpected source: Republican Governor Terry E. Branstad. It was unexpected because the ISEA and Branstad had never been friends—not while he was a legislator, not while he was lieutenant governor, and not during his first term as governor.

Branstad had consistently opposed virtually every ISEA priority. As a legislator, he had voted against collective bargaining and tenure. As governor he had vetoed the professional standards board bill and improvements in the collective bargaining and tenure laws.

When Terry Branstad ran for governor the first time, in 1982, the ISEA-PAC had endorsed his opponent, former U.S. Attorney Roxanne Conlin. In fact, when Branstad arrived at Salisbury House for his interview with the screening committee, he inquired as to whether it was really necessary to proceed, since he had observed that most of the cars in the parking lot had "Roxanne" stickers on them. A truthful answer to Branstad would have been that there was no need to proceed.

The members of the screening committee were in the same frame of mind four years later. This time the opponent was Senate Majority Leader Lowell Junkins, a "friend" of the ISEA's. Phoebe Tupper, the former ISEA president, had resigned her position before her term was up in order to join the Junkins campaign staff. Again, the deed was done before the interview. Junkins was the ISEA-PAC's candidate.

This time, however, Branstad said some strange and unusual things during the interview; at least they were strange and unusual things for Terry Branstad to say. He talked about more money for schools and, specifically, he talked about more money for teachers' salaries. The members of the interview committee were intrigued by the Governor's comments, but they did not believe him. Junkins was the candidate.

Within weeks of his re-election as governor, Branstad invited ISEA lobbyists Ron Livermore and Jan Reinicke and representatives of the Iowa Association of School Boards and the State Department of Education to meet with his chief of staff, Douglas Gross, for the purpose of hammering out the details of a legislative proposal to increase teacher salaries in Iowa by $100 million.

Agreement was reached over the Christmas holidays. The Governor would propose a mandated statewide minimum salary of $18,000. The Governor would propose that those teachers who were not affected by the new minimum salary would receive a salary increase averaging approximately $1,000 that would be funded by the state and would be paid in addition to the negotiated raises. Finally, the Governor would propose that approximately $50 million would be set aside to be paid to teachers for doing "more or better." The Governor was set to propose that teachers' salaries be increased by almost $3,000 each, on the average, over and above the negotiated increments and raises.

The legislators, both the majority Democrats and the minority Republicans, were stunned. This was out of character for Terry Branstad. The Democrats were also angry at the ISEA. The ISEA had "cut a deal" with a Republican governor without even so much as the courtesy of telling the Democrats that they were in the process of doing it. "If you think you can get a better deal, . . ." echoed under the Golden Dome.

The Governor devoted his second inaugural address to education. The address was delivered in January. House File 499, as the proposal became known, did not pass the Legislature until 2 a.m. on Mother's Day. It was one of its last acts.

Some legislators in the Democratic leadership worked throughout the session to scale back the Governor's proposal. They worked hard to pass a version at $70 million. In the end, it was a $92 million version that was enacted.

For many teachers it was the largest single raise they had ever received in their careers. A number of teachers who had planned to retire decided to stay on the job for another year or two because a raise of this size would have a significant impact on retirement earnings for the rest of their lives.

Those who thought that "pigs would fly" before the teachers and Terry Branstad would be friends started looking skyward.

The relationship between Governor Branstad and the ISEA remained cordial and productive throughout his second term. There were rumblings among the Democrats and rumors of more deals between the two. While there were many conversations, there were never any deals. Neither Branstad nor the ISEA ever offered any.

The Governor brought all of the various education organizations together to work cooperatively in developing a new school finance formula. But there were no deals.

Doug Gross, the Governor's aide, told me that the Governor, having vetoed a standards board bill during his first term, would welcome another opportunity to sign one. Another one was passed by the Legislature and this time the Governor signed it. But there was no deal.

Finally, it was election time again. Governor Branstad was a candidate for a third term. The Democrats nominated Don Avenson, the speaker of the House of Representatives, to oppose him.

The race pitted an incumbent Republican Governor with one good term in office against a Democratic challenger with a history of support for the Association's issues over the course of a long career. It was a terrible conflict for the ISEA.

In Ken Tilp's opinion, supporting Governor Branstad was the wisest choice for the ISEA. There were two powerful arguments. First, if two excellent candidates are seeking the same office and one of them is the incumbent, it is smarter to recommend the incumbent. And second, if the ISEA fails to recommend Governor Branstad for re-election after his $100 million boost in salaries, the standards board, and a number of other smaller items, then the ISEA might as well put up a sign that says "Republicans need not apply." Maybe the members who complain are correct. The ISEA only supports Democrats.

The Branstad campaign actively solicited the support of the ISEA. Doug Gross, who by now had left the Governor's staff to enter private law practice, asked, on the Governor's behalf, what he would have to say in an interview in order to secure the recommendation.

It was obvious at this point that the easiest way out for the ISEA-PAC interview committee would be to recommend both of the candidates. I suggested to Gross that the Governor tell the committee members that he felt that he had earned the support of the ISEA and that he was not interested in a co-recommendation.

Also, Avenson and the other two Democratic candidates had interviewed with ISEA-PAC prior to the primary election. There was no plan to interview him again. During his interview, in response to a question, Avenson had refused to commit himself to raising the average salary for teachers in Iowa to the national average within four years. He had said it was a worthwhile goal, something to shoot for, but not something to which he would absolutely commit himself.

I suggested to Gross that it would be very helpful to the Governor if, when the question was asked, he would state unequivocally that he would raise Iowa's teacher salaries to the national average in four years.

During the course of the interview, Branstad took both pieces of advice. He told the committee that he felt he had earned the support of the ISEA and that he was not interested in a co-recommendation. He also committed himself to raising Iowa's teacher salaries to the national average in four years.

The interview committee determined to recommend Governor Branstad to the larger ISEA-PAC Central Committee, a group of 100 or so, who would make a recommendation to the ISEA Executive Board.

In the meantime, Tilp went to work on the Central Committee and the Executive Board. It required a 58 percent affirmative vote by the Central Committee to recommend a candidate. In all likelihood, two-thirds of the committee members who would show up for the meeting would be Democrats. That meant that Tilp needed to maximize the number of Republicans who attended and make certain that they would support Governor Branstad. He also needed to persuade at least one-half of the Democrats who would be there to do the same thing.

It was a piece of political organizing unmatched in the history of the ISEA-PAC. Just as there had been no need for Branstad to show up for his interviews in 1982 or in 1986, there was no need for the Avenson supporters among the ISEA-PAC Central Committee members to show up on June 9, 1990. Tilp had methodically worked the committee roster, member by member, until he had the votes he needed. Just as the Iowa Democratic Party had come to take the ISEA for granted, so had a number of the hard core Democratic Party loyalists inside the ISEA-PAC.

Everyone had his say. The debate lasted for more than five hours. A number of the long-time observers said it was the best debate they had ever heard at an Association meeting. That is probably because both sides had a strong argument to make.

The motion was to recommend the re-election of Governor Terry E. Branstad. The vote was 56 yes and 31 no. It was 64.3 percent yes, comfortably above the 58 percent that was needed. The motion had carried. The ISEA Executive Board convened immediately thereafter. They concurred with the recommendation of the ISEA-PAC Central Committee by a vote of 22 yes to 5 no.

The Aftermath

The ISEA did not become bipartisan in its politics on that day. The ISEA-PAC has continued to recommend far more Democrats than Republicans. It probably always will. There is a Democratic bias at the ISEA. Also, Democratic candidates agree with the positions of the ISEA more often than Republicans do. Perhaps the two go together.

Everyone expected the ISEA to recommend Don Avenson on June 9, 1990.

That is what the media expected. Almost no one showed up for the news conference. It was not news that the ISEA had endorsed Don Avenson. He was the Democrat in the race, was he not? When the reporters found out that it was Terry Branstad who had been selected, they all wanted interviews.

That is what the political leaders expected to happen, both the Democrats and the Republicans. The Republicans who had warned the Governor that he would never get the support of the ISEA, no matter how many $100 millions he came up with, would have said, "I told you so." That would have been the only fallout from the political party folk.

That is what the ISEA members expected. ISEA-PAC had become predictable as far as the members were concerned. If all the Association was going to recommend was Democrats, the Association really did not have to recommend anyone at all. The members already knew the choices before the decisions were even made. The process was a farce, some thought.

The ISEA-PAC came of age on June 9, 1990. Whether the specific decision was the correct one or not will be debated for years. What is important is that the political action committee members did not take the easy way out. They faced up to a very difficult decision. By doing so, the PAC became more credible with both of the political parties. Most importantly, by doing so, the ISEA-PAC became more credible with ISEA members.

CHAPTER 17

Collective Bargaining

On February 5, 1966, the Delegate Assembly took action putting the ISEA on record in favor of collective bargaining. It was the first time.

The motion said, "The ISEA believes that local professional associations have the professional right and should have the mandatory legal right, through appropriate professional channels and democratically selected representatives, including classroom teachers, to negotiate with boards of education in determination of policies affecting professional services of teachers, including improvement of instruction, curriculum planning, salaries, and other conditions of work."

An amending motion came from Linn County to delete the word "mandatory." The amendment was defeated.

It had been coming for a long time. The first high-ranking ISEA official to openly advocate collective bargaining was Executive Secretary John Harold in 1962. "Teachers are no longer content to wait for 50 years to have things happen," Harold said. "They are restless to gain the right to bargain, the right to contribute to school policy."

"I think we need to work out a definite policy for negotiations between teachers in Iowa and boards of education," Harold continued. "I think we have to develop some sort of an approach for arbitration and specifically be opposed to such things as a strike."

Because the ISEA had not been in favor of collective bargaining before does not mean it had been oblivious to the welfare needs of the members over the years. Quite the contrary. The Association had historically advocated higher teacher salaries. The Association had also advocated that salaries be distributed to teachers in a fair and equitable manner.

The 1961 Delegate Assembly defined what a fair and equitable distribution of salaries would entail. Several decades later it is still a good statement. According to the delegates, a professional salary schedule should:

- be based upon preparation, teaching experience, and professional growth

- provide a beginning salary adequate to attract capable young people into the profession

- include increments sufficient to double the beginning salary within ten years

- be developed cooperatively by school board members, administrators, and teachers

- permit no discrimination as to grade or subject taught, residence, creed, race, sex, marital status, or number of dependents

- recognize experience and advanced education through the doctor's degree

- recognize, by appropriate ratios, the responsibilities of administrators and other school personnel

- be applied in practice.

The ISEA encouraged every local association to form a salary committee each year. The ISEA provided the local salary committees with research documents and workbooks so that they would understand the finances of their districts and how their salaries compared with the salaries paid to other teachers in the state of Iowa. All of this was to help the local salary committee prepare for its annual meeting with the school board, where the teachers would present their salary requests for the coming year.

The ISEA also held a salary school each year. It was usually held on a university campus sometime in late January. It was one of the Association's big events of the year. Hundreds of local leaders attended.

The ISEA also believed that teachers should be treated fairly in other matters, not just salary. The Association maintained a manual of model personnel policies, which it provided to school boards and administrators. Had the school boards adopted all of the model policies recommended by the ISEA and had the administrators enforced them, schools would have been happy places for teachers to work.

The problem was that teachers were not treated fairly. Schools were not happy places for teachers to work. Except for lip service and moral support from time to time, the ISEA had done very little to help. It was time, according to the teachers and the principals (surveys showed that principals supported collective bargaining, too), to put all of the flowery language into enforceable contracts. In most districts that would require a new law making collective bargaining mandatory; otherwise it would not happen. That is why the delegates voted the way they did on February 5, 1966.

The ISEA submitted its first collective bargaining bill to the Iowa General Assembly in 1967 without much enthusiasm or fanfare. It extended bargaining rights only to certified school employees. It provided for mediation to help resolve disputes. It also provided for binding arbitration, but only if both parties agreed at the time of impasse. The bill died in committee.

At the 1968 Delegate Assembly, the IACT made certain that collective bargaining became a legislative priority. The motion which passed the Assembly said that collective bargaining would be "the primary goal of the Association's 1969 legislative program."

President Elmer Gast appointed a special committee to define the parameters for the proposed legislation. Wayne Begg of Ankeny was chairman of the committee. He was joined by elected leaders Dennis Barnum, Freda Caviness, and James Freeman; Executive Secretary Kenneth Wells; staff members Duane Lodge and Bill Robinson; and attorney Marvin Adams. Their work guided the legislative effort for the next several years.

Who would be eligible to bargain and how the bargaining units would be defined were stumbling blocks in the early legislative efforts.

It was the position of the ISEA that all employees, with the exception of the superintendent of schools, should be eligible to organize for collective bargaining.

It was also the position of the ISEA that how the bargaining units were defined was a matter for the people to decide at the local level. If they wanted one big bargaining unit with all of the teachers and administrators included, that was the way it should be, according to the ISEA. However, if they wanted one bargaining unit for the teachers and another one for the administrators, that was all right, too.

The Iowa Association of School Boards thought that the position of the ISEA was a bit strange. It was the IASB's position that only non-supervisory employees should be eligible to organize. Most of the legislators, who were not anxious to sanction collective bargaining for anybody, sided with the IASB.

It was the position of the ISEA at the time that it would be better for none of its members to have collective bargaining rights than it would be for only some of its members to have them.

It was in this context that Elmer Gast said, "It would only be a matter of time before the ISEA would lose most, if not all, of its members except for the classroom teachers. Then it would no longer be an association of the profession, but merely a classroom teachers association, a much weaker association."

In the meantime, while things floundered in the Legislature, more and more local associations commenced to bargain with their school boards in the absence of a law. By the fall of 1968, 15 local associations had written agreements with their school districts. It was not bargaining as Iowans would come to know it under the law, but it was more formal than the process had been before. Slowly, more and more items were being discussed and more and more agreements were being reduced to writing.

In January, 1971, *The Communique* reported, "Davenport educators will be negotiating this year with an agreement that will allow them to discuss with the board of education the full range of educational issues including salaries, grievances, class size, teaching load, performance of non-teaching duties, teacher evaluations, and curriculum changes. The agreement is the first master contract for educators to be approved in Iowa."

CHAPTER 18

Inside the ISEA . . .

One of the more unusual developments in the history of collective bargaining with ISEA occurred shortly after the NEA Representative Assembly in 1966.

By that summer, several state legislatures had actually enacted collective bargaining statutes. Increasingly, the debate at the NEA Representative Assembly focused on bargaining, grievances, litigation, and strikes. The delegates from the larger, more industrial, states and the delegates from the urban local associations said things that made most of the other delegates feel uncomfortable.

Now, in 1966, a new issue emerged at the Assembly. It was an issue that most delegates had never considered before. Should the employees of the NEA and the employees of the state education associations be allowed to organize unions and participate in collective bargaining?

Some delegates did not like the idea of teachers bargaining with their employers, let alone their hired staff. Other delegates thought it was probably all right for the teachers to do it, but they seriously doubted that it was a good idea for the staff.

The delegates were told that it did not really matter whether they liked it or not. The staff had a right to organize and bargain if they wanted to. They were private sector employees covered by the provisions of the National Labor Relations Act (NLRA). If the employees followed the provisions of the law, the National Labor Relations Board (NLRB) would see to it that they had access to collective bargaining.

Having learned about the NLRA and the NLRB, the NEA Representative Assembly delegates resolved that the national and state education associations were encouraged to engage in professional negotiations with their employees.

At the very next meeting of the Executive Board, only two weeks later, President-Elect Elmer C. Gast raised the issue. "In light of the nationwide movement in regard to teachers' salaries and the recent resolution passed by the NEA which encourages professional negotiations by staff members, maybe," Gast suggested, "the ISEA should take a look at the possibility of developing an agreement for negotiations with our staff."

Several Executive Board members commented to the effect that the ISEA Executive Board should be the leader and should set a good example for the local affiliates.

After considerable positive discussion, Roger Blake moved that "the staff be extended the privilege of beginning to develop, in cooperation with the executive secretary, an agreement for staff organization for professional negotiations, including salaries." The motion carried.

At the Executive Board meeting on September 17, 1966, Wayne Begg, chairman of the personnel committee, reported that he and his committee had met with a delegation of staff members. "We asked," Begg said, "that the staff organize, if they so desire, in order that the Executive Board would have a group with which they could establish negotiations."

On October 21, C. William Pritchard, a member of the field staff, met with the Executive Board. He advised the board that the staff had agreed to take them up on their offer. They had organized and Pritchard was the new staff association president.

Pritchard proceeded to distribute copies of the first professional agreement. The staff had taken the liberty of preparing one on their own and he wished to explain the various provisions to the Executive Board.

Once Pritchard finished, Elmer Gast said that the agreement looked pretty good. "However," he added, "binding arbitration is not in keeping with the philosophy of a true profession." He asked Pritchard to go back to his association and rework that part of his proposal.

Executive Board member Jim Harris of Des Moines worried that perhaps this process was taking too much time and research. He asked Pritchard if he was using the ISEA equipment.

Pritchard responded, "It doesn't take much time. There are only 49 other states to compare with."

With a little tinkering here and there on Pritchard's professional agreement, the parties consummated a deal. The first professional staff contract was signed by James W. Freeman, president, on behalf of the ISEA and by C. William Pritchard, president, on behalf of the Professional Staff Education Association. It is dated January 6, 1967.

The great irony, of course, is that the union representing the professional staff of the ISEA—who for years included the Mother Jones quotation, "Pray for the dead and fight like hell for the living," on its union stationery—was organized in the beginning at the request of the school administrators who sat as members of their employer's governing board.

CHAPTER 19

The Trouble in Keokuk

"Lead the way," Paul Gaylord told the Lee County Deputy Sheriff. With that, he and three of his teaching colleagues were led away to their cells in the city jail.

Paul Gaylord was treasurer of the Keokuk Education Association (KEA). His colleagues were the other three officers of the KEA: Tom Coffey, the president; Gene Ylitalo, the vice president; and Billie Peters, the secretary.

The four were about to become the first and only Association officers ever to be jailed in Iowa for contempt of court. They had already racked up an impressive list of other "first-and-onlys." This was simply one more.

The KEA was the first and only Association in Iowa to go on strike against a public school district. One day later, the KEA became the first and only Association in Iowa to be ordered back to work by a judge. One day after that, the KEA became the first and only Association in Iowa to violate a judge's order.

For many, Keokuk seemed an odd place for all of this to happen. In the spring of 1970, the Keokuk Public Schools were looked upon across the state as a model of progressive education. They had pioneered in the area of sex education. They had a higher percentage of teachers with masters' degrees than almost any other district in the state. The local citizens were proud and supportive of their schools.

Relatively speaking, the teachers had been treated well over the years. Their salaries and benefits were generous compared to what most other teachers in Iowa received.

Their administrators had been among the more enlightened. Though he had left the school system, it was just two years before that the Keokuk superintendent, Elmer C. Gast, had served as ISEA president.

Probably the best evidence of how enlightened and progressive the Keokuk school system was lay in the fact that the school board members bargained with their teachers even though they did not have to do it. Not only that, the bargaining agreement between the Keokuk School Board and the KEA was considered to be a model by the ISEA.

A number of school districts "bargained" with their teachers in 1970, but Keokuk was one of only a handful of districts that had what the ISEA termed a "Level III" agreement.

A Level III agreement meant that the Keokuk Board of Education had formally recognized the KEA as the bargaining agent for the teachers. It meant that the parties had mutually agreed to a bargaining procedure. It also meant that the parties had mutually agreed to an impasse resolution procedure in case they might be unable to arrive at an agreement by themselves. It was the latter provision that distinguished Level III agreements from Level II agreements, according to the ISEA definitions.

While there were a number of lesser issues upon which the parties disagreed, the salary schedule index was the single major issue which seriously divided the school board and the Association.

Throughout bargaining the KEA had sought to improve the index so that the maximum salary on the schedule would be twice the beginning salary. Throughout bargaining the school board had sought to eliminate the index entirely.

Bargaining between the KEA and the school board reached an impasse in early March. Pursuant to the agreed-upon procedures, the two parties requested that a mediator be appointed by the Iowa Superintendent of Public Instruction.

Professor William Monahan of the State University of Iowa was appointed. He worked with the parties for seven days in an effort to arrive at a settlement, but to no avail. In a last-ditch effort to secure a contract, Monahan agreed to make a mediator's recommendation. He recommended that the present index be maintained and that it be applied to a base salary of $6,775.

The Keokuk Education Association accepted the recommendations of the mediator. The Board of Education turned them down.

On April 17 the school board unilaterally adopted a salary schedule of its own without an index and declared that the matter was settled. The total cost of the package adopted by the board was $21,000 less than the total cost of the package that had been recommended by Professor Monahan. The

$21,000 difference amounted to $107 for each Keokuk teacher.

The KEA leaders explained the issue to the community and they discovered that there was a considerable amount of support for their position. The teachers were the "good guys" in the dispute. They had agreed to accept the recommendations of the impartial mediator even though he had recommended less than they wanted. Many local citizens did not understand why the school board could not be as reasonable as the teachers.

The teachers met at the Trinity United Methodist Church at 5:30 a.m. on Wednesday, May 6. They voted to go on strike. Of the 196 teachers in Keokuk, only 16, 28, or 34 went to work that morning. The KEA reported 16. The school superintendent, Robert Leland, reported 28 and 34.

No classes were held that day. The school board determined that the "administrative day" scheduled for June 5 would be rescheduled for May 6. Classes were scheduled on Thursday for grades one through six and the senior class. Classes were scheduled on Friday for grades one through six only. By using administrators, teachers who had crossed the picket lines, and substitute teachers, the district was able to secure enough personnel to operate a limited program.

It appears that they had better luck securing teachers than they had securing students. The KEA asked the parents to keep their children at home. The administration reported 518 absences on Thursday, which was twice the normal number. There were widespread rumors that the senior class intended to boycott school on Friday, which is why the decision was made to cancel their classes.

Meanwhile, the action for the striking teachers shifted to district court. The school board petitioned the court to end the walkout. On Wednesday afternoon, following a one-hour hearing, Judge J. R. Leary issued an injunction "enjoining and restraining the KEA from striking and picketing around or near any school building."

According to Judge Leary, "The members of the KEA are public employees and public employees do not have the right to strike in the state of Iowa."

The striking teachers were buoyed by support from the local community, the ISEA, and the NEA. The school custodians joined the strike. The Keokuk Trades and Labor Assembly voted unanimously to support the teachers. The ISEA sent attorney Marvin Adams and staff member Neil Curtis. The ISEA also sent a check for $1,000 to help pay for the KEA's public relations campaign. The NEA sent staff member Dale Lestina.

The members of the KEA voted to defy the injunction and continue the strike. "The ethical and professional considerations and obligations outweigh the legal obligations of the injunction," said the news release issued by the KEA.

The four officers of the KEA were ordered back to court at 2 p.m. on Friday, May 8, to show cause as to why they should not be held in contempt.

Attorney Adams asked the judge for more time in order to prepare his arguments. The judge offered Adams more time, provided that the officers of the KEA would agree to call off the strike and return to school on Monday morning. Adams consulted with the officers and they refused.

The hearing went forward. It only took 15 minutes. The four officers were found to be in willful contempt of the court. The KEA was fined $250 and the four officers were ordered to jail. According to Judge Leary, "They would remain there until they ordered an end to the illegal strike."

Coffey, Ylitalo, Gaylord, and Peters were led away. They were joined at the city jail by Les Fowler and several other members of the school board. Bargaining resumed. By daybreak there was an agreement.

The parties had agreed to keep the salary schedule index and apply it to a base salary of $6,775, just as the mediator had recommended. The school board had agreed to provide each teacher with a $5,000 term life insurance policy. The teachers had agreed to give up their dependency allowance and the $140 bonus that had been paid to teachers with masters' degrees in the same field as the subjects they taught. Both parties had agreed to no reprisals. The school board would take no punitive action against the teachers who had struck and the Association would take no punitive action against the teachers who had not.

At 10 a.m. on Saturday, May 9, the officers of the KEA were free. They had been behind bars for only 19 hours. Thus ended the first and only public school teacher strike in the history of the state of Iowa.

"Now that it has happened, it probably will again," said T. E. "Ted" Davidson of Cedar Falls, the president of the Iowa Association of School Boards. "It is always easier the second time."

"There will be widespread teachers' strikes in Iowa," said Dale Lestina of the NEA staff, "as long as there is second-class citizenship for public employees."

Dale Lestina was wrong. Teacher strikes did not become widespread in Iowa. Amazingly, Ted Davidson was also wrong. It never happened again, never once.

The Association benefited from the Keokuk strike in an unusual way. Four of the strikers became staff members. The president, Tom Coffey, became a member of the association staff in Wisconsin. Gerald Ott and Clewis Walden have served the ISEA in a variety of capacities since being hired some 20 years ago. Lynn Tobin taught for another 10 years before she was hired by the Association. She served as a UniServ director until her death in 1992.

There is no doubt that what happened in Keokuk was an act of courage on the part of the teachers. Striking, even where it is legal, involves risks. Violating a court order involves grave risks. Even in places where there is a labor tradition, the state associations do not support the violation of injunctions. Judge Leary was lenient with the officers of the KEA.

As time passed, the Keokuk strike became bigger than life. It became part of the folklore of the Association. Decades later one is surprised to discover that it lasted for only three days and that the officers were in jail for only 19 hours. It must have been longer than that.

It was a little strike, but it had a big impact. The cry, "We do not want another Keokuk, do we?" was common in the halls of the state Legislature during the debate on the collective bargaining bill. Perhaps, had the teachers of Keokuk not risen up in righteous indignation at the high-handed tactics of the school board in stripping away their salary schedule index, the rest of the teachers of Iowa would have waited a little while longer than they did for collective bargaining.

CHAPTER 20

Finally...

Encouraged by success in the November elections, the ISEA determined that the time was right to secure passage of a collective bargaining law. Everyone was certain that 1973 would be the year. The Association lobbyists, George Brown and John Vint, had a lot of work ahead of them.

"Sometimes you can measure progress by the intensity of your opposition," according to Brown. By that standard, things looked pretty good for the ISEA.

A statewide committee had been formed for the first time to oppose collective bargaining. The committee, called the "Citizens for Public Rights," was worried, they said, about higher taxes and teacher strikes. Most of the names on their letterhead were farmers and building contractors, but a University of Northern Iowa professor, Wayne Truesdell, and the Harlan school superintendent, Orville Frazier, were also included.

The Iowa Association of School Boards (IASB) and the Iowa Association of School Administrators (IASA) were, of course, ready to do battle. So were the Iowa Farm Bureau, the various chambers of commerce, the Iowa Association of Manufacturers, and the Iowa Taxpayers Association. It was a formidable lot.

The IASB and the IASA were opposed to collective bargaining no matter what form it might take, but they were realistic enough to see the handwriting on the wall. Therefore, they concentrated their lobbying efforts on two issues: the scope of bargaining and the impasse-resolution procedures. It was the objective of the two organizations to define scope as narrowly as possible. It was also their objective that mediation serve as the terminal step of the bargaining process.

The two organizations were opposed both to strikes and to binding arbitration. Their position on collective bargaining was consistent with their position on teacher tenure. In the final analysis, no one should have the right to substitute his or her judgment for the judgment of a local school board. It simply was not right.

The ISEA-backed bill started in the Senate. Compared to what would happen in the House of Representatives, things went smoothly there. With support from both parties, the Senate passed a version of the bill with votes to spare. In fact, nearly two-thirds of the Senators had supported the measure.

The bill was too controversial in the House of Representatives and it arrived there too late for it to be handled during the 1973 session. Instead, the House scheduled it for floor action on February 20, 1974.

The Senate version of the bill was in good shape as far as the ISEA was concerned. It made collective bargaining mandatory upon the demand of one party or the other. It contained broad scope language and it provided for binding arbitration to resolve bargaining impasses.

The situation with the bill in the House of Representatives was tenuous at best as the 1974 session approached. There would be over 100 amendments proposed. The lobbyists knew that for certain.

In the House, as in the Senate, collective bargaining enjoyed both bipartisan support and bipartisan opposition.. The two floor managers for the bill were Democratic Representative Jerome Fitzgerald from Fort Dodge and Republican Representative Brice Oakley from Clinton.

On January 15, Fitzgerald and Oakley checked signals. Fitzgerald reported that he had 35 Democrats who would vote for the Senate bill. Oakley reported that he had eight Republicans. That left the two of them eight votes short of the 51 votes that they needed for passage.

It was their judgment that the votes were not there without some compromise by the ISEA. They met with Brown and Vint and the four of them focused their attention on two specific amendments.

The first was offered by Democratic Representative Lowell Norland. It would replace the broad scope language in the Senate bill with a "laundry list" of items that were mandatory subjects of bargaining. Norland's list was long and included almost all of the items that the ISEA considered to be important.

The second amendment was offered by Republican Representative Edgar Bittle. It would insert fact-finding into the impasse-resolution procedure between mediation and arbitration. Bittle was sensitive to the concern of the IASB about having settlements imposed on them by outside arbitrators. Bittle believed that by inserting fact-finding into the process, the number of voluntary settlements would be increased.

It was the belief of Fitzgerald and Oakley that if these two amendments were approved, they could produce 51 or 52 votes in favor of collective bargaining in the House of Representatives. The ISEA lobbyists gave their approval for the amendments.

It took 12 days of debate before the House passed the collective bargaining bill. The Norland and Bittle amendments were approved. Other amendments—crippling amendments—were moved one by one. One by one they were defeated, often by a single vote, once on a tie vote. It was as tense a battle as had ever been waged on the floor of the House of Representatives.

When it was over, 56 representatives had voted for collective bargaining: 39 Democrats and 17 Republicans. The good work of Representatives Fitzgerald and Oakley and lobbyists Brown and Vint, with the help of the Norland and Bittle amendments, had persuaded four more Democrats and nine more Republicans to vote for the bill.

The battle was still not over. The House version of the bill was headed back to the Senate. Despite the fact that a stronger version had passed there the previous year, the opponents of collective bargaining would take one more shot at it.

Their strategy was to attach at least one amendment to the House version so that the bill would have to be returned to the House. The ISEA urged the senators to vote for the measure in the exact form that it was in when it arrived back in their chamber. It was feared that if it was returned to the House, it would be bottled up by the opponents or sent to a conference committee where it would be seriously weakened.

Twelve amendments were filed in the Senate. One that would require that bargaining be open to the media and the public was believed to have the best chance for passage. Debate on the amendment came early and lasted for half a day. When the vote came, the amendment was defeated, with 19 senators voting yes and 30 voting no.

Two more amendments were offered and the first one was defeated. During the debate on the second one, the Senate majority leader and chief opponent of the bill, Cliff Lamborn, threw in the towel. He asked that the remaining amendments be withdrawn. They were. Thirty senators voted in favor of the House version and 20 voted against. Collective bargaining had been passed by the Iowa General Assembly.

It was signed into law by Governor Robert Ray shortly thereafter as everyone knew it would be. The new law became effective on July 1, 1974, and collective bargaining became mandatory on July 1, 1975.

CHAPTER 21

An Interesting Story

The legislative battle for collective bargaining was high drama. It has been the source for a thousand stories. Some of the stories are maddening. Others are humorous. Almost all of them are interesting. No story is more interesting than the story of J. Larry Mong.

J. Larry Mong was an elementary school principal in the Warren County, Pennsylvania, public school district. He was also the president of the Pennsylvania Association of Elementary School Principals.

He was a glib young man, adept at turning a phrase. He spoke forcefully about the evils of collective bargaining. As a result, he was much in demand as a speaker at conferences and conventions of school board members, school administrators, and others of like-mind on the topic at hand.

Collective bargaining was much on the mind of the IASB leaders as they planned for their annual convention in the fall of 1972. The ISEA's political action committee had made collective bargaining an issue during the fall campaign and they had done very well in the elections. No doubt the ISEA would have a bill before the Legislature in a matter of months. J. Larry Mong seemed to be the right person to give a speech at the IASB convention.

Mong spoke to a full house on November 16, 1972. He did not disappoint his audience. He said, "Now keep in mind I am not a big-city principal and I do not have militant, big-city type teachers or professional groups pushing me all the time. Still, it has come to the point where I may no longer walk or go into any of my teachers' rooms unless I have a member of the union, the building steward, with me before I talk to a teacher."

He continued, "I no longer have the privilege of asking a teacher to come into my office and speak to her about the children in her classroom, or about curriculum, or about anything that is going on in my school unless the building steward accompanies that teacher for fear I may say something that is grievable at a later time."

He added, "I must now pay my teachers $7.50 an hour to attend PTA meetings. I now pay my teachers $7.50 an hour to meet after school with parents for a parent conference because when the 3 o'clock bell rings, they are done—they teach no longer, they work no longer."

Mong's speech was music to the ears of the school board members. They made lots of copies, both on tape and in print. The copies were distributed widely. The tapes were played for service clubs and church groups. Superintendents and principals had staff meetings and played the tape for their teachers. Everyone was aghast to learn of the horrible things that could happen once teachers were given the right to bargain with their employers.

The problem was that everything J. Larry Mong said was a lie. That lie was exposed by a cooperative effort by ISEA and the Pennsylvania State Education Association (PSEA). ISEA's public relations staffer, Bill Sherman, listened to Mong's anti-collective bargaining speech. It sounded too bad to be true to Sherman who decided to purchase the cassette tapes sold by IASB. Sherman sent the tape to his counterpart at PSEA, Fred Leuschner. Leuschner forwarded the tape to a PSEA field representative who shared it with teachers in Mong's building.

Mong's diatribe enraged Warren County teachers as well as Superintendent Howard A. Thompson.

In the meantime, ISEA's Neil Curtis informed IASB's Blythe Conn that Mong's report about conditions in Warrensburg was a fabrication. Conn said he would correct this misinformation if he received a letter from Mong informing him he had lied about the relationships in Warrensburg.

Sherman informed Leuschner about Conn's comments. Soon a letter of apology arrived at IASB headquarters. Conn then wrote to superintendents and members of the Iowa General Assembly that Mong had written to him admitting the comments he had made in this IASB speech about staff relationships in Warrensburg were not true.

Superintendent Howard A. Thompson said, "It is my firm belief that the Warren County School District Board of Education and administration enjoy a very friendly, amicable, and workable relationship with the Warren County Education Association. The administering of the instructional program is in no way hampered by the negotiation process which has been in effect for several years."

John E. Eberly, a member of the board of education of the Warren County School District, agreed with Superintendent Thompson. "It is my understanding," he wrote, "that certain misinformation has been advanced concerning the Warren County School District by those who would oppose a public employees' bargaining act. The public employer - public employee relationships in the Warren County school district have advanced considerably through the use of the public employees' bargaining act. The act has provided a vehicle for the complaints of the professional employees to be made known to the board of education; consequently, we have thoroughly benefitted by this act."

Well, what did J. Larry Mong have to say in response to all of that?

Mong said that he had been misquoted. He had been talking about other school districts in Pennsylvania, not the Warren County School District.

When asked if he would like to listen to a tape recording of his speech, Mong said, "Maybe I did say those things, but unknowingly. I was talking about Pittsburgh and those places where the AFT bargains."

J. Larry Mong was had!

One can imagine Superintendent Thompson and school board member Eberly hovering over Mong while he wrote his letter to Blythe C. Conn, the executive director of the Iowa Association of School Boards.

"... The exceptionally fine educational climate in Warren County can serve as an example of the cooperation which is possible between administrative staffs, school boards, and teachers under the Pennsylvania Public Employees Relations Act," he wrote. "Teachers here are not insisting upon extra pay for attending PTA meetings, faculty representatives have not interfered with the principal's ability to run his school, and the teachers are as dedicated as they were prior to passage of the act."

After his trip to Iowa, J. Larry Mong went off the speaking circuit.

CHAPTER 22

The Next Day

Once the collective bargaining bill was signed into law by Governor Ray, the ISEA hit the ground running.

Neil Curtis had been working for the ISEA as a professional negotiations consultant since July 1, 1968, when he was transferred into that newly created position from the field services division. He had considerable experience working with those local associations whose school districts had voluntarily agreed to bargain with them in the absence of a law.

Though the outcome was by no means certain, there was great anticipation that, come February 1974, the House of Representatives would accept the version of the collective bargaining bill that the Senate had approved the previous year. Plans had been made for that happy eventuality.

Arrangements had been made with the NEA to provide special staff assistance for two years to help implement the new law. Merlin (Bud) Helstad, formerly of the Wisconsin Education Association staff, and Donna G. Walton, a teacher-leader from Michigan, arrived on the scene September 1, 1974. A year later, Walton was replaced by Nelson Okino, and Helstad was replaced by Phil Borkenhagen.

The best minds at the ISEA strategized that it would be smartest for the Association to move ahead slowly. The plan was to carefully select target districts where it was believed that good settlements could be achieved. Then, the following year, more target districts would be identified. The second wave of local associations would build upon the successes of the targets from the previous year.

The strategy did not work. There was a pent-up demand to bargain that had been released. Over the course of the next two years, some 370 master contracts would be negotiated by local affiliates of the ISEA. In just two years, 92 percent of Iowa's teachers would be protected by a legally binding, collectively bargained master contract.

The Communique reported in August, 1977: "Iowa's rapid and successful implementation of bargaining has attracted national attention. Nowhere in the country have teachers or other public employees negotiated so many contracts in such a short period of time with so few problems. We have accomplished in two years what it has taken other states eight to ten years to do."

What the Association was able to accomplish in collective bargaining in two years, from 1975 to 1977, was incredible. Still, not everything was right.

In order to secure enough votes in the House of Representatives to pass a bill, the collective bargaining proponents were forced to accept the Norland amendment, which limited the scope of bargaining to a laundry list of items.

The same article from the August, 1977, issue of *The Communique* which touted the Association's accomplishments also noted, "The current bargaining law is not perfect. For the most part, teachers have been limited to discussing mandatory economic items. They are hampered in their attempts to bargain non-mandatory items such as preparation time, class size, just cause for discharge and discipline, assignment of extra duties, and the school calendar."

Amending the law to broaden the scope of bargaining has been a legislative objective of the ISEA since the day the law was passed in 1974.

As early as March 12, 1977, the Executive Board was advised that expanding the scope of bargaining would take an "all-out, concentrated effort by all of the membership." That was good advice in 1977, and it has remained true ever since.

The ISEA has come close twice. The first time was in 1983. The lobbyists were told by the legislative leaders that an expanded scope would pass in the House, but would have tough going in the Senate. The ISEA focused its attention on the Senate.

The ISEA bill received 25 yes votes and 23 no votes. It was one vote short of passage because the rules require that a majority of the members of the chamber must support a measure in order for it to pass, not just a majority of those who are present and voting.

Senator Ted Anderson of Waterloo changed his vote from a yes to a no so that he could move for reconsideration once the 26th yes vote was found. It never was.

The ISEA came much closer in 1985. It took a conference committee working into the wee hours of the morning during the final days of the session to hammer out a compromise, but in the end, an agreement was reached. A bill providing for an expanded scope of bargaining passed both houses of the General Assembly.

In its final form, 18 new mandatory subjects of bargaining were added to the laundry list. In many cases the new items simply replaced certain topics which had been lost through court rulings and decisions by the Public Employment Relations Board. However, the addition of discipline and discharge as mandatory subjects of bargaining was a major legislative victory for the ISEA.

The bill was vetoed by Governor Terry Branstad. The ISEA has not come so close again.

The other amendment which the ISEA reluctantly agreed to accept in 1974 was the one offered by Representative Edgar Bittle. It inserted fact-finding into the impasse procedures between mediation and arbitration.

In 1991, the ISEA supported an amendment to the collective bargaining law which struck fact-finding from the process. It passed in both houses of the General Assembly and was signed by Governor Branstad.

A year later, Associate Executive Director John Vint reported to the Executive Board. "It worked as it should have," he said. "The parties are working harder to find the compromise position or settlement point, the issues in dispute were narrowed dramatically by hearing time, and it has forced school boards to bargain more than they have in the past."

Those who believed that all of the teachers' problems would be solved once they had the right to bargain with school boards were obviously wrong. Problems persist. Some of the problems that persist are the same problems that existed before collective bargaining. Some things never change, or so it seems.

At least one thing did change. And that changed for certain. Once collective bargaining became mandatory under the law, school boards and school superintendents had to listen to teachers. They had to talk with teachers about the teachers' concerns. Many of them did not do that before collective bargaining. They did not have to.

CHAPTER 23

Crackpots, Weirdos, and Perverts

The ISEA has been criticized in recent times by some who believe that incompetent teachers take refuge in Salisbury House. There are also some who believe that teachers with strange and unusual personal habits remain in their classrooms only because the ISEA has unlimited funds that it is willing to expend in order to save all of the jobs of all of its members.

Those people who think that way are wrong. The ISEA believes that incompetent teachers should find themselves another line of work. The ISEA also believes that crackpots, weirdos, perverts, child molesters, dope dealers, and others with similar strange or unusual personal habits should be in the hospital or in jail.

But the ISEA also believes that just because the "word around town" is that a teacher is incompetent does not make it so. The men and women at the grain elevators and beauty parlors are sometimes addled and confused, just as teachers are addled and confused from time to time.

Just because "rumors and gossip" about strange and unusual behavior are making the rounds of the church suppers and card parties does not mean they are true. Even if the rumors and gossip were true and a teacher's behavior was strange and unusual by church supper or card party standards, that does not necessarily mean the behavior is so unusual or so strange that firing the teacher is in order.

What the ISEA is committed to do is to make certain that every teacher who is fired deserves to be. That requires that the accused teacher know what it is that he or she is accused of doing and who it is that made the accusation. It requires that there be a hearing so that the accuser may be questioned and so that the accused may make a defense against the accusation. It requires that the final decision be made by someone who is impartial and that the decision be based only on evidence that was actually presented at the hearing. It requires that the charges must not only be true, but they must also somehow be relevant to the person's job as a teacher. The ISEA is committed to justice and due process for members.

The Old Days

There was no justice for teachers in Iowa prior to 1976. For all practical purposes a teacher could be fired anytime, anywhere, for any reason, without any recourse.

The law required that the school board notify a teacher prior to March 31 if they were contemplating his or her termination. Prior to 1967 it was not even necessary for the school board to provide the teacher with any reasons as to why it was contemplating such action. Having received the notice, the teacher had to decide in short order whether or not he or she wanted a hearing before the local school board. The teacher was entitled to a hearing according to the law, but it had to be quick. The school board only had until April 10 to make its final decision. Once the school board members' minds were made up, the matter was closed. No one or no body had the right to substitute its judgment for that of the local school board.

The law was amended in 1967. After that the school board was required to give reasons for the action it was contemplating, but any reasons would do. The law did not require that the reasons be good ones.

Some teachers took comfort once April 10 had passed without event. They believed that they were secure for one more year. They were wrong. Actually, a school board could fire a teacher anytime. Teachers who were fired after April 10 could sue the school board. But the judge had no authority to order the reinstatement of the teacher, even when the judge was convinced that the school board had the most vile of motives or the most flagrant disregard for the law. The only authority the judge possessed was the authority to assess damages after mitigation.

In other words, if the teacher who was fired after April 10 was fired from a job that paid $4,000 a year and later was able to secure a job that paid only $3,900 a year, the judge could award the teacher $100 in damages.

There was not much the ISEA could do to help teachers save their jobs in the old days. There is also not much evidence that the ISEA was troubled by that fact.

Often the ISEA staff and the Executive Board members seemed to accept the arbitrary and capricious actions of local school boards as being the way things were supposed to be. The attitude seemed to be that if a teacher was in trouble, then the teacher must have done something to deserve it.

Two examples illustrate the point.

A young male teacher from Eldora asked for the assistance of the ISEA. There were rumors of his drinking and unconventional behavior and suspicions that he was an atheist. The ISEA staff member who counseled with him recommended that he resign. "He has a brilliant mind," the staff member reported to the Executive Board. "If he can accept some of the restraints inherent in the teaching profession, he can be successful somewhere else."

Perhaps it was best for the young man to resign. The record does not divulge the extent of his drinking problem, if he had one, or the nature of his unconventional behavior, if there was any. But that is irrelevant for the purpose of this example. What is relevant are the words of the ISEA staff member, ". . . the restraints inherent in the teaching profession . . ." There was a higher standard of conduct expected for teachers than there was for everyone else. Teachers had fewer rights and privileges than did the other adults in the community. This was "inherent in the teaching profession," according to the ISEA.

The second example is from West Des Moines. Three teachers opened a pizza parlor in town. They were ordered to appear before the school board to explain why they had a right to open a business that was in competition with the businesses of taxpayers in the school district. The three teachers called the ISEA.

To the members of the ISEA Executive Board the issue was not really the business, per se. They were fairly certain that teachers had the right to own businesses in the communities where they taught. Heaven knows, many did. Farms, after all, are businesses.

No, the Executive Board was concerned about the nature of the business. What if the pizza parlor became a teenage hangout? It could damage the teachers' professional reputations. One can never be too careful when one is a teacher, according to the ISEA.

Teacher advocacy in the 1950s and 1960s meant something different to the ISEA from what it would mean later.

Martensdale

Consider the plight of the 61-year-old English teacher from Martensdale. According to the records, the lady had been teaching in Martensdale for "a good many years." "As a classroom teacher, she was excellent. No one had any complaints about her teaching," according to Frank Douma, the superintendent of schools from Ottumwa, who investigated the case for the ISEA. "That made things a little difficult for us."

The English teacher's problem was that she did not like the superintendent of schools. She told the superintendent that she did not like him. She also told other people that she did not like him.

The superintendent was a young fellow in the second year of his first superintendency. He was greatly troubled by the ongoing tension created by this nemesis. The young superintendent asked the old teacher to resign. She agreed. Then she changed her mind. The young superintendent then called the ISEA for help.

The ISEA arrived in Martensdale. Douma and ISEA staff member Ken Jonson met with the superintendent. He seemed like a nice young fellow. They met with the teacher. She seemed like a nice old lady. The men from the ISEA suggested that the two of them meet together. The superintendent accepted the offer. The teacher refused.

It was obvious now to the ISEA representatives that the teacher would have to be fired. They suggested that the best charge against her would be that she had told people, especially community people, about her feelings toward the superintendent.

The charges were filed and the 61-year-old English teacher requested a public hearing before the school board. Ken Jonson of the ISEA staff attended the hearing as an "observer."

"The community came out for the meeting. There was an audience of 30 to 40 people and most of them were sympathetic with the teacher," Jonson reported. "She was very clever. She was more able than the superintendent to present her side of the story."

When the hearing was over and the school board moved into executive session for the purpose of deliberating on what they had learned, Ken Jonson went with them.

Jonson told the school board that he was confident that the teacher had said hostile and negative things about the superintendent. For her to do so was a violation of the Code of Ethics of the Teaching Profession, according to the NEA.

According to Jonson, "That seemed to change their minds." When the school board came out of executive session to vote, three members voted to fire the teacher and two voted against.

Urbana

This story from Urbana has a happy ending. A young man fresh from the Iowa State Teachers College accepted a job teaching English to seventh- and eighth-graders. Being up-to-date on the latest teaching techniques, he determined, on his own, to dispense with the traditional workbooks which had been used by his predecessor for years.

During conferences one evening, a parent decided to rummage through a stack of workbooks that were piled on a table in the back of the classroom. She was startled to discover that the workbooks were empty. Since several months of the school year had already elapsed, it seemed quite likely to her that the year would end without all of the worksheets being completed. How could this be?

She took up the matter with the president of the school board. He, too, was alarmed. He was so alarmed that he spent one entire school day sitting in the back of the young man's classroom. The school board president was not the type of person who would form an opinion about a teacher based on rumor alone. He witnessed for himself the fact that the workbooks remained stacked on the back table, untouched by students' hands.

The school board president had seen enough to satisfy him. He informed the teacher that a special school board meeting was scheduled for Saturday evening right after the first girls' basketball game. The young man was directed to appear and was advised that the school board would be pleased to receive his resignation at that time.

The young teacher called the ISEA. The ISEA arrived in Urbana. This time it was Perry H. Grier, an elementary supervisor and Executive Board member from Waterloo, along with Ken Jonson, who made the trip.

Grier and Jonson were shocked at what they discovered. It was unconscionable for a school board president to usurp the authority of the school superintendent in a manner such as this. They counseled with the school board in order to help them come to see the error of their ways.

"We also persuaded them to give the boy another chance," Grier reported to the Executive Board. "We also suggested to the teacher that he try to do a better job of following the wishes of the community."

"As far as we know," Jonson added, "everything is all right."

Wapello

Then there was the young man who learned of a vacant teaching position in Wapello. He applied for the job. He was interviewed and offered a contract, which he promptly signed and returned to the superintendent.

Later that summer, the school board became aware of the fact that the young man was a member of the Jehovah's Witnesses. The school board, to a man, felt strongly that there was no place on the teaching staff at Wapello for one of Jehovah's Witnesses. So the board rescinded its previous action approving the contract and advised the teacher that he should continue his job search.

The young prospective teacher called the ISEA. The ISEA arrived in Wapello. It was discovered that the superintendent was chagrined by the action taken by the school board. He understood what the United States Constitution said about religious liberty and he certainly did not want trouble.

But there was another side to the story, according to the superintendent. He believed the young teacher had an obligation to disclose the fact that he was a Jehovah's Witness at the time that he applied for the job. Not to do so, the superintendent believed, was a violation of the Code of Ethics of the Teaching Profession.

The Executive Board agonized about the matter for a period of time. Its members wondered if perhaps they should refer the young man to the American Civil Liberties Union. Clearly, he had been wronged and deserved redress and the ACLU was more interested in this type of case than was the ISEA.

Finally it was decided that those Executive Board members who were also superintendents would use their many contacts to help the young man secure other employment.

Their efforts were successful. The young man was placed in a "more urban setting." He was happy. The superintendent and the school board at Wapello were happy. And the ISEA Executive Board was happy, too.

Klemme

Most often it was a teacher who was shorted by the ISEA's timidity. But every now and then a superintendent would be shorted, too.

One such case involved the superintendent of schools from Klemme. He received a letter from the president of the school board, dated April 11, advising him that he was fired. This schoolman was obviously concerned about the fact that he had fallen from favor with at least a majority of the members of the school board.

But all was not lost. Being a schoolman as he was, he knew that the notice was late. The law required that the school board notify him of its intent to fire him no later than March 31. He then had a right to a hearing if he wanted one, sometime within the next few days. After the hearing, the school board had until April 10, and no later, to tell him that he was finished.

The superintendent called the ISEA. It was an open-and-shut case. The school board had missed the deadline. The ISEA arrived in Klemme. Upon further examination it was not quite so open and shut as it might have at first appeared.

The investigators discovered that the superintendent had actually been informed during a school board meeting on February 13 that he was going to be fired. The superintendent said nothing to the school board during that meeting. He told the investigators from the ISEA that he fully expected that his official notice of termination would be late, if he ever got one at all. "These people are farmers," the superintendent said. "They do not know anything about school law."

The members of the ISEA Executive Board were aghast at the unprofessional attitude of the Klemme school superintendent. It was, Board members believed, the responsibility of the superintendent of schools to advise the school board of the proper procedures in all instances, including this one. It would be difficult to do, they recognized, but being a school superintendent was a difficult job.

The Executive Board was content to let the Klemme superintendent swing in the wind. If he had acted so unprofessionally in this instance, he had probably acted unprofessionally in other instances as well.

The Executive Board was so concerned that this type of situation might occur somewhere else that they requested that Executive Secretary Charlie Martin contact his counterpart at the Iowa Association of School Boards to urge that the IASB take steps to educate school board members about the proper procedures for terminating school superintendents.

Salisbury House has been the ISEA's home since 1954 when it was purchased from Des Moines industrialist Carl Weeks.

The plaque which dedicates Salisbury House to the teachers of Iowa appears near the south entrance of the building.

The ISEA Executive Board holds its first meeting at the Association's new headquarters building, Salisbury House, on December 11, 1954. Standing (from left) are: L. L. Pickett, Ruthven; J. L. Davies, Iowa City; J. C. Hoglan, Marshalltown; Edwin Coen, Denison; Joe L. Gettys, Oskaloosa; and Perry Grier, Waterloo. Seated (from left) are: L. L. Woodruff, Burlington; Verl Crow, Sioux City; Executive Secretary Charles F. Martin; ISEA Recording Secretary Esther Davis; ISEA President Frank L. Hildreth, Des Moines; ISEA Accountant Kathryn Hardin; Ruth Tumbleson, Des Moines; Edith Kuhl, Logan; and Margaret Meek, Leon.

At a special ceremony in March of 1960, ISEA President Ray Bryan (left) unveils a plaque honoring Carl Weeks (seated) as the Association's first Friend of Education while ISEA Executive Secretary Charles F. Martin looks on. The plaque, which is now on display in the Salisbury House Great Room, had officially been presented in absentia during the ISEA Convention in November of 1959.

The Heathershaw sisters, Lillian Darnell (left) and Jeanette, turn the deed to their property over to ISEA staff members Vesper Price, Charles F. Martin, and Dorothy Brazzle to help fund what will in several years become the Heather Manor Home for the Aged.

Vesper Price, president of the Horace Mann Home, Inc. Board of Trustees, inspects the sign erected in 1964 on the site where Heather Manor will be built.

Etta Cosner, the director of elementary education in Davenport who served as ISEA president in 1964-65, passes the gavel to the next year's president, Roger Blake, a superintendent from West Sioux.

The ISEA's first field representatives gather around a map in the winter of 1966, planning future visits to Iowa schools. From left are Bill Pritchard, Marvin Larson, and Neil Curtis.

The first ISEA Communique *is published in September of 1963.*

The covers of Midland Schools *magazines from 1959-61 feature wildlife scenes created exclusively for the Association by noted artist Maynard Reece.*

David Grosland, a high school teacher in Des Moines, staffs the Iowa Association of Classroom Teachers booth at an ISEA convention in the early 1970s.

Delegates to the 1971 Delegate Assembly arrive at the state capitol by the busloads to lobby against school spending limitations — one of many activities leading up to the ISEA's censure of the Legislature and political leaders later that spring.

The banner headline in the May 1, 1971, issue of the Des Moines Register *says it all.*

More than $1,000 is raised during the 1971 ISEA Delegate Assembly to fund the activities of the fledgling Iowa Political Action Committee for Education (IPACE). Leading the fund-raising efforts are Ken Zeising, Sioux City executive director, who is speaking at the microphone; Charles Day; and Bob Gilchrist.

IPACE representatives staff a booth at the 1972 ISEA Convention.

The May 10, 1970, issue of the Des Moines Register *announces the end of the state's first—and so far only—teachers' strike in Keokuk.*

ISEA Executive Secretary Kenneth Wells (left) thanks Iowa House leaders for their work on the Collective Bargaining Bill in 1974. From left are Brice Oakley, R-Clinton; Donald Avenson, D-Oelwein; Jerome Fitzgerald, D-Fort Dodge; and Richard Drake, R-Muscatine.

Just months after the collective bargaining law is enacted, the first master contract agreed upon under the new law is signed on December 1, 1975, by Marion Cagley, president of the Nashua Community School Board (left) and William Kunzman, president and chief negotiator for the Nashua Schools Education Association.

ISEA staff and leaders deliver a boxful of requests for impasse assistance to the Iowa Public Employment Relations Board in November of 1980.

In May of 1976, Iowa Gov. Robert D. Ray signs the landmark SF205, a bill which at long last grants teachers facing termination the right to a fair hearing.

A big apple for the teacher

Copyright 1981, Des Moines Register and Tribune Company

The March 14, 1981, Des Moines Register carries an editorial cartoon by the late Frank Miller after the Iowa Legislature slashes the allowable growth rate for schools to five percent with a minimum budget growth guarantee of three percent.

ISEA officials celebrate the ISEA-PAC endorsement of Roxanne Conlin in the 1982 Democratic primary race for governor. From left are ISEA President-Elect George Duvall of Ames, ISEA President Phoebe Tupper of Davenport, Conlin, and ISEA Executive Director Fred Comer.

The ISEA's "Mr. Freeze" becomes a popular symbol during the 1986 session of the Iowa Legislature as members across the state unite in urging lawmakers not to freeze Iowa's future.

The ISEA's colorful painting by noted American artist Joseph Stella, called "Tree of My Life," brings $2 million on the Christie's auction block in New York on December 5, 1986.

ISEA-PAC's recommendation of incumbent Republican Gov. Terry Branstad over his Democratic challenger, Donald Avenson, in the 1990 race for governor prompts the Des Moines Register's *Brian Duffy to pen this cartoon which appears in the June 14, 1990, issue.*

In a symbolic show of unity, members of the New Iowa Schools Development Corporation's (NISDC) Policy Board answer reporters' questions at an October 8, 1991, news conference called to announce the historic creation of the nation's first nonprofit organization dedicated to encouraging and supporting local school improvement efforts. From left are: Fred Comer, ISEA executive director; Ron Fielder, Grant Wood AEA administrator; Jamie Vollmer, Iowa Business and Education Roundtable director; Tim Streucker, Iowa Association of School Boards president; Don Gunderson, School Administrators of Iowa president; Gerry Ott, ISEA policy implementation specialist and NISDC executive director; Angie King, ISEA president; Ted Stilwill, Iowa Department of Education; Gaylord Tryon, School Administrators of Iowa executive director; and Wayne Leuders, Iowa Association of School Boards.

U. S. Secretary of Education Lamar Alexander (standing) chats with members of six New Iowa Schools Development Corporation network school districts while Iowa Gov. Terry Branstad looks on during a special meeting held in Des Moines in conjunction with the National Education Forum on October 27, 1991.

Officials of the state's leading education groups demonstrate a new spirit of collaboration as they lead the April 7, 1992, march to the State Capitol to protest proposed school budget cuts. From left are Gaylord Tryon, School Administrators of Iowa executive director; Don Gunderson, School Administrators of Iowa president; Patsy Partridge, Iowa Association of School Boards president; Ted Davidson, Iowa Association of School Boards executive director; Angie King, ISEA president; and Fred Comer, ISEA executive director.

CHAPTER 24

The Awakening

The first courageous action taken by the ISEA on behalf of members came in the spring of 1964. It happened in Pleasantville.

At the time, there was a sign posted on the outskirts of the village that read, "Entering Pleasantville, Iowa. Home of 1,023 Friendly People and a Few Knuckleheads." The problem was that all but one of the knuckleheads were on the school board. The other one ran a diner in town.

The guy from the diner was mostly just annoying. He distributed John Birch Society literature from his establishment and got the people riled. He preached that "Communism was infiltrating the schools through the NEA."

Elberta Gilderbloom was a much bigger problem. She was a former school teacher and a resident of Pleasantville. Gilderbloom decided that she wanted to return to teaching. She applied for a job at the local school and was turned down by the superintendent. So she ran for the school board instead and was elected.

According to the school superintendent, Fred Nus, Gilderbloom told him, "If I can't work for you, then you won't work for me."

Elberta Gilderbloom was fairly quiet during her first year on the Pleasantville School Board. But her second year was a different matter. She recruited two allies to be candidates in the fall election and both of them were elected.

Anthony Vrban was a clerk at the Veterans' Hospital in Knoxville and Oscar Renfrow did maintenance work for the Fortune Laboratories in Des Moines. Both men were ultraconservative. Neither of them ever admitted to being a member of the John Birch Society, but Renfrow came pretty close.

"I have attended their meetings," he confessed. "What I have seen of the Society, I like. I am not ashamed to say so."

Gilderbloom, Vrban, and Renfrow were the three members of a "three-to-two" school board. Anything that smacked of Communism or sex in the classrooms or hallways would be ferretted out by the three. The people of Pleasantville could count on that.

The three proceeded to make life miserable for the teachers and the administrators. Class discussions of Communism were not permitted. The physiology teacher was reprimanded for mentioning menstruation, for example. But the matter came to a head over something unrelated to either Communism or sex, at least as far as anyone can tell. The matter came to a head over the high school grading policy.

The policy had been adopted by an earlier school board upon the recommendation of the high school teachers and principal. The policy provided that a student who put forth a good effort in a class but who lacked the ability to meet the normal standards for the course would receive a "circled D" grade. The policy also provided that a student who received "circled D" grades during his or her high school career would be given a certificate of attendance at graduation rather than a high school diploma.

The parents of a student who had been issued a certificate of attendance rather than a diploma filed suit asking the district court to force the school district to grant their daughter a diploma. The court rejected the parents' claim and ruled in favor of the school district.

Shortly thereafter, the Pleasantville School Board, by a vote of three to two, directed that Superintendent Nus issue the student a diploma. The school board also directed that the high school principal, Harry Dean, go back into the records for two years and change the grades of 16 students by erasing the circles around their "Ds."

Superintendent Nus refused to issue the diploma and Principal Dean refused to change the grades. The school board prepared to fire Nus. He resigned instead. So did Principal Dean and 12 of the 18 junior high school and high school teachers. Later, five elementary teachers would also resign in support of their secondary colleagues. Altogether, 19 of the Pleasantville School District's 34 professional employees left the system in protest.

"It is difficult for a teacher to work in a school system," social studies teacher Dominic Grasso wrote in his letter of resignation, "where he or she cannot rationally teach."

Junior high school science teacher Frieda Griffin wrote that she was resigning "because of the threat that this imposes on the security of any teacher within the Pleasantville Community School."

The ISEA responded forcefully. The Delegate Assembly imposed sanctions against the school district for "conditions detrimental to education."

Teachers who were contemplating employment with the Pleasantville schools were urged to consider whether or not "the community has resolved its differences to the point where board policy and professional practice can work together" before signing contracts to work there.

The Delegate Assembly voted to offer interest-free loans for one year of graduate study to "those professional persons in Pleasantville who have resigned their positions and who do not wish to accept a teaching position for the coming year."

Probably most helpful of all, the ISEA printed brief resumes for each one of the Pleasantville teachers and mailed hundreds of copies of them to school superintendents. As a result, all of those who wished to secure other teaching positions did and most of them received a hefty increase in salary, too.

It was a scary time for the ISEA. It had never before become involved so publicly in a matter that was so controversial. Associate Executive Secretary Bill Robinson wrote to each Pleasantville teacher, "I think you have demonstrated dramatically to the community that responsible, principled educators will not work in an atmosphere of suspicion and uncertainty."

It was a portent of things to come.

The first official expression of concern by the Association about teachers' rights and job security came at the 1963 Delegate Assembly. A motion was made that directed the Association to work for improvements in the continuing contract law. And the motion was carried.

Specifically, the motion directed two things: that an amendment be added to the school code which would require that the school district, at the request of the teacher, provide a written statement of the reasons that termination was being considered and that another amendment be added to the school code which would provide for an impartial third party to whom a teacher could appeal once the school board had determined to fire him or her.

Four years later the Iowa General Assembly finally agreed to the first of the two legislative goals. It became the law that the school boards had to tell the teachers why they were being fired.

It was something, but it did not amount to much in the way of protection. A number of years later, while lobbying for a much stronger law,

ISEA President Walter L. Galvin would ridicule the "reasons" provision.

"Under the current statute any reason, no matter how ridiculous and petty, can be used to end a teaching career in Iowa," Galvin contended. "In recent months such reasons as failure to pay personal bills on time, wearing too many keys on a belt, and presenting a Christmas program that was too short have been used by Iowa school boards to justify firing teachers."

The real momentum for contracts that truly continued in force from year to year began to build in 1971. The Delegate Assembly adopted a new business item calling for legislation that established "just cause" as the standard for teacher terminations.

A more comprehensive new business item was adopted in 1972. It provided: "The ISEA shall include, in its legislative program, legislation that mandates a termination procedure for teaching contracts to include just cause, adequate notice, specific written reasons relating to job performance, prior attempts to counsel the teacher, a fair hearing before an impartial tribunal, and protection of teacher rights under the First and Fourteenth Amendments of the United States Constitution."

The teacher delegates celebrated their first Assembly without school superintendents or secondary school principals in attendance by declaring that, as far as job protection was concerned, they wanted it all.

CHAPTER 25

The Law

The ISEA made a strategic decision to concentrate on collective bargaining legislation first. Nevertheless, the ISEA lobbyists did their best over the next several years to secure passage of a piece of legislation that included as many of the items as possible from the 1972 Delegate Assembly new business item.

Once collective bargaining was enacted in 1974, the full attention of the lobbyists turned to the continuing contract legislation. The major thrust came the very next year.

The ISEA proposal provided that just cause would be the standard for terminations and that an arbitrator would be the impartial third party at the end of the process.

The major opponents of the ISEA proposal were the IASB and the IASA. To them it was an unconscionable erosion of the rights of school boards to manage the affairs of their school districts. Just cause was an impossible standard to meet. The practical impact of just cause would be that teachers could no longer be fired in Iowa. And besides, by and large, teachers had been treated fairly all along.

A goodly number of legislators, some of them friends of the Association, were unhappy also. The General Assembly had just enacted a collective bargaining bill less than 12 months before. The battle among the legislators on the bargaining issue had been ferocious. Old alliances had collapsed. Friendships were strained. Nearly everyone had a scar somewhere as a result of the fracas. Now the legislators were angry that the ISEA would come back so soon with another bill that had the potential to be as divisive as the collective bargaining bill.

Despite all that, the bill—Senate File 205—moved quickly through the Senate. It was sent on to the House of Representatives.

The outcome in the House had always been in doubt. The bill had lots of controversy built into it. Many amendments were filed and even more were threatened. Time was running out in the session.

The ISEA attempted to compromise with the school boards and superintendents, but the IASB and the IASA were unwilling to do so. All they offered was a bill that provided very minimal job protection and lengthy and expensive court appeals.

The result was that Senate File 205 was set aside in 1975 for action by the House of Representatives during the 1976 legislative session. It would be another difficult battle.

The House Education Committee took up the bill early during the 1976 session. On February 17, after 14 hours of debate, the committee voted 11 to 6 to forward the bill to the floor. The committee had amended the Senate version a number of times, but the features that were essential to the ISEA were still intact: burden of proof, just cause, and arbitration. The bill was ready for floor debate.

The bill would be amended again and again before mid-May, when it finally passed. Over the course of the legislative session, the procedures in the bill became more and more cumbersome and time consuming as the IASB and the IASA worked to extract one more technical amendment and then another one from the weary legislators.

Nervous floor managers gave away more to the school board members and superintendents than they needed as evidenced by the final vote on the measure: 88 to 5 in the House of Representatives and 32 to 10 in the Senate.

Why all of the compromises?

"The reason was simple," according to George Brown, one of the ISEA lobbyists. "Several of the House leaders doubted that it would pass and they feared using up several days of debate late in the session to have nothing gained at the end."

When the long and grueling process was over, it was still a pretty good bill, even with all of the amendments. The burden of proof rested with the party who brought the charges and the charges had to meet the standard of just cause in order to be sustained.

Unfortunately, the impartial third party at the end of the process would not be an arbitrator. It would have been simpler that way—less costly and less time consuming. Instead, the impartial third party would be an adjudicator. The adjudicator would act like an arbitrator except that his or her decision would not be binding on the parties. The law provided that if either of the parties was unhappy with the decision of the adjudicator, the matter could be appealed to district court.

It was a pretty good law and it was a great victory. For the first time, teachers were secure from arbitrary and capricious dismissal actions. A large measure of job security had been provided for Iowa's teachers.

Two subsequent efforts were made to improve the teacher termination law.

The first effort came in 1983. The ISEA sought to remove the school board from the hearing process. The local school board, which holds the first hearing after charges are filed, almost always accepts the recommendation of the superintendent no matter what the evidence shows that is presented at the hearing. Therefore, in the ISEA's view, the hearing is a waste of time. The ISEA also sought to replace the language in the law which provides that the charges must be supported by a "preponderance of the evidence" with language that established a "substantial" evidence test.

Both of the changes sought by the ISEA were approved by the General Assembly. Later, they were both vetoed by Governor Terry Branstad.

A year later the ISEA was successful in securing legislation that requires that separate contracts be issued to teachers: one for their teaching assignments and another for their extracurricular duties.

Prior to the effective date of the change on July 1, 1985, teachers could be required, for example, to coach a sport whether they wanted to or not. Teachers were offered a single contract. If the contract included coaching assignments which were unacceptable to the teacher, he or she could refuse to sign the contract. But by doing so, of course, the teacher was resigning from all employment with the district, not just from coaching.

Worse yet, a good teacher could be fired from a school district because he or she was a poor coach. It was all one contract. The school district had the burden of proof, of course. It was incumbent upon the employer to prove that the person was a poor coach. But having established that, the person was out of a teaching job as well as a coaching job.

It was a terrible situation. Teachers could be required to accept coaching assignments that they did not want, perhaps because they knew they would make poor coaches. Then, in just a matter of a few months, they could be fired from their teaching jobs because they did, as they knew they would, a poor job at something they did not want to do in the first place.

It still made sense to the IASB. "What would they do if none of their teachers wanted to coach?" But it no longer made sense to a majority of the members of the General Assembly or to the Governor. The bill was passed and signed into law.

CHAPTER 26

The New Days

The passage of the new teacher termination bill resulted in more changes than just the obvious one—the fact that teachers felt more secure in their jobs than had been the case.

Many of the changes that resulted occurred at the ISEA. At best, the ISEA had been timid and cautious in the past. At worst, it had refused to advocate on behalf of the interests of the teachers. Now the ISEA was aggressive, perhaps, at times, overly aggressive.

One is left with the impression, after reading the communications of the day, that the staff and leadership looked forward to the mistreatment of teachers. It was necessary in order for the Association to advocate on their behalf. It was not unlike the fireman who looks forward to fires so that he can put them out.

It used to be that the decisions about whether or not to fund litigation were soberly pondered, sometimes for a long period of time. Most often the decision was no. The ISEA rarely funded litigation.

A member with a concern would call the ISEA. A team of two—an Executive Board member and a staff member—would travel to the local site and conduct an investigation. The two would then report to all of the members of the Executive Board at the next scheduled meeting. Most often the two would report that the problem had been solved or that there was nothing that the ISEA could do. Once in a while, the team would recommend that the Executive Board consider litigation.

The matter would then be forwarded to an attorney for an analysis and a recommendation. In the early days the attorney was Peter Janss. Later, it was Marvin Adams. Most often the attorney would meet with the Executive Board to explain his analysis and recommendation. When all was said and done, the ISEA funded one or two pieces of litigation each year.

Now the requests came fast and furious. It was both impractical and unnecessary to seek the approval of the ISEA Executive Board. It was impractical because there simply were too many requests. It was unnecessary because this 1970s model Executive Board would have approved almost all of them anyway.

So the power to authorize litigation was transferred from the Executive Board to a member of the staff at the state headquarters. The Executive Board was concerned, not that the staff person might authorize too much litigation, but that he might authorize too little. So it established a process through which denials could be appealed.

A member who had been denied access to an ISEA-paid lawyer by the member of the staff could appeal the decision to the executive director. The executive director often overruled the member of the staff. A member who had been denied access to an ISEA-paid lawyer by the executive director could appeal the decision to the Executive Board. The Executive Board almost always overruled the executive director.

Later, a committee of the Executive Board was substituted for the entire Executive Board as the body to receive the appeals based on denials by the executive director. The executive director's decisions have been sustained by the committee more often than was the case when the appeals were heard by the full Board.

During this period the ISEA relied solely on retained counsel. As the years went by and the number of cases increased, so, too, did the number of lawyers who made their livings from the ISEA. In the 30-year period from 1960 to 1990, the amount of money expended by the ISEA for lawyers' fees increased from just over $6,000 a year to just under $600,000 a year.

By the mid-1980s the amount of money being paid to lawyers each year became a matter of concern for the leadership and management of the Association. The Delegate Assembly would adopt a budget that provided for a generous increase in the legal services line items. At the end of the fiscal year the line item would be over-expended. The next year the Delegate Assembly would approve another generous increase and at the end of the fiscal year the line item would be over-expended again.

It was becoming commonplace for the Executive Board's budget committee to pare back appropriations for other programs in order to pay for the Association's legal service bills.

It was decided, as part of the Association's long-range plan, to experiment with in-house counsel. At about the same time, a member of the staff completed his law studies at Drake University and was admitted to the Iowa Bar. In February, 1987, William Unger became the first attorney to practice law as a member of the professional staff of the ISEA.

The Association monitored the experiment carefully for the next several years. It was determined that it was significantly less expensive to employ lawyers at an annual salary than it was to retain them at an hourly rate. A decision was made to hire more lawyers.

Polk County Democrats, who are not always a discerning lot, gave the ISEA a boost. They went to the polls for their primary election in the summer of 1990, where they unceremoniously dumped most of the incumbent office-holders in county government. While they were angry at the members of the County Board of Supervisors who had committed large sums of public money to a race track in Altoona that was on the verge of going belly up, they took their frustration out on everyone.

One of the victims was James A. Smith, the long-time and highly regarded County Attorney. Smith was in search of a job and the ISEA was in search of an attorney. The management and Executive Board took advantage of Smith's availability and experience to create a new staff division at headquarters called "the Office of Advocacy Services," with Smith as the associate executive director in charge.

Smith hired another attorney, Gerald Hammond, who had worked nearly full time on Association cases as a member of the downtown Des Moines law firm of Sayre & Gribble. Since September, 1991, most of the ISEA legal cases have been handled by the three staff attorneys: Unger, Smith, and Hammond. At the end of the fiscal year, the amount of money expended for legal services had actually decreased from the previous year, the first time that had ever happened.

Controlling expenses is the best that the ISEA can ever hope to do, for as long as there are grain elevators, beauty parlors, church suppers, card parties, school boards, and teachers, there will be rumors and facts and teachers to defend. At least now teachers have a fighting chance. That wasn't always the case.

CHAPTER 27

The Emerging Profession

As state associations came to look and act more and more like labor unions, most divested themselves of all the trappings of a professional association. Bargaining, grievances, politics, and litigation grabbed the interest and filled the time. There was not much of either left over for issues such as teacher preparation, licensure, in-service education, and professional development.

A schism developed inside of the state associations around the country between the younger, more militant, union-oriented teachers and the older, more passive, professionally oriented teachers. The "union types" in the association made jokes about TEPS. Every state association had a TEPS committee. TEPS stood for "Teacher Education and Professional Standards." The "professional types" worried quietly among themselves about the changes that were under way inside their profession and inside their association.

Where the battle was engaged, the unionists won. They were younger, more aggressive, and better organized. They were also addressing issues of fairness and equity which had never been addressed before.

Advocacy on behalf of fairness and equity was not "professional," according to the superintendents who had controlled the associations. Therefore, when the insurgents took over, much like an invading army, they destroyed everything in their paths that had been tainted by the term "professional."

That did not happen at the ISEA. There were strains and stresses inside the ISEA. Some argued, correctly, that the focus of the Association was on bargaining and grievances and that the professional programs were getting the short shrift in terms of staff time and budget. But even then, the ISEA never abandoned the professional issues.

The credit is due, once again, to the IACT. The IACT led the fight for fair representation for teachers in the governance of the ISEA. They brought the resolutions to Delegate Assemblies that put the Association on record in favor of collective bargaining and tenure. The IACT also supported ethical standards of professional practice, higher requirements for entry into teaching, and improvements in teacher preparation programs.

The IACT offered impressive programs for in-service and professional development. The IACT drive-in conferences and Mobile In-Service Training Laboratories (MISTLs) were models. Staff and leaders came from other state associations to observe the IACT at work.

When Roy Karlson, president of the ISEA, and Jim Knott, president of the IACT, negotiated the agreement between the two organizations which led to the disbanding of the IACT in 1973 as a separate department, they paid considerable attention to the preservation of the professional programs of the IACT.

The creation of the Instruction and Professional Development (IPD) unit inside the ISEA was part of the deal. *The Communique* reported to the members on August 29, 1973: "The IPD unit of the ISEA was formed to aid the Association in continuing to meet the needs of Iowa educators. Through the merger of activities conducted by the former IACT and the activities conducted by the ISEA, the new unit will be responsible for organizing, developing, and implementing programs and activities concerned with instruction and professional development."

Because of the strong influence of the IACT, the ISEA positioned itself to address both the welfare needs of the members and the professional needs of the members at the same time. Most other state associations did not do that.

The two men who cut the deal for the ISEA and the IACT, Roy Karlson and Jim Knott, epitomize the unique character of Iowa leadership. Roy Karlson would become a UniServ director, and Jim Knott, a long-time member of the Executive Board. Over the years, both would maintain that for the Association to truly serve its members, it had to address both concerns.

The ISEA has accepted, on behalf of its members, the responsibility for improving education. It has been the view that promoting quality and productivity results in better schools, stronger communities, and a more vital Association. Teachers also feel better about themselves and the work that they do.

CHAPTER 28

The Standards Board

Almost since the day that the ISEA was born in 1854, it has held to the position that self-governance is the essence of a profession.

The right to determine how prospective members of the profession are trained and educated, the authority to determine the criteria for certification and licensure, the authority to issue and revoke certificates and licenses, and the right to establish standards of ethical practice, are all legitimate responsibilities of the profession itself. In fact, only professionals themselves have the knowledge, understanding, and experience necessary to make the expert judgments these responsibilities require.

Yet, among all the professions and trades, only teachers were denied the right of self-governance. Throughout history this reality has been more demeaning to teachers than any of the other indignities that they have suffered.

It is a public profession, some argued. But hundreds and thousands of accountants, lawyers, doctors, and nurses are public employees, also. It is a unionized profession, some argued later. But hundreds and thousands of accountants, lawyers, doctors, and nurses are unionized, also. The fact of the matter is that, over time, the state and nation institutionalized the control of teachers by lay people. The public expected teachers to act like professionals, but they denied teachers the rights of professionals.

In Iowa, the authority to regulate the profession resided with the State Board of Education. It was this collection of lay people, political appointees of the Governor, who determined what a person must know and be able to do in order to teach. They determined who was qualified enough to be certified to teach. They determined what constituted ethical practice. The same people who asserted that teachers should clean up their own ranks denied them the authority to do it.

The creation of an autonomous standards board had been part of the ISEA's legislative agenda for generations. Finally, in 1984, a bill passed both houses of the General Assembly. It was not a model bill, but it was a start.

It created a nine-member independent board: four classroom teachers, one faculty member from a college of education, and four members from the public. The board was given the authority to approve standards for teacher education programs and to issue both initial and renewal certificates.

Most of the organized opposition came from inside the education community. The administrator organizations opposed it because they worried that it would enhance the power of the ISEA at their expense and there were no provisions made for administrator representation on the board.

The most vigorous opposition came from the deans of the colleges of education, especially from Virgil Lagomarcino, dean of the college of education at Iowa State University. Publicly, Lagomarcino argued that the college could not submit itself to external control. To do so would compromise the integrity of the institution and violate the basic precepts of academic freedom.

In truth, the real issue was which outside agency was going to approve the university's programs, not whether some outside agency would do it. The State Board of Education already had the authority. The bill transferred it to the standards board. Dean Lagomarcino was comfortable that he could control and manipulate the lay board members. He was less comfortable with his ability to manipulate the teachers who would be members of the standards board.

Oddly enough, the IASB urged the Governor to sign the bill. Still, Governor Branstad vetoed the measure. "Nobody is in favor of it," he said, "except the ISEA and the IASB."

President Phoebe Tupper called the veto a serious mistake. "It is a major setback in the adoption of educational reforms needed to improve the learning opportunities for Iowa's half-million students," she said.

Five years later, Governor Branstad asked the ISEA to propose the measure again. It passed once more, this time in a better form than was the case in 1984. It would be called the Board of Educational Examiners. Of the 11 members, nine would hold valid licenses to teach. It would have the right to establish criteria for licensure. And it would have the authority to license all professionals: teachers and administrators.

In the process of compromise, which is always necessary in the halls of the capitol, especially when a major piece of legislation is involved, the

ISEA reluctantly agreed that the authority for the approval of teacher education programs would remain with the State Board of Education. Transferring that authority to the Board of Educational Examiners remains a legislative objective of the ISEA.

The bill was signed into law by Governor Branstad. Shortly thereafter, his office requested that the ISEA provide him with the names of 10 members. From that list he would select five for appointment to the new board. The first five ISEA members to serve on the autonomous standards board were Virginia Garnjobst of Burlington, Cal Halliburton of Ames, Dan Martinez of Red Oak, Rachel Stewart of Fort Madison, and Maureen White of Cedar Falls.

CHAPTER 29

The Reports

In more recent times, the NEA and many of the state associations have been viewed by politicians and the media as impediments to change and improvement in the schools. The ISEA, however, has worked hard to position itself as the leading advocate for school improvement in Iowa.

One example is the response of the ISEA to the 1983 report of the President's Commission on Excellence in Education, commonly referred to as *A Nation at Risk*.

While most of the education establishment responded defensively to the Commission's recommendations for things such as a longer school day, a longer school year, more required courses (in science, mathematics, and foreign language), merit pay, competency testing for teachers, and the like, the ISEA saw it as an opportunity.

"Despite the negative publicity it has aroused, ISEA members should welcome the recommendations made by the recently released report," said ISEA President Phoebe Tupper.

"We welcome this and other similar studies because they help emphasize our continuing efforts to strengthen and upgrade public schools," Tupper noted. "I am particularly pleased that the Commission communicates the same sense of urgency we have felt to make improvements in the quality of education for students in Iowa and across the nation."

Within five months from the time *A Nation at Risk* was issued, the ISEA issued a major report of its own. It was entitled *Achieving Excellence in Our Schools: Major Areas for Renewal*.

According to President Tupper: "Ours is not just another report. It is a comprehensive proposal developed by practitioners to focus attention on what we believe will enhance Iowa's public education system. The ISEA's proposal encompasses all facets of the education arena. We have resisted the temptation to respond to singular issues such as merit pay and teacher competency tests. Rather we have developed a package of interrelated proposals which address the complex nature of educational renewal."

The report offered 15 pages of recommendations. It proposed sweeping changes in teacher preparation, certification, professional authority, performance evaluation, the learning environment, professional development, and compensation.

Achieving Excellence set the tone and the agenda for the political debate that followed. While teachers in other states were consumed by fending off the half-baked ideas of their politicians, Iowa's politicians were consumed by responding to the constructive proposals of the ISEA.

At the end of her tenure in office, Phoebe Tupper looked back with pride: "We were the first state in the country and the only group in Iowa to come out with a comprehensive plan for achieving excellence in education. Because of the leadership role we assumed, Iowa education has been spared some of the irresponsible, quick-fix reform measures that other states have had imposed on them.

"Because we've taken a positive approach and have been willing to fully discuss issues such as teacher testing and merit pay," she continued, "we can be assured that any plan that does come out will be well thought out and will have the involvement of our members."

Three years later, another major national report was issued, this one by the Carnegie Forum on Education and the Economy. This provocative report, entitled *A Nation Prepared: Teachers for the 21st Century*, proposed major changes in the role of the teacher and the manner in which schools are structured.

The response from the nation's education establishment was much more positive toward this report than it had been toward *A Nation at Risk*. Still many expressed their reservations. Mary Hatwood Futrell, the president of the National Education Association, who had served as a member of the Forum, attached her exceptions to the back of the report.

But once again, the ISEA demonstrated its willingness to take risks on behalf of change, especially when it believed the change would enhance the profession of teaching and improve the education of students. The ISEA Executive Board voted to endorse the recommendations of the Carnegie Forum without reservation. The vote was unanimous.

The ISEA prepared another major report in 1991. This one, entitled *Time for a Change: A Report to the People of Iowa from the Teachers of*

Iowa, was prepared following more than a year of research.

The Association started with a scientific sample of Iowa's teachers. From responses to a questionnaire of 100 items, four major concerns were identified. These were put in question form and taken to groups of teachers, selected at random. Discussion in each "focus group" was transcribed and analyzed. A summary was drafted and submitted to state-level teacher leaders who adopted recommendations.

A report was then drafted and submitted to leaders of local teachers' associations. Recommendations were returned to the state leaders group for review. Many were incorporated into a draft which was approved by the ISEA Executive Board.

The results of the research, particularly the focus group research, were startling. It uncovered growing frustration among teachers with a rapidly deteriorating educational environment in their schools and districts resulting from factors over which they had little or no control.

Quoting from the research report, "Iowa teachers are likely to have as their personal visions, schools where they can teach children under the best possible circumstances . . . they are likely to believe that they, as well as others, are responsible for addressing the problems of the school."

The researchers continue: "Iowa teachers are likely to perceive their dedication and the rewards they have associated with working with children as steadily eroding in recent years. Their perceptions of a growing lack of respect for teachers and for education among students, parents, and the community, as well as a general decline of parental values and control of children, are the major problems teachers are likely to be contending with in Iowa's public schools."

ISEA President Angie King explained the reason for the 1991 report: "Iowa has a good record in educational reform. Ours is the only state to finance decentralized change through the Educational Excellence Act. We involve many groups, organizations, and sectors in our schools. Our students consistently out-perform others nationally; and Iowa's teachers are known nationally for educational quality, reform, and innovation."

"However," King continued, "even in Iowa, schools today are the same as they were at the beginning of the 'excellence movement.' Permanent structural changes in schools have not occurred. In part, this is because the recommendations of teachers have not been heard clearly. While many issue reports about education, few ask teachers for information. In this report, Iowa's teachers say clearly what must be done to improve schools."

Time for a Change might more appropriately have been titled, "Time, for a Change" because the lead statement says, "Our greatest need is time, time to educate every child fully. We need time to change our teaching styles so that we can work with individuals rather than groups. We need time to prepare for classes and instruction. We need time just to 'catch up,' let alone to prepare. And, we need time for professional improvement."

The report recommended that teachers and principals be given greater authority and more responsibility. It recommended that the first efforts at school transformation be directed toward the early elementary grades. It recommended more and better uses for technology. In all, the report offered 20 pages of recommendations.

One paragraph toward the end of the report captures its essence: "America needs schools where all children succeed. Such a school provides personalized learning, educates rather than trains, and applies the best that is known about teaching in theory and practice. It creates an environment conducive to learning and is a safe place where the mind may grow. It is collegial rather than corporate and is a place where teachers and administrators shape the learning environment through shared decision making. It is based on the school building. And it has enough money, technology, and people to provide excellence to everyone."

The ISEA has always been a thoughtful Association. The reasoned and rational recommendations and reports have served everyone well. The politicians, the press, and the public expect the ISEA to offer a vision of what education should be like and the ISEA does not disappoint them.

CHAPTER 30

The Projects

The ISEA has done much more over the years than write reports and offer recommendations. The ISEA has been a hands-on player in school building, school district, and statewide initiatives to change and improve schools.

The ISEA joined with the NEA in sponsoring the Mastery in Learning Project at a site in Iowa.

The program, under the direction of the NEA's Dr. Robert McClure, was an unusual kind of school improvement project. Instead of professing to be the one-and-only model for school reform, it provided teachers with the latest research and support so that they could determine how to best meet the needs of their students and how they might restructure themselves in order to meet those needs.

In the fall of 1986, Paul Norton Elementary School in Bettendorf was selected as one of 28 Mastery in Learning sites in the nation. The following June *The Communique* reported, "Teachers at Paul Norton used to swap casserole recipes during lunch. Now they discuss developmental learning theory. That is just one of many changes occurring since the school was selected to take part in this unique project."

The Communique visited again in September of 1988. "Among the many innovations they've come up with," the newspaper reported, "is organizing a pool of parent volunteers to help relieve teachers of secretarial and classroom chores so that they have more time to spend with individual kids. They also brought in an expert on developmental learning theory to help them determine whether their teaching units are age-appropriate, they've rewritten the science curriculum, and they've worked with a personal inventory instrument to help them better match their teaching styles to students' learning styles."

"These are our ideas," said teacher Bette Kulas. "Everybody is involved because they see that we can make a difference. We're committed."

Early in 1988, NEA President Mary Hatwood Futrell appointed a committee of NEA Executive Committee members, members of the NEA Board of Directors, and state association presidents for the purpose of developing a long-range plan for the "total restructuring of our nation's public schools." I was invited to serve as a consultant to the group.

One of the recommendations of the NEA committee was the creation of "learning laboratories." It was envisioned that each state association would identify one school district which, with the consent of the local association, the administration, and the school board, would become a laboratory for educational innovation.

The ISEA responded quickly and enthusiastically to the NEA challenge. The Executive Board made a $30,000 commitment to the project. It was agreed that the Learning Lab district would received $10,000 a year from the Association for each of three years. A committee was appointed to develop the selection criteria, receive and screen applications, and recommend a winner to the Executive Board.

Four school districts were selected as finalists: Bettendorf, Denison, Marshalltown, and South Tama. Following visits to each community by members of the committee, the Marshalltown Community School District was recommended to the Executive Board as the Iowa Learning Laboratory. The Board concurred.

On May 13, 1989, NEA Executive Director Don Cameron announced that Marshalltown was the first Learning Laboratory in the United States. That summer, Marshalltown was joined by the second, third, and fourth Learning Labs—Chaska, Minnesota; Westerly, Rhode Island; and Memphis, Tennessee—in being honored at the NEA Representative Assembly.

That fall *The Communique* visited Marshalltown. "From the outside it looks like business as usual in the Marshalltown School District," it was reported, "but teachers, administrators, and school board members there are planning to turn everything inside out and downside up."

"As the nation's first school district to be designated as an NEA Learning Lab, Marshalltown has embarked on at least a five-year effort to redesign how learning takes place," according to *The Communique*. "Although they have only begun to map out their strategy, at the heart of the plan is the mutual desire to shift decision making about instruction and curriculum from the central office to the school building and individual classrooms. It is based on a belief that teachers, who are most closely affected by decisions, ought to be making those decisions."

Gerry Ott, whose official title at the ISEA is implementation specialist for education policy, had consulting with the Marshalltown Learning Lab as part of his job responsibilities. While attending a workshop in that capacity, Ott met W. P. "Pat" Dolan of Kansas City, Missouri.

Dolan, who runs a nationwide consulting business, had 15 years of experience working with major corporations and labor unions in restructuring how they do business with each other.

One of Dolan's success stories is the Ford Motor Company and the United Auto Workers. When Dolan began working with them in the late 1970s, the quality of Ford products had deteriorated and the corporation was in serious financial difficulty. Both the corporation and the union were in trouble.

But by turning the organizational structure and the union-management relationship upside-down and by giving employees the authority and the responsibility for making important business decisions, Ford has rebounded as a leader in building quality automotive products.

According to Dolan, the way schools are currently structured is a major block to what is, and what can be, in the classrooms.

At the heart of the problem, he says, is that the current military model—or organizational pyramid, as he calls it—does not allow for improving both quality and productivity.

For example, the traditional pyramid functions by putting people in charge at the top and giving them the authority and responsibility to control the workers who are at the bottom. The result is a top-down, authoritarian hierarchy, controlled from above, and responded to from below.

Dolan says that under this model, any degree of change tends to force everyone to "seize up" and become paralyzed.

"The goal is to make the structure open and free enough to allow it to move—to allow it to become unstuck," he explains. "You cannot make a difference if the structure is not flexible."

"The new system has to be designed by the users themselves," Dolan continues. "The top must be willing to change from a monitoring role to becoming more accessible and supportive."

Dolan was right for Marshalltown and he was right for Iowa, according to Ott. Based upon his recommendation, the ISEA, with the assistance of the NEA, sponsored a conference in September of 1990, the likes of which had never been seen before. Former ISEA President Ken Tilp came back to observe. He described it as "his first religious experience in 25 years."

The ISEA invited teams to participate from 28 different school districts. It was a three-day conference and it was all at the Association's expense.

The most unusual aspect of the conference was the fact that the members of the teams were not solely teachers. The UniServ director was part of the district's team, as was a principal, and the superintendent of schools, and a member of the school board. The "family" was back together for what most thought would be a one-time-only reunion.

The conference participants heard the gospel according to Pat Dolan.

"We need a dramatic reversal in the pyramid," he said, "where all roles and relationships change. The top group of administrators has to stop monitoring and controlling and begin providing leadership, support, vision, and direction."

Teachers need to change, too, Dolan said, as must the relationship between the Association and the administration.

"Instead of the traditional, confrontational, power-driven relationship, we need to develop a new collaborative relationship in which both parties jointly address the major issues and begin to restructure their schools," he said.

He emphasized that this new relationship is not designed to replace collective bargaining. "Bargaining is a powerful tool and there is a role for it," he explained. "But we need to create a parallel model to the collective bargaining process—a new arena in which you can solve problems that cannot always be addressed through bargaining."

The participants committed themselves to continue the search for new relationships and structures when they returned to their home communities. They asked for a follow-up conference in February, this time much of it at their own expense. Five months later 22 of the original 28 districts returned. Most would come back again and again. A second wave of "Dolan schools" were identified and then a third wave.

The ISEA's efforts impressed others. Jamie Vollmer, the director of operations for the Iowa Business and Education Roundtable told the first conference participants, "The role that the ISEA has played in fostering collaboration is breathtakingly unique. It is a great service to education in Iowa."

Director of Education William Lepley also spoke to the group. Although he acknowledged that the Department, with its rules and regulations, can sometimes be an impediment to change, he pledged his support for both statewide and individual school district efforts to transform education.

The ISEA had given birth to a revolution. Teachers, administrators, and school board members from dozens of school districts were working cooperatively to reform or transform their schools. They had the spirit and the plans. What most of them lacked was the money.

Once again, the ISEA led the way. On October 8, 1991, history was made when the state's education groups joined with business and political leaders to form the nation's first state-level corporation designed to promote school transformation from the inside out.

The New Iowa Schools Development Corporation (NISDC) was created as a private, non-profit organization. Its primary purpose was to collect and disseminate funding and coordinate the sharing of resources and information for the growing network of Iowa school districts that were exploring various ways of restructuring themselves.

The board of directors of the new corporation included the presidents and executive directors of the ISEA, the IASB, and the SAI. Also included were the director of operations for the Iowa Business and Education Roundtable, representatives from the Department of Education, the Governor's office, the Area Education Agencies, and the chairs of the House and Senate Education Committees. ISEA's Gerry Ott was named the group's executive director.

Most of the members of the NISDC board of directors attended the news conference which was called to announce the formation of the corporation. A reporter asked, "Since NISDC doesn't have any money, what are you going to do, go hat in hand?" "No," Ott responded. "We are going to go hand in hand."

Go hand in hand they did. The first major contribution came from the State of Iowa. Governor Terry Branstad proposed funding for NISDC as part of his 1992 state budget and the Legislature appropriated $250,000.

Shortly after the NISDC was formed, United States Secretary of Education Lamar Alexander came to Des Moines. He met with the NISDC board members and representatives from six of the "Dolan" districts: Cedar

Falls, Des Moines, Fort Dodge, Indianola, Iowa City, and North Scott.

They apparently had quite an impact on Alexander, who told reporters in a news conference held after the session, "Iowa has an extraordinary commitment to excellence in education. My meeting with the six teams was the most interesting hour-and-a-half that I've spent in some time."

Lamar Alexander also told reporters, "There is more creativity in one square mile of Iowa than there is in all of Washington, D. C."

CHAPTER 31

The Reunion

The formation of the NISDC marked the first formal working relationship among the teachers, administrators, and school board members since the administrators walked out of the ISEA in the early 1970s.

The administrators left in anger and most of the teachers were happy to see them go. For the next decade the superintendents and school board members were the bitter enemies of the teachers. Most of the battles between the state organizations were fought in the halls of the State Capitol.

The battles between the ISEA and the SAI and the IASB were replicated at the local level in most districts. There were a few school districts where the teachers, administrators, and school board members were able to maintain a friendly working relationship, but in most districts they were not.

There were relatively few issues that divided the groups. Collective bargaining and tenure were the big ones. Yet they refused to work cooperatively on the issues upon which they agreed, even though it was in their self-interest to do so.

Often the battles, especially at the local level, were personal and nasty. People said things about one another and did things to one another that were hurtful. Some scars still remain.

Obviously, something had changed.

It was actually the IASB that took the first step. IASB President James M. Adams, President-Elect Helen Van Steenhuyse, and Executive Director Ted Davidson came to Salisbury House in 1982 for a conversation with President George Duvall and me.

The atmosphere was tense, but polite. Their message to us was that perhaps the time had come to open the lines of communication between the two organizations. While there are issues about which we have serious disagreement, there are also issues upon which we agree. Their point was that perhaps we should cooperate with one another when we could.

One conversation led to another. Soon the officers and executive directors of the two organizations were meeting on a regular basis. The Iowa Association of Secondary School Principals merged with the Iowa Association of Elementary School Principals. Eventually the merged association of principals would join with the Iowa Association of School Administrators to form the School Administrators of Iowa (SAI). Their officers and executive director joined in.

The first cooperative project was the creation of a program to recognize outstanding schools. A committee of representatives from all of the organizations established the criteria for the awards, received and evaluated the applications, and determined who the winners would be. The program became known as the FINE (First In the Nation in Education) Schools Recognition Program.

The defining moment, as far as the ISEA was concerned, came in November of 1986 when the annual convention of the IASB supported a resolution calling for an increase in taxes and higher salaries for teachers. Further, the convention directed that the IASB staff work cooperatively with the ISEA staff to secure both.

The IASB and the ISEA worked cooperatively with Governor Branstad to secure passage of the Governor's $100 million pay proposal. Even though they were not included, the SAI also supported the proposal. Neither the IASB nor the ISEA advocated the inclusion of the administrators in the plan. In retrospect, the leaders of both organizations recognize that to omit them was probably a mistake.

Some in the ISEA believe that perhaps the principals should return to the Association. President Phoebe Tupper and I met with Gaylord Tryon and Ken Lemke, the executive director and president of the principals' association, in 1986. President Tupper shared with them a willingness to commence discussions, without any preconditions, that might lead to the return of the principals.

The time was not right, for the principals were already engaged in merger discussions with the Iowa Association of School Administrators. President Lemke was grateful for the overture. "If nothing ever comes of this," he said, "I still want you to know how much your offer means to us."

President Ken Tilp told the Iowa delegates to the 1989 NEA Representative Assembly that he expected the principals would return to the ISEA within five years.

His prognosis was overly optimistic. The ISEA's disinterest in the school superintendents returning to the organization along with the principals is a roadblock. So is the unwillingness of the NEA to make any concessions in terms of national dues. Most principals would wish to maintain membership in their national associations. Also, being required to pay full dues to the NEA is a deterrent to their return to the ISEA.

The relationship among the ISEA, IASB, and SAI has continued to grow. During the 1992 legislative session, the three organizations held joint briefing sessions every Tuesday morning. They also held several joint news conferences.

During the darkest days of the session when the state's financial crisis threatened funding for education, the three organizations called their members to Des Moines. More than a thousand came. They marched together from East High School to the Capitol.

Patsy Partridge and Ted Davidson, president and executive director of the IASB; Don Gunderson and Gaylord Tryon, president and executive director of the SAI; and President Angie King and I of the ISEA marched side-by-side as we led the parade. A decade earlier, such a show of unity in a time of crisis would have been unthinkable.

The ISEA will do battle with administrators and school boards in the future, much as it has in the past. There will be collective bargaining impasses and arbitrators' awards. There will be grievances and more arbitrators' awards. School boards will fire teachers and the ISEA will defend them. Occasionally, a local association will do what it can to get a principal or a superintendent fired or a school board member defeated on election day.

The ISEA will seek legislation to expand the scope of bargaining and to make members more secure in their jobs. The IASB will oppose those efforts.

Teachers, administrators, and school board members do have some disparate interests. It is legitimate for each to act in an appropriate fashion to advance those interests. What is different now is that each organization respects the right of the others to act on their own behalf and in their own interest.

What is also different is that teachers, administrators, and school board members now recognize that there is more that unites them than there is that divides them. Strong, vital public schools; a quality education for every child; adequate funding; and competitive salaries and benefits for all educators are powerful, unifying issues.

All that has happened since Irving H. Hart wrote *Milestones* 40 years ago had to happen. It is the coming of age of the ISEA. Teachers as proud, powerful, independent professionals are free to cooperate with others for the common good. Only those who have trust and confidence in themselves can truly have trust and confidence in others.

CHAPTER 32

Salisbury House

Salisbury House is quite a place: a 42-room Tudor mansion in the middle of 10 acres of virgin timber in the middle of Des Moines. It was built by cosmetics baron Carl Weeks as a residence and ostentatious display of his personal wealth. He gave it to Drake University. Drake University gave it back. Together, they sold it to the ISEA.

Since the deal was closed on Monday, September 27, 1954, Salisbury House has dominated the ISEA. Year after year, Executive Board after Executive Board, Delegate Assembly after Delegate Assembly, the teachers of Iowa have been haunted by the House.

Salisbury House is both a corporate office and a national historic site. It is private property but it serves a public purpose. It is ISEA's asset and it is ISEA's liability. It is a blessing and it is a curse. Salisbury House is an enigma.

For Carl Weeks, Salisbury House was his public pronouncement that a poor boy from Toddville, Iowa, had made it in the big city. Weeks said, "With four little boys at home, Edith needs a bigger place than the one on 39th Street." But there were lots of bigger places available. No, for Carl Weeks, Salisbury House was an irrefutable statement.

Carl Weeks never attended high school. He was tutored by an uncle while he worked as a drug store clerk. The uncle persuaded him to enroll at the Highland Park College of Pharmacy. He did and apparently did well.

Upon graduation, he worked in various drug stores. Weeks was impressed with women's seemingly insatiable demand for cosmetics, particularly imported face powders. For several years he experimented with making a face powder which he hoped to market as a domestic competitor for the imported powders. Finally, Weeks mixed cold cream and face powder and the foundation for Salisbury House was laid.

The company was called "Armand," named for a hero from an English romance novel. Armand grew to be a giant in a grossly profitable industry. Weeks competed with the Hudnuts of Indianapolis for market share. They were so competitive that Weeks' youngest son was called "Hud" because he was so naughty he was told he had to be a Hudnut rather than a Weeks.

It was Carl Weeks' net worth that outgrew the house on 39th Street more than the size of his family. Salisbury House cost Carl Weeks $1.2 million in the mid-1920s, lot not included. The furnishings and works of art were valued at over $600,000 at the time ISEA purchased the house. "It was all built on the vanity of women," he was fond of telling acquaintances.

The Weekses shopped for a lot for over a year. One day they drove down Tonawanda Drive and Weeks said, "If there is a level spot on top of that hill, I will buy it." No one remembers whether the hill was for sale at the time. Having purchased the land, the Weekses then retained architect Byron "Ben" Boyd to design them a house, something in a Spanish motif, which was popular at the time.

While Boyd was at work, Carl and Edith Weeks went to Europe. They visited Turin first, then Paris, and finally Salisbury, England. Carl had been there before but Edith had not. Carl's purpose for the visit was to share with Edith the Salisbury Cathedral, which had impressed him greatly.

This time it was the King's House that captured his fancy. While Salisbury House is not an exact replica of the King's House, there is somewhere in Salisbury House every principal feature of the King's House. Weeks no doubt placed a trans-Atlantic call to Boyd. "Hold the Spanish motif, Byron, I have got another idea." Had it not been for a trip to Salisbury, England, by Carl and Edith Weeks, the ISEA might today be headquartered in something resembling the Alhambra.

The House was finished in 1928 and the Weeks' attention turned to furnishings: canvases, marbles, bronzes, heraldry, Buddhas, china, oriental rugs, and a bejeweled Madonna once owned by Enrico Caruso—something representing every age since 600 B. C.

"The Brothers LaBochere" by Sir Thomas Lawrence, the 19th-century English portraitist; "The Tree of My Life" by Joseph Stella, the important American modernist; "Cardinal Domenico da Rivarola" by Sir Anthony Van Dyke, the court painter to Charles I; and a hundred other works of art were selected to decorate the house.

The Weekses and their four sons settled in.

It is said that during the early planning stages Carl and Edith Weeks agreed that the House would someday be given to an institution or organization that would preserve it. In 1934 they gave it to Drake University for use as a college of fine arts, retaining their right to use it as a residence during their lifetimes.

In 1954 Drake University gave it back. Dr. Henry G. Harmon, president of Drake University explained: "We in education are well aware of the increased responsibilities involved today in the development of an efficient educational program. That is why we have decided in cooperation with Mr. Weeks, to sell the property." Obviously Salisbury House did not fit in Dr. Harmon's efficient scheme of things.

At the same time the ISEA was house hunting. Since 1926 the Association had been headquartered in the downtown Shops Building. In 1943 Executive Secretary Agnes Samuelson suggested that the time was right to buy or build an office. In 1948 the Delegate Assembly authorized an annual appropriation of $10,000 for a building-reserve fund. In 1952 the Delegate Assembly approved the purchase of a building site at 2150 Grand Avenue. In 1953 the Delegate Assembly approved two fund-raising campaigns, one for business and industry and the other for members. In 1954 the Executive Board bought Salisbury House.

It was proper for the Executive Board to make the purchase. Under the Articles of Incorporation the Executive Board members are trustees of the corporation and are the only persons authorized to purchase or dispose of property. The problem was that delegates to the annual Assembly were led to believe they had something to say about it. They created a building fund, authorized purchase of a site, and sanctioned a fund-raising campaign. No doubt the delegates envisioned a contemporary office facility, something akin to a modern elementary school, perhaps. When they were told that they owned a 42-room Tudor mansion, they were very angry.

Allan Whitfield, a Des Moines attorney and mutual friend of Carl Weeks and ISEA Executive Secretary Charles F. Martin, arranged the sale. The three of them persuaded the Executive Board. The Board members, most of them school superintendents, believed they had acted prudently. They were professionally trained to spend money wisely and they took their responsibilities seriously. For $200,000 they had purchased a $2 million value. How could anyone be upset by that?

How indeed? "Who authorized this?" was the question. It was asked early and it was asked often. It was asked often enough that *Midland Schools* editorialized on the subject in its November, 1954, issue:

"There's no glossing over it. There is a feeling of unrest among ISEA members at a time when the spirit of unity and cooperation should be at its best. This situation has been brought about by the fact that the ISEA Executive Board felt it necessary to make some far reaching decisions at a time when it was not practical to poll the membership for individual opinions."

At the December 1954 meeting of the Executive Board, J. C. Hoglan from Marshalltown reported that the appraisers had determined that the value of all the various furnishings and works of art was $619,000. "This is confidential information," President Frank Hildreth cautioned. "It might hurt our cause if it were generally known."

"That is right," Hoglan agreed, "People have been criticizing us for buying too much art. While the fact remains that all those things were thrown in, my feeling is that it should not be publicized."

Two years later, in the fall of 1956, the anger was unabated. Joe L. Gettys, superintendent of schools at Oskaloosa and vice president of the Association bemoaned the fact. "The most serious thing bothering our Association is Salisbury House," he told his Board colleagues. "In the last few years it has thrown dissension into our ranks. It is a disconcerting influence in our Association and we need to give it considerable attention."

The members of the ISEA were not the only ones angry. The "South of Grand" neighbors were just as angry. The neighbors have proven to be a surly lot where Salisbury House is concerned.

Carl and Edith Weeks were good neighbors, or at least they were good for the neighborhood. It is not known whether the folks next door knew of the arrangement between the Weekses and Drake University. If they knew they did not complain. A school of fine arts conjures up images of string quartets playing pleasing music on warm spring evenings. But now? Salisbury House was to become an office building. Not if the neighbors could help it! They found a lawyer, which was not difficult since many of the neighbors were lawyers, and delayed the purchase for months.

It was necessary for Salisbury House to be rezoned in order for it to be used as an office. The neighbors fought the rezoning. When it became apparent that the Zoning Commission was interested in striking a compromise between two powerful adversaries—Carl Weeks, Drake University, and the ISEA on the one side; and the "South of Grand" neighborhood on the other—bargaining commenced.

Agreement was reached. It was sanctioned by the Zoning Commission and made official in the form of an order by the district court. Salisbury

House could serve as the offices of the ISEA. However, there were a number of restrictions imposed. There could be no printing presses on the premises. There could be no more than 35 employees. There could be no more than 50 people at meetings except for four times a year when the limit would be 200. The parking lot could be no more than 12,500 square feet. The east driveway would be closed, and all traffic would use the south driveway. There could be no exterior alterations to the building except for a one-story addition in the garage area and that had to conform with the existing design of the building. The kitchen facilities on the first floor were to be dismantled. There could be no sleeping accommodations on the premises. And finally, the variance applied only to the ISEA. If ISEA were ever to sell the property, the zoning would revert to single family residence.

The members were angry. The neighbors were upset. And Edith Weeks was not too happy either. It is not known how often Carl Weeks consulted with Edith on business matters. But it is known that she was hospitalized during the period of time when serious negotiations took place between her husband and Charlie Martin leading to the deal for the House and its contents.

Edith was not upset about the sale of the House. Carl and she had given it away 20 years earlier. But she was obviously upset that certain of her valued personal possessions were included on the inventory of items that Carl had sold to ISEA.

One can imagine Edith, having regained her strength a bit, finally reviewing the agreed-upon inventory and the ensuing conversation between Carl and her. Weeks called Charles Martin and asked if they could talk about a trade. "I have given away some things that are important to Edith," he said, "but I doubt they are of much interest to you."

Weeks wanted five single beds, a table and chest from his bedroom, a gate-legged table from William's room, a table from Edith's sitting room, three trefoil stands, and eight shawls—six paisley and two cashmere. In exchange he offered a lace cover for the dining room table, a collection of cups and saucers, a china cabinet to put them in, the autographed letters from the library, and "The King of the Beggars"—a painting by Joseph Stella. It was a very good deal. No one knows what became of the eight shawls—six paisley and two cashmere—but "The King of the Beggars" is one of the most popular paintings in the Salisbury House collection, worth tens of thousands of dollars.

The ISEA moved in, in mid-October. On December 11, 1954, President Frank Hildreth welcomed the Executive Board members to their first meeting at Salisbury House. "It is a real thrill," he said, "to end the centennial year in such an auspicious way."

Immediately, the Board turned its attention to fund-raising since Salisbury House was not paid for. It figured the total cost for the project would be $400,000 or so, considering the purchase price, the cost of the addition which was planned from the beginning, and office furnishings appropriate for a 42-room Tudor mansion. They were over $300,000 short.

John Yourd, the Decorah High School principal, was named chairman of the committee to raise the money. He had a formidable task ahead of him but he was the right person for the job. He was realistic and creative.

He told the Board, "I do not think the teachers will give very willingly to buy this new ISEA headquarters." He was realistic. "But they will give," he said, "to remember a teacher who helped them." He was creative. Thus, the "Teacher Appreciation Fund" was established rather than the "Salisbury House Fund."

The internal rallying cry was "sharing from every member by the 6th of November." An intricate plan was established through which every member would have an opportunity to give. The vehicle was a solicitation card. It read:

"As an expression of appreciation for the teachers who have enriched my life and for the purpose of underwriting the Memorial Headquarters Building, I hereby contribute the sum of _____ to the Teacher Appreciation Fund. Because of one teacher's special help, guidance, and understanding, I hereby request that my above subscription be dedicated to_____. By doing so, I have caused that teacher's name to be permanently inscribed in the Book of Memories as one of the teachers for whom the Memorial Headquarters Building is especially dedicated."

Yourd was a pretty smooth operator. Salisbury House was unpopular so it was renamed for fund-raising purposes as the "Memorial Headquarters Building." One wonders if there was a member somewhere who contributed saying, "I am glad to do this, but I would not give any money to that Salisbury House." Yourd was adamant with the Board, "The primary objective is to sell teacher appreciation. It is not to raise money."

Members were encouraged to give as much as they could afford, but it cost $20 to get a teacher's name permanently inscribed in the Book of Memories. Also, recognizing that there may well have been more than one teacher who had a significant impact on the life of a potential donor, multiple $20 contributions were encouraged so as not to have to choose, from among many, the one teacher to be permanently remembered.

It did not work. Not only did they not have a contribution from every member by the 6th of November, they never came close. In fact, some members pledged $20 or more, causing a name to be "permanently" entered in the Book of Memories, then did not make good on their pledges.

These deadbeats were a source of great irritation to the Executive Board. At a meeting in the spring of 1957, Clyde Lindsley from Cedar Rapids moved that "if the pledges are not met, the name of the person memorialized will be removed from the Book of Memories and the person so memorialized will be notified of the removal." The motion failed, but the minutes of the meeting note that there was considerable sympathy for its intent.

Teachers Appreciation Fund solicitation continued through the end of the 1956-57 membership year; then the Executive Board shut it down. By the last accounting $153,339.74 was raised, an average contribution of $4.75 per ISEA member or enough to cause 7,666 names to be permanently entered in the Book of Memories, which is safely ensconced in the "Memorial Headquarters" Building.

The campaign to raise funds from business and industry did not fare as well. Publishing baron Gardner Cowles made a substantial contribution, as did Ed Burchette, chairman of the board of Valley National Bank, who headed the campaign to raise funds among the rich and powerful in Des Moines.

Burchette did his best. He mailed hundreds of letters soliciting contributions. The take from the letter campaign was $1,006.96. He and Mrs. Burchette hosted an elegant affair at Salisbury House. Many of the guests commented that the place looked better than it had when the Weekses lived there. When the campaign was over Burchette raised less than $30,000. He blamed Joe Rosenfeldt of Younkers for his lack of success. According to Burchette, "Rosenfeldt believes the ISEA is a profit-making organization and is not in line for fund-raising. He has opposed us consistently up and down the line and has had a lot of impact in the loop area."

In the midst of all this, ISEA was dealt another blow. From the first conversation among Allan Whitfield, Carl Weeks, and Charles Martin until October 10, 1956, when the district court said otherwise, Martin and the Executive Board members believed they would be free from property taxes at Salisbury House. The ISEA lawyer had argued that the House was a public art gallery. In the opinion of the court, Salisbury House was first and foremost an office building and somewhere down the line it was a public art gallery. Owners do not pay taxes on public art galleries, but they do pay taxes on office buildings. ISEA was stuck.

The Executive Board contemplated almost every alternative. Peter Janss, their trusted legal counsel who had argued the tax case, suggested they give it back to Drake University. He laid out a scenario whereby ISEA would lease the property back from the University. ISEA would be responsible for upkeep and the care and exhibition of art objects. He suggested the rent could be calculated so as to provide a reasonable interest return upon an assumed value of the property so as to make the matter attractive to Drake. At the same time, he speculated that the rent would be less than the current tax burden on the land, house, and art objects.

Selling the lot north of the east driveway was a possibility. In December, 1957, it was listed with a realtor at a price of $10,500. It did not sell.

That same month the Executive Board members discussed the possibility of selling some of the furnishing and art objects. The Board members seemed to be dissuaded not so much because they treasured the objects or wished not to break faith with Mr. Weeks. Rather, they were dissuaded by Mr. Burchette's argument that it would be impossible to raise money from businesses in the community if ISEA started selling the contents of the building.

The delegates to the 1958 Assembly were concerned, also. They inquired as to whether or not it might be possible to sell some art in order to pay for the building. D. R. Lillard, an Executive Board member from Winterset, set the tone for the next three decades. He responded, "They can be sold but remember that while the main purpose in purchasing Salisbury House was to secure a headquarters building, there was the other very important aspect of acquisition: the maintenance of a cultural center consistent with the ideals of an organization of teachers. To sell the art objects would be breaking faith with the ideals of those who initiated the project and with those many teachers who have contributed because they appreciate the cultural aspects of the headquarters."

The possibility of raising dues temporarily with the increase earmarked for the mortgage was contemplated and rejected. "It would not be fair to those who already contributed."

In the end regular dues money was used. On February 1, 1961, the mortgage was burned in an ISEA urn that predates the birth of Jesus Christ.

In the fall of 1961, ISEA conducted an internal opinion poll and it was determined that a majority of the members no longer objected to Salisbury House.

For the next decade Salisbury House was rarely an issue. Occasionally a delegate to the Assembly or a member of the Executive Board would inquire as to whether or not Salisbury House was cost effective or whether or not it was an efficient office facility. They were assured that it was cost effective and that it was efficient.

Someone suggested that having staff in little cubby holes throughout the building inhibited their ability to work together. Kenneth Wells, executive secretary when the issue was raised, responded that he knew of office buildings without any walls where the staff did not get along, so that probably was not the reason.

The University of Iowa offered to buy the rare book collection. The Executive Board turned it down. The lot north of the east driveway was put on the market again, this time for $25,000. This time it was sold.

From the mid-1960s to the mid-1970s the members and leaders of the ISEA had other things on their minds. There were bigger issues than Salisbury House.

Then a bunch of things went wrong all at the same time, or so it seemed. Heavy rains came and washed away a retaining wall. A contractor was consulted and he reported that the building was leaking in so many places it looked like a sieve. In the contractor's judgment the days of patching were past. Major repairs were needed soon. *The Des Moines Register* reported that valuable works of art were being allowed to deteriorate by the ISEA.

Executive Secretary Wells consulted a realtor about the possibility of selling Salisbury House. He was told "the salability of Salisbury House is practically nil." The realtor suggested that it might be possible to give it away, perhaps to the city of Des Moines or the state of Iowa. Wells solicited the opinions of his management staff and reported that they were divided. One thought it should be given away. One thought it should not. The third did not know for sure.

The severity and immediacy of the problem was communicated to the members and they responded. The William G. Robinson/Salisbury House Preservation Fund was established in 1975 for the purpose of restoration and preservation of Salisbury House artifacts. Bill Robinson, who had recently died of cancer, was a long-time member of the ISEA management staff. No doubt he was the one who opposed giving it away.

Members were able to contribute to the Preservation Fund by checking it off on their membership form each fall. Over the next decade they would contribute in excess of $330,000. By 1981 *The Des Moines Register* art critic Nick Baldwin was able to report, "Thanks to the teachers of Iowa, art objects at Salisbury House are being saved from deterioration with restoration projects that already have returned many of the mansion's treasures to their pristine condition."

Over the years the Association had relatively little success in securing private funds for the purpose of preserving Salisbury House other than those from its members. So the leaders now pursued public funds.

Salisbury House was determined to be a National Historic Place and was listed in the National Register of Historic Places. With this distinction Salisbury House became eligible to receive federal matching grants in aid for the preservation of the property. Also, National Register status permits the owner to secure FHA home improvement loans.

The Association had no more success slopping at the public trough than it had at the private one. It received a single small grant for the purpose of installing a humidity control system needed for the protection of the paintings and books.

The renewed Association commitment to Salisbury House was managed by a preservation committee created by the Delegate Assembly. Seventeen members were appointed. Some were members of the ISEA and others were appointed because of their special interest or expertise. Among those appointed were an art collector, an architect, an expert on rare books, and another on rugs and tapestries. Also appointed was "Hud" Weeks, the "naughty" son of Carl and Edith.

It was the committee's job to familiarize itself with Salisbury House and the collection, to determine what items needed restoration and how badly. Then the committee would match the funds available from contributions with the items most in need and recommend projects to the Executive Board.

The Salisbury House Preservation Committee did an excellent job. The members of the committee approached their responsibilities with dedication and vigor. They monitored the restoration of the major paintings; "The Brothers," "The Cardinal," and "Tree of My Life." Valuable rugs were relocated to avoid wear. The walls, floor, and ceiling in the dining room were reconditioned. Valuable tapestry upholstery was removed from antique furniture, cleaned, and reapplied. A 16th-century Flemish tapestry and four Beauvais tapestries were cleaned and restored. The giant player organ was reconditioned at a cost of $25,000.

As time passed the members of the preservation committee became increasingly frustrated by the limited funds available for restoration projects. They believed that contributions would increase if they were tax deductible. So the preservation committee took steps to create a foundation. They called it the Iowa Society for the Preservation of the Arts. Contributions would be made to the "Society" rather than to ISEA. Thus, they would be tax deductible.

The members of the Board of Directors of the "Society" were to be the same people appointed by the Executive Board of ISEA to sit on the Preservation Committee, at least at the outset. Since there was a need to "keep an arm's length relationship" between the "Society" and ISEA, vacancies on the foundation board would be filled by the remaining members. Therefore there was no guarantee that the membership of the two boards would always be the same.

In some regards the preservation committee worked too well. It took issue with decisions made by the officers and management of ISEA. On occasion it was able to generate sufficient pressure to reverse some of those decisions. Clearly the preservation committee was motivated by what was good for Salisbury House as a museum and the collection of artifacts that it contained. But they demonstrated little understanding or concern for the need of the Association to establish and maintain an efficient office operation.

The differences of opinion among members of the preservation committee and the officers and managers were tolerable. But the move to create the "Society" was not. For now the ISEA faced the possibility of losing control of the money that was contributed for the purpose of restoring its assets.

The matter came to a head for the first time at an Executive Board meeting on the eve of the 1984 Delegate Assembly. John Mesicek of Ankeny moved that "all contributions received from members for the restoration and preservation of Salisbury House and its contents shall be retained by ISEA and shall not be transmitted in whole or in part to the Iowa Society for the Preservation of the Arts and that all activity pursuant to seeking IRS tax-exempt status for the society shall cease." The motion carried.

For all practical purposes Mesicek's motion killed the Iowa Society for the Preservation of the Arts. Shortly thereafter the Executive Board also killed the preservation committee itself. The Board eliminated the large committee of members, staff, and outsiders with special interest or expertise and replaced it with a committee of five members of the Executive Board.

While the old preservation committee was attending to the restoration of painting and tapestries, real trouble was brewing.

First of all, the roof, eaves, and downspouts were in a serious state of disrepair. Fixing the roof at Salisbury House is not a project for a weekend handyman. The tiles are slate—17th-century slate. Each one must be removed individually, carefully lowered three stories to the ground, safely stored, and then returned individually once the repair work is complete.

Then one day the insurance agents came by and announced that they would no longer insure the contents of Salisbury House. In their judgment Salisbury House was not secure. Upon reflection it was nearly everyone's judgment that Salisbury House was not secure. There were a few electronic beams on the first floor in the museum area and a caretaker lived in the cottage across the courtyard. A professional thief or even a reasonably able amateur thief could master the electronic beams. Bats could not. They fly about the House at night and would occasionally trigger the alarm. Bill Sherman, the Association's long-time public relations specialist, could not. He once tried to jump over the beam and triggered the alarm. Salisbury House art works were secure from bats and PR men, but not from professional thieves. Also, the caretaker once had his snowmobiles stolen from in front of the garage behind the cottage, which is across the courtyard from Salisbury House.

The insurance agents said the Association would have to install a modern, computerized, electronic surveillance system throughout the entire House, not just in the museum area. Estimated cost: $125,000. In the meantime it would be necessary for the Association to employ security guards. Once the system was in place, the agents were certain that the treasures would be insurable but that in all likelihood the premiums would be twice what they had been in the past.

Finally, in the mid-1980s, Americans were terrorized by asbestos. It had been widely used as an insulator during the first half of the 20th century. Now it had been determined that asbestos, along with almost everything else, caused cancer. One day a concerned employee remarked, "I will bet those pipes are wrapped with asbestos." One thing led to another. The Executive Board authorized $10,000 to retain a consultant to determine whether or not asbestos was a problem at Salisbury House and, if it was, to suggest what needed to be done to correct it. The consultant determined that asbestos was a problem. Some of it could be sealed. The rest would have to be removed. Estimated cost, $70,000.

Phoebe Tupper from Davenport was president at the time and I was executive director. We were depressed. Water was seeping between our 17th-century tiles. Our treasures were uninsurable. Our pipes were wrapped in asbestos. It was enough to try the patience of Job.

Also, we were out of money. The bottom fell out of the agricultural economy in the United States during the early 1980s. Iowa was hit harder than most. Ag land values dropped. Prices paid for farm commodities dropped. Unemployment in agriculture-related industries rose. So did the number of farm foreclosures and bank failures. The health of the Iowa economy is dependent on agriculture. The well-being of public schools is dependent on the health of the state's economy. The large number of school employee layoffs had a significant negative impact on the resources of the ISEA.

Those were desperate times. Everything was considered, including the possibility of selling the furniture and artifacts one by one, dismantling the building and selling it piece by piece, and subdividing the land and selling it lot by lot. Everyone agreed that ISEA would realize the maximum return from the sale of assets if they were disposed of piecemeal rather than as a whole. A real estate authority advised that the land was worth more without Salisbury House on it than it was with it.

The whole matter was dropped in the lap of the 1986 Delegate Assembly. It was a long and emotional debate. Some delegates wept. In the end four key decisions were made.

It was decided that Salisbury House should be maintained as the ISEA headquarters. Seventy-three percent of the delegates agreed.

It was decided that certain of the valuable assets should be sold. The take from the sales should be invested and the annual earnings placed in a restricted account to be used to maintain Salisbury House and its contents.

Salisbury House is bordered on the east and south by nearly four and one-half acres of forest. It was decided that the forest land should be sold. Eighty-nine percent of the delegates agreed.

ISEA owned four paintings by contemporary artist Joseph Stella. The most valuable of the four, "Tree of My Life," had recently been appraised at $1 million. Two others, "The Birth of Venus" and "The Apotheosis of the Rose," were believed to be worth $1.5 million together. It was decided that these three Stella paintings should be sold. Sixty percent of the delegates agreed. The fourth Stella painting, "The King of the

Beggars," the one traded to ISEA by Carl Weeks in exchange for his wife's valuables, was to be retained.

The officers and managers were happy. It was believed that the sale of the land and paintings would realize about $3 million. That sum, prudently invested, would produce annual earnings of $250,000 to $300,000, enough each year to care for the House and the artifacts that were left.

Their happiness would soon become euphoria. It was decided that the paintings would be sold at auction in New York City by Christies, one of the two prestige auction houses in the world. Christies officials recommended that "Tree of My Life" be sold first. "The Birth of Venus" and "The Apotheosis of the Rose" should be sold later, perhaps two or three years later. There was a pent-up demand for Stellas. Selling a single, valuable Stella painting would take maximum advantage of the demand.

December 5, 1986, was set as the date for the auction. Bill Pritchard, associate executive director for administration, packed his bags and accompanied the painting to New York. He called on the eve of the sale to report that more than one party appeared interested in our painting—which is good news at an auction. "Christies," he said, "believes that, at a minimum, ISEA will realize the appraised value of the painting." Those who remained behind began to contemplate a sale price of $1.1 million or maybe even $1.2 million.

The sale occurred shortly before noon. It took less than a single minute. When the gavel fell, the Association had sold "Tree of My Life" to a contractor from St. Louis, Missouri, for $2 million. It was, at the time, the second highest price ever paid for a work by an American artist.

Back home in Des Moines, some who had opposed the sale were heard to say that they had never really liked the painting that much anyway.

The sale of the land was another matter entirely. Orange surveyor stakes appeared in the forest mid-summer and the neighbors saw red. ISEA was desecrating the memory of Carl Weeks. The Association was about to destroy the only stand of virgin timber left inside the city limits of Des Moines. What about those teachers whose names were permanently entered in the Book of Memories?

Most of the neighbors perceived the forest as their private preserve. Some thought it was a city park. Two of the many attorneys in the vicinity emerged as the "pro bono" spokespersons. Edgar Hansell and Addison Parker represented the aggrieved neighbors.

Their mission was to have Salisbury House declared a city landmark. Landmark status meant that the owner of a property could make no substantial alteration without prior approval. Prior approval came from the Historic District Commission, whose decisions were appealable to the Plan and Zoning Commission, whose decisions were appealable to the City Council, whose decisions were appealable in court.

That is the same process through which a property is declared to be a landmark. It is recommended by the Historic District Commission to the Plan and Zoning Commission to the City Council which decides.

The matter of Salisbury House was unique. It is customary for the owner of a property to seek to have it declared a landmark. Supposedly it is desirable to be a landmark. There is status and enhanced property value that accompanies such designation. In the case of Salisbury House it was the neighbors who sought landmark status. The owner, ISEA, vigorously opposed it.

It did not matter. The Historic District Commission sided with the neighbors with but one lone dissenting vote. The Plan and Zoning Commission was worse. They sided with the neighbors without a single dissenting vote. The matter was headed for the City Council, where the dynamics were considerably different.

Commission members are appointed to office and serve for a variety of reasons, some known only to themselves. City Council members are elected to office. They are politicians in the true sense of the word. They wish to be re-elected to office and some, if not all, covet loftier positions. The Council members knew of the money and influence of the neighbors. They also knew of the thousands of ISEA members who lived and voted in the City of Des Moines, its legislative districts, and the 4th Congressional District of which Des Moines was a part. The Salisbury House matter was cut and dried before the Commissions. It was not cut and dried before the City Council at all.

The first hearing was held before the City Council on December 7, 1987. ISEA was represented by President Ken Tilp, Associate Executive Director Bill Pritchard, and attorney James Sayre. The neighbors packed the chambers and pulled out all the stops. "Hud" Weeks spoke, though he said he did not know what he was supposed to say. A Weeks granddaughter came from somewhere out of state. Frank Hildreth, the ISEA president from 1954, reappeared. Edgar Hansell, Addison Parker, and neighbor after neighbor addressed the Council. They spoke of architectural integrity, memories of times past, the heart and soul of the city, and acres of virgin timber.

The City Council deferred action until January. In January they deferred it again. Eventually, they deferred it indefinitely. Some Council members declared their positions. Others spoke to the issue in a fashion that allowed one to conclude what their position was. Two Council members, Connie Cook and Mike McPherson, were Des Moines Public School administrators. They sided with the Association. So did Elaine Szymoniak who was a candidate for the State Senate at the time. Mayor John "Pat" Dorrian and Council member George Flagg sided with the neighbors. No one ever knew for certain how Archie Brooks and Ric Jorgensen would vote if they had to, but it was believed that Brooks would vote with the Association and Jorgensen would vote with the neighbors.

Council member Jorgensen was in the most difficult position of all. Salisbury House and all the neighbors are in the middle of his ward. That probably explains why he asked his colleagues on the Council to defer action in order to allow him time to work with the parties in an effort to arrive at a compromise that would be satisfactory to both the Association and to the neighbors. The Council was pleased to defer.

The ISEA Executive Board watched the developments closely. By January 1988 its members were angry, almost to a person. Nancy Schmidt of Pleasant Valley moved that "ISEA shall maintain control of its property as a private property owner; therefore the neighbors' proposal is out of order." It passed. It did not mean much except as an outlet for the members' frustration.

Janet White of Marion made a more significant motion on behalf of the Board's Preservation Committee. She moved that "ISEA explore the possibilities of selling Salisbury House in its entirety in the event it becomes necessary to maintain the integrity of the House, contents, and grounds." White's motion also passed.

Preservation Committee members explained that they intended to pursue all options in order to resolve the current problem with the neighbors. It was not their intent nor their desire to sell the building, but they believed strongly that it should be sold if there was a danger of losing control of it.

Following the Executive Board meeting, the neighbors were advised that ISEA would consider an offer to purchase Salisbury House for $7.5 million. Word travels fast. Reporters called and were advised that the rumors were true.

On March 8, 1988, I received a call from Marcus Abels, a young attorney. Abels indicated that he was calling on behalf of a client who wished to make an offer for the purchase of Salisbury House. An appointment was made for the next morning.

The next morning Bill Pritchard, Ken Tilp, and I waited in the conference room with great anticipation for the arrival of the mystery buyer. We were excited both to learn his identity and the amount and terms of his offer. We were certain that we would recognize him. He had to be the chairman of the board or president of one of Des Moines larger corporations. Who else could afford to buy Salisbury House?

As it turns out we did not recognize him, nor had any of the three ever heard of him. His name was H. Bryan Hughes. He was young, tastefully groomed, and expensively dressed. He was president of a West Des Moines company named Bryton Capital Management, Inc. He offered $6 million for Salisbury House. He confided that much of the money would come from the sale of artifacts. It was a bonafide offer, but until the deal was closed his identity and the identity of the corporation were to be kept confidential. Not even the Executive Board was to know.

We explained ISEA governance to Hughes and Abels. We offered to call a special meeting of the Executive Board. We agreed to recommend to the Board that it transmit the offer to Delegate Assembly, which was scheduled to convene on April 7. Hughes and Abels agreed.

The Executive Board met in special session on March 20. A motion was adopted for transmittal to Delegate Assembly that provided for a number of things, including that "the Executive Board is authorized to negotiate the sale of Salisbury House at such terms and conditions, including price, as the Executive Board deems appropriate."

The media got wind of the fact that a deal was in the works. They were barred from the Executive Board meeting and told that no announcement would be made until Monday morning, two days hence, when a news conference would be held at Salisbury House.

The news conference became a bit of a circus. A fairly rowdy group of neighbor ladies occupied a hallway demanding access to the news conference. Bill Pritchard persuaded them to leave Salisbury House voluntarily upon threat of calling the police and having them thrown out. President Tilp started the news conference by jokingly telling the reporters that he would like to give them the name of the buyer, but could not because he did not speak Japanese. After the gasps subsided, Tilp announced that a bonafide offer had been received, that the buyer was local, that the identity of the buyer was confidential until all terms and conditions were set, that further discussions were contingent upon Delegate Assembly authorization, and that the Delegate Assembly would consider the matter on April 7.

Four days later, Bryton Capital Management, Inc. withdrew its offer. According to Hughes, upon further consideration, he had determined that it was not in his best interest nor in the best interest of the company to become embroiled in a long and heated battle with the neighbors of Salisbury House.

Bryton Capital Management, Inc., did not want to buy Salisbury House but maybe someone else did. It was decided to carry the Executive Board motion to the Delegate Assembly even though there was no live buyer on the string.

Again it was a long and emotional debate. Six different amendments were offered to the main motion. Each would have limited the Executive Board's prerogatives or placed conditions on the sale. Each, in turn, was defeated. When the vote was taken, the outcome was clear. There was no call for division. The delegates overwhelmingly voted to sell Salisbury House.

The negotiations started by City Council member Ric Jorgensen continued and continued and continued. Finally, in the fall of 1989, an agreement was reached. The neighbors agreed to collect $600,000. The money would be given to the Iowa Natural Heritage Foundation. The Foundation would invest it. The annual earnings from the investment would be given to the Association to be used for restoration projects or to offset some of the costs of operating Salisbury House as a museum. In return, the Association agreed that a preservation easement would be placed on the land, protecting it from development.

The neighbors had up to two years to fulfill their part of the bargain. All of the deadlines passed. No one in the Association knows how much they actually collected, but all are certain that they never came close to $600,000.

So there sits Salisbury House. It is still quite a place after 65 years: a 42-room Tudor mansion in the middle of ten acres of virgin timber, in the middle of Des Moines. It is the home of the ISEA.

Much of the interior of the building has been remodeled. It is as efficient an office building as it will ever become. Major repair work remains to be done on the roof, but a modern, computerized, electronic security system has been installed and the asbestos has been sealed or removed.

The other two Stella paintings, "The Birth of Venus" and the "Apotheosis of the Rose," were never sold. They were taken to Christies in New York City to be auctioned but there were no bidders this time.

A fellow in a moth-eaten sweater and funny-looking hat rode up on his bicycle one day and offered to buy Salisbury House for $7.5 million. He left a check for $400 as earnest money. Another time, a man on the $2 tour offered to trade his dump truck and garbage business for Salisbury House. It is fair to say that the Association has received no serious offers for the purchase of Salisbury House since the Delegate Assembly said it should be sold.

The Association has contemplated making another attempt to sell the four-and-one-half acres of forest land. The neighbors would not like it, but no one at Salisbury House much cares what the neighbors like.

In February 1992 the Executive Board decided to make a long-term commitment to Salisbury House. A motion was made and passed that says, "The Executive Board directs that the Salisbury House Preservation Committee develop plans for replacing the roof, complete other repairs which have been delayed, and offer a plan for adding office space which would meet the needs of the Association beyond the year 2000."

Even though the motion passed unanimously, one could sense that there was more resignation than enthusiasm in the voices of the members when they voted. One suspects that a legitimate buyer with a bonafide offer could probably consummate a deal with ISEA for the purchase of Salisbury House in pretty short order.

Salisbury House is now a National Historic Site. Its historical significance is that it stands as an example of the excesses of the rich and powerful during the Roaring Twenties, a period in our history remembered for its excesses. Carl Weeks spent nearly $2 million of his fortune to build and furnish a 42-room Tudor mansion that today can neither be sold nor given away.

Salisbury House is quite a place.

CHAPTER 33

Heather Manor

Next to Salisbury House, Heather Manor has been the ISEA's most troublesome edifice.

As the early promotional materials described it, Heather Manor is "a 12-story, twin-towered apartment building, designed to include well-planned facilities for comfort and recreation. The residents will enjoy, as they choose, the privacy of their own home or the companionship of others with mutual interests."

As Heather Manor has evolved, it has become a "life-care" facility. Older people buy or "endow" apartments. Some will become unable to live without assistance. When they do, assistance is provided. Some will become unable to live on their own at all. When they do, a nursing home or health center, as it is called, is attached. When a resident dies or it is determined that a move to the health center is permanent, the apartment is re-endowed and the cycle begins anew.

It is really a pretty good deal for the residents, especially in these days when older people worry about the availability and cost of nursing home care. For the price of an apartment and a monthly fee, one is guaranteed care for life no matter what the circumstance.

It has not been such a good deal for the ISEA.

Heather Manor's official birthdate is October 30, 1970. It was dedicated on that date. The twin towers—12 stories each, 147 one-room and studio apartments, all located on three and one-half acres of land in downtown Des Moines near the business loop and the state Capitol—were dedicated in style.

NEA President Helen Bain paid recognition to several members who had worked to ensure construction of the home. She used the opportunity to announce that the NEA would employ a special consultant to assist other groups interested in developing similar homes.

Governor Robert D. Ray praised the ISEA for helping this type of home become a reality.

Mabel Iowa Robbins spoke to the 300 guests about the joys and comforts of Heather Manor living. Robbins was president of the Iowa Retired Teachers Association and the first official resident of the home. She was 79 years of age at the time. On February 26, 1991, Robbins celebrated her 100th birthday as Heather Manor's longest continuous resident.

It was a grand day for Heather Manor, perhaps its grandest. The 20 previous years had been difficult ones for those who saw the possibilities. The years to follow would be even more difficult for those who had to deal with the realities.

The idea was conceived by the Delegate Assembly in 1950 with the adoption of an item calling for an investigation into the need for a teachers' retirement home in Iowa. The issue was discussed for over five years.

There was no clear concept as to what the home should be. Some talked of the need for a home for impoverished retired teachers, an alternative to the county farm, as it were. The California Teachers Association maintained several facilities where a few aged, destitute teachers could live out their last years with a modicum of dignity. Some considered this the model.

Others envisioned building a home where teachers with modest means could afford to spend their retirement years living securely and comfortably.

While some viewed building a retirement home for teachers as an act of charity, others viewed it as a special service, akin to travel programs or life insurance, something that members could benefit from if they could afford to.

The charitable view was prevalent in the early years of planning. Mary Jane Graham, a young teacher from Greenwood Elementary School in Des Moines, made the first voluntary contribution to the project. She gave $2. "It is a definite advantage," she said, "to teach in a state with the added security that this home will provide."

By the time the corporation was formed in 1958, the retirement home was clearly viewed as a special service program. The Horace Mann Home for the Aged, Inc., was established as a non-profit corporation. But for contributions to the corporation to be tax deductible, it was necessary for the trustees to agree to accept some persons who could not afford to pay their own way. It was agreed that the benefits from contributions being tax deductible outweighed the drawbacks from government-mandated charity.

When Heather Manor opened in 1970 it was no longer exclusively a home for teachers. It was advertised as a residence for retired teachers and "their friends over the age of 62." Soon the pretense of Heather Manor being a teacher retirement home was dropped completely. It became an apartment facility for any older person who could afford the endowment and monthly fees. Some wished it could be otherwise, but serious financial problems made the change necessary.

The Board of Trustees of the Horace Mann Home for the Aged met for the first time on January 31, 1957, at Bishop's Cafeteria in Des Moines. Those who wished to, met for dinner at 6 p.m. The meeting commenced an hour later. The 11 trustees were joined by Charles F. Martin, the ISEA executive secretary who would serve as a consultant, and by Dorothy Brazzle, an ISEA research analyst who had been assigned by Martin to serve as executive secretary for the trustees. The board elected Vesper Price, a Des Moines teacher, to serve as the first president of the corporation. For the next decade, she and Brazzle would be the driving forces behind the home.

The Board of Trustees of the Horace Mann Home for the Aged, Inc., met with the Executive Board of the ISEA for the first time on June 14, 1958. The trustees made their initial request for assistance and the Executive Board approved it. From that date until construction was completed, every request for help, whether financial or otherwise, was granted, most without question. The ISEA—the officers, management, Executive Board, and Delegate Assembly—were behind the project.

The trustees needed an attorney to draw up a working plan and get it approved by the tax authorities so that contributions to the home could be tax deductible. The Executive Board authorized the use of ISEA legal counsel to serve the Horace Mann Home for the Aged, Inc. Charles Martin assigned Marvin Adams and the assignment lasted for nine years.

The trustees had expenses and no money. They needed a checking account with, say, $10,000 in it for starters. The Delegate Assembly approved a $10,000 non-interest-bearing loan to be paid back when the Horace Mann Home for the Aged, Inc., was able.

The trustees needed $9,000 along with the official sponsorship of the ISEA to forward to the Federal Housing Administration (FHA) as part of their application for a loan. At this point Dr. William Anderson, Cedar Falls superintendent of schools and a member of the ISEA Executive Board by virtue of being ISEA past-president, did raise an issue or two.

On September 19, 1964, Anderson wondered what "sponsorship" entailed. He was told by Marvin Adams that it meant that the ISEA would promote the Horace Mann Home, that its officers would have the authority to make the arrangements for the loan, and that the Association would collect the entrance fees and hold them in escrow.

Anderson also questioned "whether or not sponsoring such a home was the responsibility of the profession." But in the end, he seconded the motion made by George Fischer of Des Moines directing the executive secretary to draft the necessary documents, in consultation with Marvin Adams, for the sponsorship of the Horace Mann Home. "The most the ISEA could lose," Anderson noted, "would be $19,000." There was a dissenting vote, which was unusual for motions dealing with the Horace Mann Home for the Aged, Inc. The name of the dissenter was not recorded in the minutes of the meeting.

The trustees needed $2,850 to accompany their application for mortgage insurance. The Executive Board authorized it.

The trustees needed $35,000 to hire an architect. On March 19, 1966, the Executive Board approved a motion "directing the executive secretary, on behalf of the Association, to join with the Horace Mann Home for the Aged in the execution of a contract with Wetherell, Harrison, and Wagner for architectural services in connection with the retirement housing facility to be built by the Horace Mann Home for the Aged."

As best as can be determined, in the nearly eight-year period from June 1958 through March 1966, the ISEA spent some $80,000 on various aspects of the Horace Mann Home project. The figure does not include the cost of the time spent by Charles Martin, the executive secretaries who followed him, Dorothy Brazzle, and the rest of the ISEA staff.

While $80,000 is a significant commitment to make to any project, it is small potatoes compared to the commitment the ISEA was about to make.

On September 18, 1965, attorney Adams had a different answer to Dr. William Anderson's question of what "sponsorship" entailed. "There is no way of knowing the exact requirements which would be set out by the FHA," he said, "but before they will finally insure any loan, a portion of that loan must be guaranteed by the sponsor, which in this case would be the ISEA."

Adams said he had researched the Articles of Incorporation and he believed that the Executive Board had the authority to obligate the Association as guarantor. However, the Executive Board thought perhaps it would be better if this matter was referred to the Delegate Assembly.

M. M. Rogers, a member of the Executive Board from Sumner, made the report to the delegates on the affairs of the Horace Mann Home for the Aged, Inc. "If you accept this report," he said, "you will authorize the Executive Board to execute a guarantee agreement in an amount of approximately $707,600, which in turn will permit the Horace Mann Home for the Aged to secure FHA approval of a mortgage in the tentative maximum amount of $1.95 million." "There naturally will be some risk," he added, "but I believe it will be very slight."

Upon completion of his remarks, Rogers moved "the adoption of the report of the Horace Mann Home for the Aged, Inc., including authorizing the ISEA, as sponsor, to execute a guarantee agreement as required by the FHA."

Incredibly, the minutes of the 1966 Delegate Assembly show that Rogers' motion carried unanimously.

As time went by, the amount of the loan and the amount of the loan to be guaranteed by the ISEA got bigger and bigger. The $707,600 figure reported to the Delegate Assembly next became $921,000. By early 1967, it was up to a cool $1 million.

Not only had the amount of the guarantee increased, but officials of the Association now understood that their obligation would continue for the entire term of the mortgage. Since the mortgage was for 40 years, they would be encumbering assets of the Association for a period of time extending well into the 21st century. The Executive Board paused for a moment to contemplate the significance of its commitment to the Horace Mann Home for the Aged, Inc.

At the Board meeting on March 18, 1967, a motion was made that "the ISEA reaffirms its sponsorship and takes action to underwrite the Horace Mann Home project." The motion carried unanimously by those present and voting.

By October 18, 1967, the amount of the guarantee had risen to $1.15 million. A motion was made "to take all the necessary steps to proceed with the Horace Mann project." Again, the motion was carried unanimously by those present and voting.

By January 31, 1968, the deal was done. ISEA President Elmer C. Gast and Executive Secretary Kenneth P. Wells had committed the Association to the Horace Mann Home for the Aged until the mortgage was paid in full. At the Executive Board meeting on that date a motion was made "to ratify, approve, and confirm all contract agreements and guarantees entered into by

Elmer C. Gast and Kenneth P. Wells." The motion was carried unanimously by those present and voting. The construction of Heather Manor commenced shortly thereafter.

How did the Horace Mann Home for the Aged become Heather Manor? It all began, as far as the name is concerned, in 1959, when the Heathershaw sisters—Lillian, Mae, and Jeanette—gave their family's farm on Fleur Drive in Des Moines to the Horace Mann Home for the Aged, Inc.

Both Lillian and Mae were retired teachers. They had, no doubt, at some time or other been moved by the descriptions of the sorry plight of some of their former colleagues. They became aware that the ISEA, through the Horace Mann Home for the Aged, Inc., shared their concern and was trying to do something about it. The Heathershaw sisters wished to make a contribution.

The farm, or what was left of it by then, consisted of 3.5 acres of land and a house at 4501 Fleur Drive. The property was valued at $75,000. The house was still occupied by Jeanette Heathershaw and she wished to remain there until her demise. The property had already been rezoned for commercial use so converting it for multiple housing purposes would be a fairly simple matter.

Midland Schools reported, "This gift of a valuable, beautiful site has given tremendous impetus to fulfilling the need of a home for retired teachers in Iowa."

The FHA approved the site for construction of the Horace Mann Home for the Aged. But the FHA suggested that because of its close proximity to the Des Moines Airport, Federal Aviation Administration (FAA) approval of the site should also be secured. The FAA decided that the construction of two, 12-story apartment houses along the flight path for incoming and outgoing jets was not in the best interests of the residents of the apartment houses or the passengers on the jets. FAA approval was denied.

The site on Fleur Drive was sold and the search commenced for a new location. The trustees purchased property on East Fifth Street in downtown Des Moines.

This time *Midland Schools* reported: "The Board of Trustees was fortunate in securing a site high above the city of Des Moines with a magnificent view of the city and surrounding countryside. The location is in the River Hills urban renewal area, which is now a beehive of activity."

Since the home had not been built on the Heathershaw property, the trustees thought it fitting to recognize the generosity of the sisters in some permanent manner, lest it be forgotten over the years. They thought about naming the home "Heathershaw Manor," but decided, in the end, that "Heather Manor" had more of a ring to it.

Seldom has a project gone sour so soon. The twin towers opened for business in the early part of June, 1970. By the time the ISEA Executive Board met on October 21, nine days before the facility was to be dedicated by the president of NEA and the Governor of Iowa, it was obvious there was serious trouble.

Potential customers had viewed the property but very few had purchased apartments. Executive Board members expressed their concern about the small number of residents. Charles Godfrey had been hired by the Board of Trustees of the Horace Mann Home for the Aged, Inc., to manage the property. The Executive Board directed that he develop a plan for recruiting residents and report it to them by December.

A written report was given to the Executive Board at its November meeting. The members requested that "a more meaningful report" be prepared and sent within one week. "Further," the members said, "in the future, monthly reports should include the number of occupants, the number of additional commitments on which a down payment had been received, etc., so that we can keep ourselves more current on the financial picture."

Charles Godfrey and Dorothy Brazzle met with the Executive Board in December. They reported that as a temporary, stop-gap measure, they had secured the permission of the FHA to rent apartments on a month-to-month basis until such time as they could be sold.

Finally the situation became so desperate that it was decided to consult with someone who knew something about the retirement home business. On February 3, 1971, the Executive Board met with Dr. Kenneth P. Berg, president of Christian Home Services, Inc., of Kansas City, Missouri. Christian Home Services was a corporation that specialized in setting up and filling retirement homes.

Berg explained that there was a demand for retirement homes like Heather Manor. "There has to be something wrong with yours," he said, "if you are unable fill it."

Berg had a number of suggestions. Something needed to be done to make the interior of Heather Manor more attractive to prospective buyers. A professional should be hired to decorate the model apartment units. The hallways should be carpeted. The recreation areas should be decorated and furnished.

"Most retirement homes like Heather Manor have infirmaries," Berg explained. He suggested that one be added as soon as possible and speculated that an infirmary was likely to cost $100,000 or so.

Berg also recommended that Christian Home Services should be retained as the sales agent for the apartments at Heather Manor. The Executive Board took this suggestion and all of the others.

By the end of August the Christian Home Services salesperson was able to report that all but five of the one-bedroom apartments had been sold. She was hopeful that they would be gone by February, 1972. She was not so optimistic about the sale of the efficiency units.

On March 18, 1972, the Executive Board authorized entering into a contract with Ringland, Johnson, and Crowley for the construction of a 10-bed infirmary. It would cost $170,000 rather than the $100,000 that Berg had estimated earlier.

The ISEA was heavily invested in Heather Manor. Not only was the Association on the hook for the duration of the 40-year mortgage, but it was also directly supporting the day-to-day operations of the facility with cash from its own coffers. In March, 1971, the Executive Board members expressed concern about the fact that the ISEA had borrowed an amount of money equal to one-half of its annual budget. It was pointed out that the amount that ISEA had borrowed was about the same amount that it had advanced to Heather Manor. It was decided that once all the apartments at Heather Manor were full, the cash picture at the ISEA would return to normal.

Two years later the situation had not improved at all. If anything, it was worse. The Executive Board members were advised that all but five of the apartments were sold, but that the deficit from operating the facility had continued to grow and it was now at a point where something dramatic needed to be done. Dr. Robert Creighton from Shenandoah moved that the ISEA "rid themselves of this obligation" at the earliest possible moment. His motion carried. In just three short years "the gleaming twin towers" had become "this obligation to be rid of."

It was not possible to be rid of this obligation. Who else would assume it? But there were some things that could be done.

For one, the Association took control of Heather Manor away from the Board of Trustees of the Horace Mann Home for the Aged, Inc. It happened on February 17, 1973. The trustees were told that from now on they would meet once each year to attend to the formalities that the law required of them.

In the future, the real decisions would be made by the ISEA Executive Board, management, and staff. The trustees acquiesced.

Some immediate steps were taken by the ISEA management. The purchase price of the apartments was raised and the monthly fees were increased. The charge for meals was raised so that the dining room could operate on at least a self-sustaining basis. Also, the size of the Heather Manor staff was reduced.

A major step was taken on December 15, 1973, when the Executive Board approved a contract with Christian Home Services, Inc., for the professional, day-to-day management of Heather Manor.

Things got worse and then after awhile they got better. At one point the members of the Executive Board were so desperate that when the management staff of the ISEA would report that a resident of Heather Manor had died, some would applaud because the apartment could now be re-endowed.

Today, Heather Manor is not a special service or benefit for the members of the ISEA. Very few of the residents were ever teachers. Plainly and simply, Heather Manor is an apartment house, restaurant, and nursing home for older persons who have the means to live there.

If Heather Manor profits, there is no benefit to the ISEA. If Heather Manor fails, there is a terrific price to be paid by the ISEA. There is always a risk. In the meantime, a significant portion of the assets of the Association are encumbered until the year 2011.

From the Delegate Assembly in 1950 when the idea of a retirement home for teachers in Iowa was first proposed until this day, there has never been a time when Heather Manor was an asset to the ISEA.

Heather Manor was quite a mistake!

CHAPTER 34

A Personal Reflection

The history of the ISEA since 1954 is the story of an organization coming of age. It is also the story of a profession coming of age.

It is a story about tenacity, courage, and upon occasion, reckless abandon. Most important of all, it is a story about teachers who never became president or executive director of ISEA—teachers like Ruth Foster, Maxine Henry, Lydia Reida, Doris Mauer, and Stanley Van Hauen. It is a story about teachers who, throughout long and distinguished careers, never lost sight of the vision of a profession and a professional organization committed to quality and equity for themselves and for the students they taught.

For me, writing the history of the ISEA was an emotional experience. It enabled me to relive my career. Most often the emotion that I experienced was anger. At the age of 50 I no longer get angry very often. When I do, I am usually riled by a politician or the author of a letter-to-the-editor. Now, most often, I am able to control my emotions. Twenty-five years ago I was visibly angry much of the time.

The minutes of the Executive Board meetings provided me with the most valuable information and the greatest insight. Dorothy Helmick, who served as secretary to the Executive Board until 1973, was a court stenographer. Her minutes are lengthy. Often the dialogue is printed verbatim. It was much of this dialogue that made me angry.

A classic example is the September, 1965, meeting between the Executive Board and the officers of the IACT. The demeanor of Roger O. Blake, ISEA president and superintendent of schools at Hawarden, brought to mind again the fact that in the "old days," classroom teachers were patronized, insulted, and threatened with impunity by administrators and school board members.

Dick VanderWoude, the IACT president-elect in 1965, is the only one that I know personally who was present at the meeting. He and his wife, Pam Ryan, have since become dear friends. Both are NEA staff members and Dick served for a number of years as the executive director of the Nevada State Education Association. Knowing Dick, I assume the meeting made him more determined than it did angry. He is soft spoken and gentle by nature. As I read the account, I was cheering for someone, preferably Dick, to punch Blake in the nose, but no one did.

My earliest recollection of the Association was as a high school student in Davison, Michigan, during the late 1950s. Some of the high school teachers in this Flint suburb were AFT supporters. Others—I am certain a large majority—were loyal to the NEA. The unpleasantness between the factions was known to the students. My analysis as a "future teacher" was that the younger, more daring, less conforming teachers were the Federation sympathizers. Therefore, I decided that I would be one, too.

This early decision was reinforced by my college experiences at Central Michigan University. Many of my education professors were dull and boring. To a man, they were former school superintendents and active Association supporters. The one notable exception was a stunningly attractive, extremely articulate woman named Dr. Ann Galbraith. She, too, may have been an Association supporter, but I doubt it. She said things like, "What teachers need is a leader who combines the talents of Jesus Christ and Jimmy Hoffa." She was the first teacher advocate that I ever met.

I was especially amused by Bill Anderson's concern expressed to his ISEA Executive Board colleagues in 1962 regarding the debate he witnessed between Association and Federation representatives at the State College of Iowa. "It would be better for the NEA to decline to participate in these things," he said, "if they cannot send someone who knows how to debate."

I was amused because I witnessed a similar debate at almost the exact time. It was a massacre as far as I was concerned. To this day I remember the name of the AFT representative. He was Clair White, a teacher from Bay City, Michigan. I do not recall the name of the Association representative. I have often wondered if it was someone I later came to know and, in all likelihood, respect.

White took the offensive early and was relentless in his attack. "The Association is a private club for school superintendents," he charged. "They don't give a damn about teachers! They want the teachers' money. That's all they care about." I was persuaded.

I never actually joined the AFT, but I did refuse to join the Association upon arriving in Fennville, Michigan. Fennville is a small, rural community in southwestern Michigan. They grow fruit and shoot ducks in and around Fennville. It is quite possible that in 1964 there was not a single union member among the 705 residents of the village, let alone one among the teachers in the school system.

I did call the local AFT office in Grand Rapids to inquire as to whether it would be interested in having a member in Fennville. Apparently it was not, for no one ever returned my call.

I was not the only non-member. Jim Walz, the iconoclastic librarian, and his wife Grace, the history teacher, were not members, either. At the beginning of my second year of teaching, my friend Willie Armstrong came to Fennville to be the band director. He did not join the Association. Also, Sally Ost arrived to teach biology. She had actually been a Federation member the previous year while teaching in the small community of Biwabik on Minnesota's Iron Range. She did not join the Association.

Three months later Sally and I were married at Jim and Grace's house. Willie was the best man. The five of us spent the remainder of the year harassing the Fennville Education Association. Four years later I would be a negotiations consultant for the Michigan Education Association (MEA) and Fennville would be one of my locals.

Collective bargaining came to Michigan 10 years before it came to Iowa. It passed the Legislature and was signed into law by Governor George Romney in the spring of 1965. By winter, most local associations were bargaining with their school boards. However, my personal experience as a bargainer commenced more than a year prior to the enactment of the law.

The mark of success on my college campus in the spring of 1964 was $5,000. Those graduating seniors—prospective teachers—who signed a contract for $5,000 or more had made it. They were successes. Those who signed for less lied about it.

I was offered a contract by the Lake Orion Public Schools, not for $5,000, but for $5,100. I was also offered a contract by Fennville, where I was student teaching at the time, for $4,600. It was a dilemma for me. The $5,100 at Lake Orion was pretty good money for a beginning teacher in 1964. But I really wanted to teach in Fennville.

I agonized for days. Then it occurred to me, "This isn't an either-or matter. I can bargain. If they want me in Fennville they will have to pay me!"

This was real bargaining that I was thinking about; man to man, take it or leave it, down and dirty.

The next morning I went to the superintendent's office. Henry Martin was his name. I inquired of the secretary as to whether or not Mr. Martin would see me for a minute or two. I hoped that he would not. What had seemed so exciting the night before had become very scary to me in the light of day. I really hoped that he would not be able to see me for days or even weeks.

As my luck would have it, he was in and he had a minute or two. I was ushered into his office. It was one of the few times in my life that I have experienced terror. My knees were shaking. My hands were cold and clammy. My voice was trembling. I mustered up all of the courage that I could. "Mr. Martin," I said, "I really want to teach in Fennville, but Lake Orion has offered me $5,100 and I just can't teach here for $4,600."

There! I had said it and I was relieved if only for a second. My mind was racing. "What is he going to say?" I wondered. "I know he is going to say $5,100 is a pretty good salary, young fellow. You are going to enjoy Lake Orion. Have a good life!"

But he did not. Instead, he asked, "What would you have to have to teach in Fennville?" It had never occurred to me that he might ask me that question. I had given the matter no thought at all. "What would I have to have to teach in Fennville?" I inquired of myself, hurriedly. "$4,700," I blurted out. "We have a deal," said Henry Martin.

Ed Carrigan was the principal of Fennville High School during my first year of teaching. He was a wonderful, caring principal who conscientiously nurtured his beginning teachers. The only negative comment on my first performance evaluation had to do with the fact that I had chosen not to be a member of my professional Association. All else must have been in order because I received a "merit" raise in my second contract.

As in Iowa, many districts in Michigan bargained with their teachers before they were required to by law. Fennville was not one of those districts. In many other districts where they did not bargain, the school board unilaterally established a salary schedule. Fennville was not one of those districts, either. There was no known minimum or maximum salary in Fennville. In fact, Henry Martin would occasionally ask what I am certain was a rhetorical question, "Isn't it nice to teach in a system where there is no limit as to the amount of money a teacher can make?"

Late in January it was announced that the school board had determined that the standard raise for teachers for 1965-66 would be $200. Shortly thereafter, I received a letter from Henry Martin advising me that my raise would be $215 reflecting the excellent contribution that I had made to the school district.

In a matter of days, I received another letter from Henry Martin advising me that the school board had decided to take away the $15 merit bonus from those who got it. It seems that some people could not keep the information to themselves and it had caused hard feelings.

It was one piece of bad news after another or so it seemed. Not long after I lost my $15, I lost my principal, too. Ed Carrigan announced that he was moving on to bigger and better things. He was replaced by JTMcM.

The book, *Up the Down Staircase*, was a best seller at the time. JJMcH was the infamous memo-writing principal at that New York City high school. Not only did JTMcM actually initial his memos "JTMcM," but he also reminded most of us of JJMcH in other ways as well.

JTMcM had retired as principal of Steinmetz High School in Chicago. Being principal of Fennville High School was expected to be a piece of cake for an eminent educator from the city of Chicago. Snaring someone of JTMcM's stature to be the principal of Fennville High School was the defining moment of Henry Martin's career as a school superintendent.

JTMcM brought most of the teachers closer together. The more generous among us thought that perhaps, in a place like Chicago, JTMcM could be successful. We guessed that at Steinmetz High School there was an army of assistant principals, department heads, and guidance counselors who made all of the little everyday decisions that kept the school running. Most likely, the principal of Steinmetz High School was only responsible for the big decisions.

The problem was that at Fennville High School there were no really big decisions, only the little everyday ones that kept the school running. We had no assistant principals or department heads and only one counselor. Once JTMcM arrived, no one made any decisions.

We met JTMcM the first day of school and after that we rarely saw him. Had it not been for his memos and intercom messages we might have come to believe that he did not exist at all. There was a certain "Wizard of Oz" quality about his management style.

Not only did he communicate with the students via the intercom, but it was also his preferred medium for communicating with teachers. "Certain teachers have been seen leaving school early. You know the rules!" "Grades were due in my office at noon. The following teachers are tardy: Mr. Comer, Mrs. Comer! . . ."

Toward the end of the year I wrote a long letter to Henry Martin. It was not intended to be the letter of resignation which it turned out to be. Simply put, my message was, "If JTMcM stays, I go." He stayed and I went.

It was a rash act on my part, but not quite as rash as it might at first appear to be. Sally stayed on in Fennville. The Comer family had one steady income, small as it may have been.

Rather than attempt to secure other employment, I enrolled as a full-time graduate student at Western Michigan University. That was a rash act!

It was the summer of 1966 and President Lyndon B. Johnson had directed a major escalation in the commitment of United States troops to South Vietnam. As a teacher at Fennville I had enjoyed an occupational deferment from the military draft. As a graduate student at Western Michigan University I was reclassified 1A. I received notice of my reclassification one week and my orders to report for a physical exam the next.

I was determined to dodge the draft. I called my draft board in Flint and inquired about what I needed to do. "You have two options," the voice at the other end of the wire told me. "Get another teaching job or become a father."

The prospects of securing another teaching job seemed dim. The possibility of becoming a father seemed much brighter. Sally was most helpful. In addition, she was a biology teacher. She understood reproduction and all of its nuances much better than I, a government teacher and debate coach.

Through the magic of science and mathematics she was able to calculate the precise moment at which she would be most likely to conceive. Not to be overconfident, we decided that we should give the effort our very best for two days prior to the moment and for two days after.

At the time we were renting a small, old house. The linoleum was loose, the roof leaked, and the walls between the rooms were paper thin. It was a dump, but it did not matter that much to us prior to the moment when my parents called to say that they would arrive on Friday and depart on Sunday. That Saturday was the day!

It is probably the second most amazing story of its kind. Our daughter, Allison Lee Comer, who is now the fourth generation of school teachers in her family, was conceived that Saturday evening in a fashion so quiet and subdued that her grandparents slept peacefully in the adjoining bedroom without a suspicion as to what was transpiring nearby.

My problem with the draft board may have been solved, but now we had other problems. The Fennville School Board policy required that pregnant women resign from their teaching positions at the end of the semester in which they became pregnant. Sally had until the end of the third week in January and then she was finished.

We decided that there was no compelling reason to share our special secret with either Henry Martin or JTMcM. Sally would be four months pregnant by the end of the first semester. With a little luck and bulky sweaters, we figured she could make it into February before Henry Martin noticed. It was, of course, possible that she could make it through the entire second semester without ever seeing JTMcM.

We were not certain what Henry Martin and the school board would do once they happened upon our sin of omission. It was possible that she would be fired. We thought it was more likely, though, that she would be permitted to finish the year. Certified science teachers were hard to find in 1967. They were especially hard to find in Fennville in February. That is what happened. Sally was permitted to finish the year and Allison was born on June 14.

We had one more problem. There was no such thing as employer-paid fringe benefits at Fennville then. The payroll clerk would begrudgingly withhold insurance premiums from our paychecks if we wanted her to, but it was our money, not the school district's, that purchased the protection.

Neither Sally nor I had health insurance. We could not afford it, or so we thought. Also, we were young and healthy and would not need it anyway, or so we thought. But now we were planning to need it. Since one had to be covered for nine months prior to the birth of a baby in order for the insurance company to pay the costs, it was imperative that we become insured immediately.

Sally signed up for health insurance and the first monthly premium was deducted from her September paycheck. We were covered. But, come October, there was no deduction. I called the payroll clerk to call to her attention the fact that she had forgotten to withhold our premium.

"Oh, I didn't forget," she said. "The September deduction was a mistake. Since you were eligible to be part of our group last year and weren't, you aren't eligible this year until November 1. I shouldn't have withheld anything in September. I'll take it out again in November."

I wanted to scream into the telephone, "You dumb, stupid, incompetent fool! Sally is pregnant. We don't have any insurance coverage. It is all your fault!" But Sally and I had a secret. Instead, I said, "OK."

I did visit with a lawyer. It occurred to me that perhaps the district had some liability since we were misled by the payroll clerk's error. The lawyer did not think so. It was her assessment that there was no liability since the district was simply doing us a favor. "Perhaps if the district was obligated to withhold insurance premiums, it would be a different matter," she said.

So the expenses for Allison Lee Comer were on us. She cost $300—total! We had health insurance 18 months later when Justin Arthur Comer was born. He cost over $700. I learned something about doctors, hospitals, and health insurance.

Since reproduction is an inexact science, it seemed ill conceived to put all of our eggs in that one basket so I commenced to peruse the Western Michigan University placement bulletin. To my pleasant surprise, I happened upon a social studies vacancy at Wayland Union High School, just 30 miles or so away.

An unexpected surge in student enrollment had produced a serious overload problem at Wayland. Some classes had nearly 50 students and several teachers had agreed to forgo their preparation periods and were teaching extra classes. They were looking for someone immediately. The superintendent agreed to hold the job for me until January so that I could complete my semester of graduate study.

Things were different as I commenced my second job. I asked to join the Association on my first day in Wayland. Daryl Fleser was the WEA president at the time. He was not certain how to sign up someone in the middle of the year. Nor was he certain whether I would be required to pay full annual dues or whether they would be prorated. It would just be easier, Daryl thought, if I waited until the fall to join. So I did.

I was confident that I had not changed my views at all in the 2 1/2 years since I started teaching in Fennville. It was the Michigan Education Association (MEA) that had changed. Its affiliates were bargaining contracts now and some had gone on strike. It was all very exciting to me. The fact of the matter is, at some point it occurred to me that the MEA was really a better organization than the Michigan Federation of Teachers. It was and it still is.

Not only did I join the Association for the first time in September of

1967, but I was also appointed to the bargaining team. My career as an Association staff person was launched. I loved the fight. Wally Wakeman, a local school board member, represented the district. To me, he was the devil incarnate. He was the oppressor and I was the liberator. I have since sat across the table from literally hundreds of bargainers. Rarely, if ever, have I met one as gentle and reasonable as Wally.

I was once physically removed from a school building in Godwin Heights by the local police. At the time I was defending the inalienable right of women teachers to wear pantsuits to school.

On another occasion, this time in Hopkins, an obese milk truck driver who was also on the school board blocked my entrance to a bargaining session. I tried to explain the law to the gentleman, but he was not really too interested in the law at the time. I spent the evening in the bushes under an open window eavesdropping on the session. I entered the building and joined the teachers for their caucuses.

Most often, I have thought of Wally late at night or early in the morning while at impasse somewhere over nickels and dimes. "When we get within $25,000 of each other we have a settlement," Wally would say. "I don't have time to haggle over petty cash."

At the same time I was learning about collective bargaining I was learning about the real world of partisan politics. Politics had been my passion since I was ten years old. I watched the national conventions on our family's new 17-inch Emerson television set and I was hooked.

My book-learning was nearly complete. My undergraduate major was political science. My graduate degree was also in political science. But I was about to learn some things about politics that they do not teach in college classrooms.

My opposition to the war in Vietnam became more and more strident as time went by. I came to loathe Lyndon Johnson. When Senator Eugene McCarthy of Minnesota announced his candidacy for the Democratic nomination for president in opposition to Johnson, I had a candidate.

I was joined by my friends from the Wayland Education Association bargaining team. Lindy Anderson and Dick Miller were even younger than I was. As members of the bargaining team we youngsters were plotting the overthrow of the school board. At the same time we were plotting the overthrow of the Allegan County Democratic Party.

Today all three of us are Republicans. But in 1968 our politics were left of center. Both Lindy and Dick still live in Wayland. Lindy is mayor of the city and an assistant principal at the high school. Dick teaches American history, coaches tennis, plays golf, and skis in Colorado. They are country-club mainstream, no doubt about it.

The Allegan County Democratic Party was free for the picking. Most county party organizations are. Delegates to county political conventions in Michigan were popularly elected during the primary elections. If one's name was on the ballot, one got elected. If one's name was not on the ballot, but one could round up three or four write-in votes, one almost always got elected. If one was not popularly elected but showed up at the convention, one almost always got seated as a delegate because so few people attended.

I do not recall what the maximum number of delegates could be to the Allegan County Democratic Convention. I do recall that we were able to ascertain that the usual number who actually attended ranged from 20 to 30. It seemed to be a simple matter. We needed to get 31 or more of our like-minded friends elected as county convention delegates and the party was ours. We could then elect a McCarthy slate as delegates to the state convention.

We were optimistic as the evening of the convention drew near. We had successfully elected some 40 to 50 delegates. We also had some others, from precincts where no one had been elected, who agreed to attend the event hoping to be allowed to fill vacant seats.

Our only worry was that perhaps the "party regulars" had figured out that something unusual was happening, given the extraordinary interest in the position of county convention delegate in the primary election that year. If they had, perhaps there would be more than 20 or 30 of them. If there were 50 or 60, we were in for a fight. If there were more than 60 of them we were dead.

Before the evening was over we would be in for a fight, but it had nothing to do with the numbers. There were the usual 20 to 30 party regulars who showed up. They were pleased to see us. In fact, several remarked how nice it was to see that young people were taking an active interest in politics and government.

We introduced the resolutions that we had prepared ahead of time, but we played our other cards close to our vest. We allowed the county chairman to be elected as chair of the convention. He proceeded through the resolutions. We came to the one that condemned the war in Vietnam. The debate was spirited. The resolution was adopted. Finally, the party regulars realized that something was amiss.

Next in order was the resolution endorsing the candidacy of Senator Eugene McCarthy of Minnesota for the Democratic nomination for President of the United States. The convention chairman left the podium and conferred with several of his compatriots. The delegates were atwitter. He returned and announced that there was a tornado warning. The convention was adjourned. It would reconvene the next evening. He and 20 to 30 of his close associates left the auditorium. We assumed their number would grow before next evening.

The rest of us stayed on. We elected a new chairman, adopted the resolution endorsing the candidacy of Senator McCarthy, and elected a McCarthy slate of delegates to attend the state Democratic convention. We celebrated late into the evening.

There is ample evidence that the regulars returned the next evening, for two slates of delegates from Allegan County showed up at the state convention. There was a credentials committee fight and a floor debate. On a close vote, our McCarthy slate was seated.

Other than the politics of the situation, there were two issues to argue. There had been a tornado watch, not a tornado warning. Also, state law set the date for county conventions and there were no provisions for it to be held at any other time. Had the county chairman recessed the convention rather than adjourning it, he might have had a stronger case.

We basked in our victory until election day. I left school that snowy Tuesday in November and Sally and I headed for the Watson Township Hall to cast our ballots. Upon arrival, we were shocked to discover that neither of us was registered to vote. "That can't be! Check again!" "No," we were assured, "There is no c-o-m-e-r or c-o-m-b-e-r or k-o-m-e-r . . ."

We were directed to the residence of the township clerk. He seemed like a decent fellow, honestly concerned about how something like this could have happened. No, he had no idea at all. Finally, it began to come back to him. "I think maybe Ed Holtoff told me you moved. He told me somebody moved."

Ed Holtoff was right. Sally and I had moved that fall. With Allison as part of the family and Justin on the way, our "mobile home" was a bit crowded. We had left the trailer park adjacent to the Martin Speedway for a roomier 900-square-foot home in a subdivision in Middleville. But that was no excuse. We had not lived in Middleville long enough to establish residency. If we were going to vote in November of 1968, it was in Watson Township or nowhere.

"Who is Ed Holtoff?" I inquired.

"He's the justice of the peace." I was told.

"Do you always remove people from the voting roles when Ed Holtoff tells you they have moved?" I asked.

There was no answer.

Then it occurred to me. I asked if Ed Holtoff was a Democrat. He was. I had been had.

The township clerk agreed to call the county clerk to find out what could be done, if anything. The county clerk did not know. She agreed to call the secretary of state's office in Lansing. The word she sent back was that the township clerk should return with us to the township hall. Sally and I were to be allowed to vote unless there was a challenge.

The Republican challenger had no problem, but the Democratic challenger did. Sally and I would not be allowed to vote.

I raised my voice. The township clerk was concerned. "Please, please, no violence in the polling place!" he implored. Sally, eight months pregnant at the time, placed herself between me and the fiend who had challenged us. She and Justin nudged me toward the door.

It had been just over four years since I entered a classroom as a teacher for the first time. In less than a year I would be a staff member of the MEA. Though I am always proud to tell people that I am a teacher by profession, my career was very short. But I learned so much.

I share my experiences because in many ways I typify the teachers of my generation. My father was a school custodian. I was the first person in my family to receive a bachelor's degree. I was raised in the vicinity of Flint, Michigan. Many of my friends' parents or grandparents had participated in the sit-down strikes in the auto plants in the 1930s. As teenagers we drank beer and sang "Solidarity Forever." I worked my way through college, but I also received government help through the National Defense Education Act and the Michigan Higher Education Assistance Authority.

The words "fairness," "justice," and "equality" took on new meaning for my generation. Birmingham Sunday, Bull Connor, Lester Maddox, and George Wallace at the schoolhouse door—all penetrated our consciousness and heightened our senses. It was no longer acceptable to decry injustice; it was important to do something about it.

When John F. Kennedy urged Americans to do something for their country, it was directed at this "new generation"—my generation. We responded. Thousands joined the Peace Corps. Others joined VISTA. Thousands and thousands became teachers. Teaching was not just a profession or a career; it was a mission.

I was only 22 years old when I arrived in Fennville in 1964. But I was a college-educated, degreed, licensed, professional school teacher. I expected to have authority, responsibility, and respect. I was prepared to demand them if they were not offered. So were most of the others who entered the profession of teaching with me.

We relished the battles. We were prepared to struggle against unfairness and injustice wherever we found them. There was no question but that this new generation of teachers intended to control its own destiny. It would not be denied.

EPILOGUE

That is the story of the ISEA since 1954. It is the story of a new generation of teachers for whom teaching was a mission: a college-educated, degreed, licensed, professional bunch with a different sense of fairness and justice. They came looking for a fight. They relished the battle. And they won. They would not be denied.

When the Executive Board determined to undertake this writing project several years ago, many expressed the importance of communicating the past to today's younger generation of teachers. "They do not understand all that we have been through. They take what we have accomplished for granted," some said. "They do not have the same feelings of commitment that you and I had when we were their age."

There was hope that if we could tell this younger bunch the stories about Roger Blake, the Executive Board, and the IACT officers, they would feel the anger for the first time that we older teachers felt again when we relived the moment.

It is my hope that the younger teachers who read this book will appreciate what we have accomplished. It is important that younger teachers understand the history, traditions, and culture of their profession. Reading this book will not cause younger teachers to have the same feelings of commitment to the same issues that we older teachers had when we were their age. All of that *is* history. Rather, it is important that each generation of teachers build upon the successes of the preceding one and to have deep feelings of commitment to their own issues.

The challenge for those of us from my generation who remain in positions of responsibility within the ISEA and within the family of NEA is to mold the organization so that it meets the needs of the next generation of teachers. It is not our challenge to mold the next generation of teachers so that it meets the needs of the Association as it exists today.

Should we attempt to do the latter, the next volume of the history of the ISEA will chronicle how this newest generation of teachers threw us out. The story might be remarkably similar to this one.

ISEA Presidents Since 1954

Frank L. Hildreth. 1954-55. English teacher, Roosevelt High School, Des Moines. Born in Trenton, Nebraska. BA, Hastings College. MA, Colorado State College of Education. Taught in Giltner, Lushton, Lyons, and Grand Island, Nebraska; and Monte Vista, Colorado. Served on the Des Moines Board of Education following his retirement.

L. L. Woodruff. 1955-56. Superintendent, Des Moines County. Born in Grandview, Iowa. BA, Parsons College. MA, University of Iowa. Taught in Packwood and Oakville, Iowa. Superintendent in Sperry, Iowa.

Harold Weber. 1956-57. High school principal, Clinton. Born in Muscatine, Iowa. BA, University of Iowa. Taught and was assistant high school principal in Muscatine. Center, University of Iowa football team.

Joe L. Gettys. 1957-58. Superintendent, Oskaloosa. Born in Des Moines, BA, Grinnell College. MA, University of Iowa. Taught in Creston. Principal in Alta. Superintendent in Marathon, Sibley, Harlan, and Atlantic.

Oscar E. Thompson. 1958-59. Professor of education, State College of Iowa. BA, Moorhead State Teachers College. MA, University of North Dakota. PhD, University of Iowa. Taught in East Grand Forks, Minnesota; laboratory school, University of Wyoming; laboratory school, University of Iowa. Principal in Ortonville, Minnesota, and Sauk Centre, Minnesota.

Ray Bryan. 1959-60. Department head, vocational education, Iowa State University. Born in Bavaria, Kansas. BS and MS, Kansas State University. PhD, University of Nebraska. Taught in Burdick, Kansas. Principal in Longton, Kansas. Superintendent in Manchester, Kansas. Education department head at Kansas Wesleyan University and Nebraska State Teachers College. Bryan was hired to be executive director of ISEA in 1961, but decided to remain at ISU instead.

Ray Nyhan. 1960-61. Principal, Anson Junior High School, Marshalltown. Born in Waterloo. BA, Iowa State Teachers College. MA, Drake University. Taught in Marshalltown and was elementary principal in Marshalltown.

Verl Crow. 1961-62. Dean of students, North Junior High School, Sioux City. Born in Monroe, Wisconsin. BA, Morningside College. MS, Drake University. Taught in rural Woodbury County schools, Holly Springs, Alton, and Sioux City.

William A. Anderson. 1962-63. Superintendent, Cedar Falls. Born in Coin. BA, Tarkio College. MS, Iowa State University. PhD, University of Nebraska. A teacher, high school principal and superintendent in Villisca, Superintendent at Clarinda. Retired as Des Moines superintendent and joined the faculty at Iowa State University.

Kenneth Wells. 1963-64. Athletic director and football coach, Ames. Born in Lake View. BS, Iowa State University. MA, Colorado State College. Taught in Grundy Center. Served as ISEA executive director, 1964-75.

Etta L. Cosner. 1964-65. Director of elementary education, Davenport. Born in Centerville. BA and MA, University of Iowa. Taught in Centerville.

Roger O. Blake. 1965-66. Superintendent, West Sioux. Born in Marshalltown. BA, State College of Iowa. MA, Drake University. Teacher and was high school principal in Lytton. Superintendent in Le Grand.

James Freeman. 1966-67. Industrial arts teacher, Harding Junior High School, Cedar Rapids. Born in Newhall. BS, State College of Iowa. MS, Iowa State University. Taught in Dinsdale and Goodell. Superintendent in Wadena and Latimer. Served as president of the Cedar Rapids Federation of Teachers.

Elmer C. Gast. 1967-68. Superintendent, Keokuk. Born in Hardin County BA, Cornell College. MA, University of Chicago. Taught in Dysart. Superintendent in Keystone and North Fayette. Gast was the last superintendent to serve as ISEA President.

Wayne Begg. 1968-69. High school principal, Ankeny. Born in LeMars. BA, Westmar College. MA, Colorado State University. Taught in Blencoe and Correctionville. Begg was the last administrator to serve as president.

Jack L. Hudson. 1969-70. Chemistry teacher, West High School, Davenport. Raised in Cedar Rapids. BA, University of Iowa. MA, Miami University (Oh.). Youngest person to serve as president of ISEA.

Reynard M. Satory. 1970-71. High school counselor, LeMars. Born in Storm Lake. BA, Buena Vista College. BS, Iowa State University. MA, University of Alabama.

Walter L. Galvin. 1971-72 and 1974-75. History teacher, Technical High School, Des Moines. Raised in Burlington. BA, University of Northern Iowa. MA, Drake University. Taught in Martelle. Galvin was the first full-time president of ISEA. He retired in 1992 as the UniServ director for the Des Moines Education Association.

E. L. "Roy" Karlson. 1972-73. High school history teacher, Coon Rapids. Born in Waterloo. BA, University of Northern Iowa. MA, Northwest Missouri State University. Taught in Alta. Karlson serves as UniServ director for the Northeast Iowa Education Unit.

Robert Creighton. 1973-74. High school band director, Shenandoah. BA, San Jose State University. MA and EdD, Columbia University. Taught in Davenport. Pacific Coast heavyweight boxing champion. Creighton served as mayor of Shenandoah following his retirement.

Nancy George. 1975-76. Media specialist, Longfellow Elementary School, Iowa City. BA, University of Northern Iowa. MA, University of Iowa. Served a few years as JDC UniServ director following her term as president.

Richard G. Staver. 1976-77. High school English teacher, Lewis Central. BA, Loras College. MA, Northwest Missouri State University. Taught in Dunlap and Holstein. Now superintendent in Perry.

Robert J. Gilchrist. 1977-78. Junior high school mathematics teacher, Linn-Mar. Born in Walker. BA, University of Northern Iowa. MA, University of Iowa. Gilchrist is the only person in the history of the ISEA to serve in all four leadership positions: president, vice president, treasurer, and NEA Director.

George Duvall. 1978-79 and 1980-82. High school mathematics teacher, Ames. Born in Ames. BA, University of Utah. MA, Iowa State University. Taught in New Market, Stratford, Belle Plaine, Algona, and Independence. Duvall was a state championship golf and basketball coach.

Ken Pfile. 1979-80. Language arts teacher, Kennedy High School, Cedar Rapids. Born in Baxter. BA, State College of Iowa. Since his presidency, Pfile has served as a UniServ director in Wisconsin and Michigan.

Phoebe J. Tupper. 1982-86. Counselor, Wood Junior High School, Davenport. Born in Milbank, South Dakota. Tupper received her undergraduate education in South Dakota. MA, University of Iowa. Tupper was the first person to be elected to two two-year terms as ISEA president. Since her presidency she has served on the staff of the Service Employees International Union.

Ken Tilp. 1986-90. High school French teacher, West Des Moines. Born in Dubuque. BA, Loras College. MA, Northeast Missouri State University. Since his presidency Tilp is now a UniServ director in Michigan.

Angie King. 1990- . Third grade teacher, King-Perkins Elementary School, Des Moines. Born in Des Moines. BA, Iowa State University. MA, Drake

University. King is the first elementary teacher to be elected president of ISEA. She is also the first person since 1947 to be elected president without first having served as vice president.

ISEA Executive Directors Since 1954

Charles F. Martin. 1946-61. Superintendent, Jackson County, 1927-46. ISEA president, 1945-46. Martin served as ISEA associate executive secretary for three years following his tenure as executive secretary. He retired in 1964 at the age of 75. He died in 1970 at the age of 81.

John W. Harold. 1961-64. Superintendent, Cedar Falls. Born in Cedar Rapids. BA, Coe College. MA, University of Iowa. Taught in Cedar Falls. Superintendent in Oakland, Hartley, and Carroll. Left ISEA to become a high school principal in American Samoa.

Kenneth Wells. 1964-75. Athletic director and head football coach, Ames. Born in Lake View. BS, Iowa State University. MA, Colorado State College. Taught in Grundy Center. ISEA president, 1963-64. Retired in 1975.

Neil R. Curtis. 1975-79. Negotiations specialist, ISEA. Born in Seymour. BA, Northeast Missouri State University. Taught English in Seymour and Centerville. Also served as field representative for ISEA. Left ISEA to become executive director of the Arizona Education Association, where he served for about two years.

Beverly Wolkow. 1979-81. Executive Director, Student NEA. Born in De Smet, South Dakota. BS and MS, South Dakota State University. Taught English and speech for 12 years. Served as South Dakota Education Association president. Left ISEA to become Michigan Education Association executive director.

Fred R. Comer. 1981- . Associate executive director, Michigan Education Association. Born in Lapeer, Michigan. BS, Central Michigan University. MA, Western Michigan University. Taught social studies and coached debate for 5 1/2 years. Also served as negotiations consultant, UniServ director, and assistant executive director for the Michigan Education Association.

Vice Presidents of the ISEA Since 1954

L. L. Woodruff, Des Moines County	1954-55
Harold Weber, Clinton	1955-56
Joe L. Gettys, Oskaloosa	1956-57
Oscar E. Thompson, State College of Iowa	1957-58
Ray Bryan, Iowa State University	1958-59
Ray Nyhan, Marshalltown	1959-60
Verl Crow, Sioux City	1960-61
William A. Anderson, Cedar Falls	1961-62
Kenneth Wells, Ames	1962-63
Etta L. Cosner, Davenport	1963-64
Roger O. Blake, West Sioux	1964-65
James Freeman, Cedar Rapids	1965-66
Elmer C. Gast, Keokuk	1966-67
Wayne Begg, Ankeny	1967-68
Jack L. Hudson, Davenport	1968-69
Reynard M. Satory, LeMars	1969-70
Walter L. Galvin, Des Moines	1970-71
	1973-74
E. L. (Roy) Karlson, Coon Rapids	1971-72
Robert Creighton, Shenandoah	1972-73
Nancy George, Iowa City	1974-75
Richard G. Staver, Lewis Central	1975-76
Robert J. Gilchrist, Linn-Mar	1976-77
George Duvall, Ames	1977-78
	1982-84

Ken Pfile, Cedar Rapids 1978-79
Phoebe J. Tupper, Davenport 1979-82
Ken Tilp, West Des Moines 1984-86
Steve King, Algona 1986-90
John Mesicek, Ankeny 1990-

Treasurers of the ISEA Since 1954

Leslie D. Olsen, Des Moines 1954-65
M. M. Rogers, Sumner 1965-66
J. R. Ingraham, Clinton 1966-68
Elmer C. Gast, Keokuk 1968-69
Neil J. Boyle, Bennett 1969-71
Robert D. Hoogeveen, Sheldon 1971-72
Robert J. Gilchrist, Linn-Mar 1972-76
Ronald Muilenburg, Webster City 1976-81
Marlene Lottridge, Sioux City 1981-82
Dan Hargrave, Centerville 1982-87
H. O. Maxey, Cedar Rapids 1987-

NEA Directors from Iowa Since 1954

Joe L. Gettys, Oskaloosa 1954-55

Verl Crow, Sioux City 1955-61

J. E. Smith, Emmetsburg 1961-64

Leland J. Gritzner, Osage 1962-63

Arvil C. Parks, Estherville 1963-66

Bernice Reida, Sac City 1964-67

James Harris, Des Moines 1966-73

Walter Schnelle, Iowa City 1967-70

1971-73

Dennis L. Barnum, Ft. Dodge Comm. College 1970-71

Jane Strong, Council Bluffs 1973-74

Gary Mitchell, Sioux City 1973-81

Fred Shearer, Corning 1974-76

Calvin Halliburton, Ames 1976-82

Robert J. Gilchrist, Linn-Mar 1981-87

John Mesicek, Ankeny 1982-88

Patricia Shipley, Corning 1987-91

Wayne Bauman, Des Moines 1988-

H. O. Maxey, Cedar Rapids 1991-92

Jolene Franken, Denison 1992-

ISEA Friend of Education Award Winners

This award was created by ISEA to recognize citizens who work to improve educational opportunities for students.

1959 Carl Weeks, Des Moines, creator of Salisbury House
1960 W. Earl Hall, Mason City, newspaper editor
1961 J.W. Hunt, Guttenberg, former State Board of Public Instruction president
1962 Kenneth Mac Donald, Des Moines, newspaper editor
1963 Frank Nye, Cedar Rapids, newspaper managing editor
1964 Sterling Martin, Melrose, former state Board of Public Instruction member
1965 J.W. Fisher, Marshalltown, industrialist & philanthropist
1966 Charles Penningroth, Cedar Rapids, judge & school board member
1967 LeRoy H. Petersen, Grimes, state legislator
1968 David A. Dancer, Lamoni, State Board of Regents secretary
1969 Lloyd D. Fark, Sioux City, chairman of school bond issue committee
1970 Kenneth M. Freeman, Davenport, coordinator of tutoring program
1971 Jack W. Peters, Council Bluffs, school board member
1972 Mrs. Lou Lyons, Clinton, PTA leader
1973 Mrs. Beverly Siekman, Burlington, local PTA leader
1974 Otis Tuttle, Norway, school board member
1975 Mrs. Doris Jungmann, Saydel, board member
1976 John S. Murray, Ames, state senator
1977 Robert & Frances Bickelhaupt, Clinton, arboretum creators
1978 Al Schrock, Marshalltown, broadcaster
1979 Eustolia Partida, West Liberty, Spanish-speaking liaison
1980 Hugh Wood, Moulton-Udell, school board member
1981 Barbara Colehour, Mt. Vernon, school board member
1982 Ralph Lynn, West Des Moines, gifted & talented supporter
1983 Marilyn Kollmorgen, Urbandale, school board member
      Dave Bitterman, Davenport, parent volunteer

1984 Barbara Canova, Ankeny, community education leader
1985 Millie Kruse, Carlisle, parent volunteer
1986 IllaBelle Brennan, Dunkerton, retiree volunteer
1987 Frank Schlue, Davenport, school volunteer
1988 Charles & Judy Rhinehart, Dallas Center-Grimes, fine arts supporters
1989 Mary Eastman, Riceville, school board member
1990 Sumner Heman, Fort Dodge, artist & school volunteer
1991 June Schroeder, Davenport, volunteer
1992 Dave Elder, Washington, newspaper editor & school volunteer

Charles F. Martin Award Recipients

The Charles F. Martin Award has been presented annually since 1972 as ISEA's top honor to a member who has made a significant contribution to the teaching profession through Association involvement over at least a ten year period. The award was named in honor of Charles F. Martin who served as ISEA President in 1945 and then as ISEA Executive Secretary from 1946-61. Mrs. Martin provided funding for the establishment of the award.

1971 Phyllis Oetken, Mason City
1972 Alline Stavely, Charles City
1973 Virginia Meskel, West Union
1974 Joyce Grubb, Council Bluffs
1975 Lois Mae Whitson, Fremont Mills
1976 Helen Brooks, Brooklyn
1977 Charles T. Williams, Davenport
1978 Doris Mauer, Cedar Falls
1979 James Knott, Carroll
     Marlene Lottridge, Sioux City
1980 Judy Fossell, Waterloo
1981 Ruth Foster, Des Moines
1982 Maxine Henry, Indianola
1983 Glen Wehrkamp, Hartley-Melvin
1984 Sue Quail, Davenport
1985 Liz Tracey-Engen, Turkey Valley

1986   Robert Gilchrist, Linn-Mar
        Wilbur Grove, Kirkwood Community College
1988*   Pamela Schmidt, Dunkerton
1989   Jean Seeland, Waterloo
1990   Doreen Rick, Mason City
1991   Joseph Tollari, Dubuque
1992   Linda Nelson, Council Bluffs
1993   Janet White, Marion

*ISEA Executive Director, Fred Comer, requested that the year of future Martin awards be changed to more appropriately correspond to the date of presentation. Initially, the award was presented in February at the ISEA Delegate Assembly. In the early 1980s the date of the Assembly was shifted to April.

ISEA TEAM Award Honorees

The "Together Educators and Administrators Make it happen" (TEAM) Award was established by the ISEA Executive Board in 1990 to honor school administrators who are exemplary in the creation of a collaborative, collegial environment for all staff.

1990   Dr. Peter Flynn, Superintendent
        Davenport Community School District

1991   Joyce Caprata, Principal
        Longfellow Elementary School, Clinton

1992   John Villotti, Principal
        Emerson Hough Elementary School, Newton

At a Glance

The '50s

- The ISEA purchases Salisbury House in 1954.

- The 1956 ISEA Delegate Assembly approves a "Ten-Point Program" calling for among other things "securing a high degree of understanding and cooperation between teachers and school boards," "securing direct state support of total public school costs in an amount equal to at least the national average," and "attaining units of school administration of sufficient size and valuation to provide adequate elementary and secondary educational opportunities for all Iowa children."

- In 1957, Iowa's average teaching salary of $3,928 ranks 33rd in the nation, and the ISEA's call for a 10 percent salary increase makes headlines in newspapers across the state. In October of that year, ISEA hits the airwaves with its "Midland Schools of the Air" weekly radio program broadcast on Station WOI in Ames.

- The 1958 ISEA Delegate Assembly adopts a bold three-point legislative program that calls for increasing state aid to schools from 14 percent to 25 percent, securing financial support for the State Department of Public Instruction, and amending continuing contract and sick leave laws in order to grant teachers preliminary termination hearings and allow boards to grant more than 35 days of accumulated sick leave. One year later, the Iowa General Assembly approves two of the three measures.

- In 1959, the ISEA commissions popular wildlife artist Maynard Reece to create covers for issues of *Midland Schools* and makes "full-color" reprints available to members for 25 cents each. In that year, the ISEA also launches a "help wanted"

1950 - 1960

• Senator Joe McCarthy was censured by the Senate following a televised witch-hunt

• Blacks in Montgomery, Alabama, staged a successful bus boycott • The Salk Vaccine offered hope for an end to polio

• The Suez Canal reopened after Egypt's Nasser seized it • The AFL-CIO expelled Hoffa's Teamsters Union

• Rival street gangs

fought in Broadway's West Side Story • Alaska and Hawaii became states • de Gaulle was proclaimed president of France • Readers savored Breakfast at Tiffany's • A public relations conscious Khrushchev toured America and visited Coon Rapids to talk about farming with Roswell Garst

---

1960 - 1970

• The word "laser" entered the vocabulary • Teenagers learned to twist • Alan Shepard became the

public relations campaign designed to tell parents and taxpayers that the schools need and want their help.

The '60s

• ISEA's Employment Information Service reports that in 1960, 65 percent of Iowa's school districts reported vacancies, including an all-time high of 2,771 teaching and 213 administrative positions. Also in that year, the debt on Salisbury House is retired following a final payment of $40,000 to Drake University.

• In 1961, the ISEA convenes a committee to study the Association's organization and governance structure.

• The 1963 ISEA Delegate Assembly calls for improvements in the continuing contract law to require school districts to provide a written statement of reasons why a contract termination is being considered and to provide for an impartial "state authority" to which a teacher "might appeal" if his or her contract is terminated by the local board; and it affirms its support for a single salary schedule "admitting no discrimination as to grade or subject taught, creed, race, sex, marital status, or number of dependents."

• A new publication, the *ISEA Communique*, is launched in September of 1963—the 8 1/2" x 11" "newsletter" serves as a supplement to the popular *Midland Schools* magazine. In November of 1963, the ISEA Committee to Study County Councils recommends that a field service office be established in each ISEA district with a full-time director and secretary and that school districts within counties may apply for independent association status.

• In the midst of a severe teacher shortage, the 1965 average Iowa teacher salary has passed the $6,000 barrier, but is still far below the national average; men continue to earn "heads of household" bonuses of $100 to $500 more than women; meanwhile, the ISEA launches a comprehensive "Proportionate Sharing Plan" campaign, complete with newspaper ads and broadcast media spots, to convince the public and legislators to increase state aid to schools from 10.4 percent to 40 percent.

- By the end of 1966, there are four "Professional Negotiation Agreements" in the state: WACO and Bettendorf—level one, which recognizes the Association as the organization representing teachers; Keokuk—level two, which recognizes the Association and outlines possible negotiation procedures; and Burlington—level 3, which recognizes the Association, outlines possible procedures, and includes a provision to resolve an impasse.

- ISEA's field staff grows to five in 1967. It is also a good year for education-related legislation with the passage of several long-time Association goals including the establishment of a Professional Practices Commission, a change in the continuing contract law to allow teachers to request the reasons for their dismissal, and an increase in the salary figure used for calculating IPERS benefits from $4,800 to $7,000.

- 1968 sees the election of Iowa's own George Fischer as NEA President and the relocation of five ISEA field staffers to various offices across the state.

- The 1969 ISEA Delegate Assembly directs the Association to investigate the feasibility of organizing a political action arm; teachers receive average salary increases of about 9.6 percent, although the *maximum* amount a teacher with an MA degree can actually earn varies from $10,000 to $12,000.

The '70s

- During the 1969-70 school year, the ISEA's Association of Classroom Teachers launches a year-long instructional improvement project which introduces a cadre of specially trained facilitators and includes the first Mobile In-Service Training Labs

first American in space, but he came after Soviet Cosmonaut Gagarin • In Jerusalem, Nazi war criminal Adolf Eichmann was sentenced to death by hanging • The U.S. Court of Appeals found Mississippi's Governor guilty of contempt for resisting university integration • President Kennedy stood up to Soviet aggression in Cuba • The Reverend Dr. Martin Luther King declared that he had a dream • The

Warren Commission shared its findings on the Kennedy assassination • Student demonstrations began against the "war" in Viet Nam • Malcolm X was shot in New York • Dr. Christiaan Barnard performed the first heart transplant • Mickey Mantle hit his 500th home run • The Beatles' Sgt. Pepper album confirmed the group's pop music genius • Sirhan Sirhan was convicted of murdering Robert Kennedy • Neil Armstrong walked on the moon

(MISTL), instructional seminars, and a statewide educational improvement workshop.

• The ISEA begins phasing out the Library Service in 1970 citing the influx of trained school librarians who have made the 18-year old program unnecessary; members begin selling badges and bumper stickers featuring the slogan, "Keep Education Alive and Well in Iowa" to raise funds for the fledgling Iowa Political Action Committee for Education (IPACE); and the ISEA gets NEA approval to begin hiring staffers for an innovative new field service program called UniServ.

• In January of 1971, the ISEA releases a comprehensive school finance study outlining 21 "principles" that should be included in legislation; during the legislative session, the Association emerges as a credible news source and gains statewide media visibility, culminating with its public censure of the Governor, Lt. Governor, and the Iowa Legislature for their lack of support for school funding and other educational issues. The censure action prompts the passage of a landmark new school aid formula which pumps more money into districts while reducing the local property tax burden.

• The 1971 ISEA Delegate Assembly approves the addition of a staff member to serve higher education members, and the school administrators and secondary principals vote to disaffiliate with the ISEA effective July 1 of that year.

• In the fall of 1971, the ISEA challenges the Nixon Administration's wage-price freeze and is successful in convincing school districts to pay teachers based on their 1971-72 contracted salaries.

• On February 1, 1972, Diane Harrington, a first-grade teacher in the Olin district, is allowed to return to school after the birth of her baby instead of being forced to resign, thanks to ISEA's involvement on her behalf; what's more, she is allowed to use 21 of her 23 days of accumulated sick leave for her recovery. The ISEA steps up its efforts to protect teachers who are unjustly fired and begins making the case for an improved teacher termination law.

• On May 6, 1972, the ISEA's political action arm, IPACE, emerges as a powerful political force when it announces its endorsements of candidates in the primary election at a political rally held in Monticello; endorsement decisions are made following candidate interviews, an analysis of their voting records, and public statements made at the rally.

• After 54 years, 86 volumes, and 456 issues, the final edition of ISEA's *Midland Schools* is published in the summer of 1972, falling victim to budget constraints caused by increasing member field service needs.

• The 1973 ISEA Delegate Assembly adopts a plan which allows for the creation of both autonomous "cluster" UniServ units and state units. Also in that year, Jim Harris, a Des Moines junior high teacher, is elected as the NEA vice president, president-elect; and the state's first teacher strike is settled in Keokuk.

• In the fall of 1973, ISEA President Bob Creighton of Shenandoah embarks on the first statewide President's Tour; the Iowa Association of Classroom Teachers becomes the ISEA's new Instruction and Professional Development Unit; and the ISEA launches the nation's first teacher image media campaign called "It's the Kids that Count."

• Elementary principals vote to disaffiliate with the ISEA effective July 1, 1973.

• After 10 years of lobbying, ISEA members in 1974 witness the historic passage of the collective bargaining bill for public employees. Also in that year, legislation creates 15 area education agencies to provide special education and media services to school districts.

• The 1974 ISEA Delegate Assembly approves the restructure of UniServ from 9 to 19 units;

1970 - 1980

• *Cigarette commercials were banned from U.S. television*

• *Amtrak began passenger rail service*

• *Governor George Wallace was shot and partially paralyzed*

• *Vice President Spiro Agnew resigned*

• *Americans faced gas shortages as the energy crisis began*

• *Alexander Solzhenitsyn was stripped of Soviet citizenship and exiled*

• *Streakers wore sneakers and little else*

• *The Watergate*

affair came to a close with Nixon's resignation • Sylvester Stallone slugged away in "Rocky" • Saigon was renamed Ho Chi Minh City and America's shores teemed with waves of new Southeast Asian immigrants • Novelist Alex Haley's "Roots" was a mega-hit • President Carter pardoned nearly all U.S. draft evaders • The disco craze hit and millions caught "Saturday Night Fever" • The U.S. dollar plunged to

and as cases of teachers being fired for no reason—or any reason—continue to mount, the Association launches an all-out media campaign to create an awareness of the need to change what it calls the "phony" teacher dismissal law. Among the many components of that effort are the production of a film and a booklet of news clippings detailing the ridiculous reasons school boards used to fire teachers.

• As more and more of the Association's resources are committed to preparing its local associations for bargaining, the 1975 Delegate Assembly moves to abolish the annual ISEA Convention; and after more than three years of litigation, the ISEA wins an Iowa Supreme Court ruling in the spring of 1975 clarifying that teachers can use sick leave for pregnancy-related leaves of absence. NEA later provides legal assistance for a successful appeal before the U.S. Supreme Court which provides full maternity rights for teachers.

• The 1975 Iowa Legislature enacts the most significant improvements in IPERS since the program began; a long sought-after bill to provide teachers with due process rights when they're threatened with termination passes in the Senate, but is stalled in the House.

• The ISEA hires a bargaining specialist and the NEA provides two full-time staffers in the summer of 1975 to help the Association keep up with the demand for bargaining training and assistance. By the end of September, 216 local associations are eligible to begin and 100 have actually started bargaining under the new law. The ISEA purchases a computer for its research needs.

• In 1974 and 1976, the ISEA produces two films to create understanding and support for students with special needs—"I Would if I Could" spotlights the problems faced by students with learning disabilities; and "Children of Promise" addresses the challenges posed by gifted and talented students.

• In December of 1975, IPACE urges members to support Democratic Presidential candidates Birch Bayh or Morris Udall in the January 19 precinct caucuses but takes no action in the Republican race between President Gerald Ford and Gov. Ronald Reagan. It is the group's first foray into national politics and it serves as a catalyst for unprecedented member political involvement at all levels.

• By the spring of 1976, 303 local associations bargain their first master contract under the law; the 1976 Iowa Legislature passes SF205 capping a 13-year Association battle to protect teachers against "arbitrary and capricious" firings.

• A 1977 ad hoc committee calls on the ISEA to adopt a goal of raising the leadership involvement of women and minority members to a level "more commensurate" with their actual numbers; the 1977 ISEA Delegate Assembly calls for the creation of a Salisbury House Preservation Committee.

• Following a massive ISEA media campaign, the 1978 Iowa Legislature provides $28.5 million in new money to help districts cope with the effects of declining enrollment and the "phantom student" concept becomes an important component of the school funding formula.

• A growing shortage of teachers prompts the ISEA in 1979 to call for higher teacher salaries. The average beginning salary in that year is $10,230, while the overall average is about $14,000, ranking Iowa 25th in the nation. Meanwhile, school employees are finding it tough to keep up with the effects of skyrocketing inflation.

The '80s

• The 1980-81 allowable growth rate is set at 13.59 percent, and local association bargaining teams win salary increases averaging 12.5 percent.

• In the fall of 1980, the ISEA launches the

---

record lows against foreign currencies and "Proposition 13" led to an unprecedented tax revolt

• *Soviet troops invaded Afghanistan*

• *Margaret Thatcher became the first woman to lead the British government*

• *Rampant inflation drove investors from banks and into gold, silver, antiques, and art* • *Three Mile Island Nuclear Facility created a nightmare*

1980 - 1990

• *John Lennon was*

shot on a New York street corner • Television audiences wondered "who shot J.R.?" • Iran and Iraq became locked in a merciless blood bath • Voyager I transmitted the first close-up photos of Saturn's rings • The hostage crisis ended as Ronald Reagan assumed office and militants almost simultaneously released captives • Brezhnev's death was announced by Moscow • Britain and Argentina went to war

"Take Pride in Iowa Schools" media campaign to create an awareness of Iowa's high-quality educational system and to fight back against a growing anti-public education movement of the conservative right wing. At the same time, the Association makes an all-out effort to defeat a proposed constitutional convention to rewrite the state's constitution to provide, among other things, a limitation on taxes and government spending. Also in that year, ISEA begins organizing a number of Educational Support Personnel local associations.

• In 1980, IPACE changes its name to ISEA-PAC in order to comply with Federal Elections Commission regulations.

• The ISEA gears up to fight a proposal to cut some $41 million in promised allowable growth money with a comprehensive Save Our Schools (SOS) campaign in 1981, and more than 1,000 persons show up to protest at a legislative public hearing. In the aftermath, an estimated 3,000 teachers and other school employees receive termination notices.

• The ISEA sponsors a statewide conference in October of 1981 to help members understand and deal with right-wing attacks on teachers and public education.

• Some 600 teachers receive lay-off notices in the March Massacre of 1982, but the ISEA helps them fight back by developing and delivering a comprehensive training program.

• In April of 1983, the infamous *A Nation at Risk* report warns of "the rising tide of mediocrity" in public education; two weeks later, the ISEA convenes a meeting of the various Iowa education groups to explore the possibility of developing a common response to the issues raised in that report. That meeting helps form the basis for a long-standing coalition between the groups.

• In November of 1983, the ISEA becomes the first organization in the state and in the nation to issue a proposal for reforming Iowa schools called, *Achieving Excellence in Our Schools: Major Areas for Renewal*. That report helps set the tone for the extended debate on school reform that follows.

• The 1984 Iowa Legislature enacts another in a series of across-the-board cuts in education funding—this time it's 2.8 percent. The average Iowa teaching salary of $20,149 ranks 28th in the nation, down some $1,800 from the national average.

• In September of 1984, the ISEA releases its second major report called, "Funding Excellence: The Forgotten Factor," which, through a series of meetings and public forums across the state, is designed to create an awareness that achieving excellence in education requires a massive infusion of resources into school districts.

• The 1985 Delegate Assembly tackles long-range planning and gives the Association the authority to sell certain Salisbury House artifacts to help underwrite the increasing costs of doing business.

• In the face of a proposed freeze on school funding in 1986, ISEA's "Mr. Freeze" snowman becomes a popular symbol during the legislative session as ISEA members, in an unprecedented lobbying blitz, urge lawmakers not to freeze Iowa's future. In March of that year, more than 600 members and friends trek to the steps of the state capitol to dramatize the funding crisis. Although the freeze ultimately thaws, Iowa's average teaching salary plummets to an all-time low 38th in the nation—more than $3,900 below the national average.

• The 1986 Delegate Assembly expands the ISEA Executive Board to include representation for area education agency and educational support members.

• At 3 a.m. on Sunday, May 10, 1987, the Iowa Legislature passes the historic three-phased, $100

over possession of the Falkland Islands

• *Millions of moviegoers befriended "E.T."*

• *The personal computer revolution was in full swing*

• *Sally Ride became the first American woman to travel in space.* • *Video and rock joined forces on MTV* • *Black involvement in politics was epitomized by Jesse Jackson* • *Geraldine Ferraro became the first woman chosen for a top elective office by a major U.S. political party*

• *Americans watched*

in horror as the space shuttle Challenger carrying teacher Christa McAuliffe exploded • The Chernobyl meltdown gave the world its worst nuclear accident • The nation was riveted by Oliver North's congressional testimonial on his role in the Iran-Contra scandal • American televangelism was exposed • A Cedar Rapids teacher appeared on the cover of TIME magazine that featured the story headlined "Who's

million Educational Excellence Bill to pump more money into teachers' pockets. Within 40 hours, the ISEA holds the first in a series of training sessions to help local leaders make sure that teachers get their fair share. Nearly every ISEA local affiliate submits Phase III plans under extremely tight deadlines and all are approved by the Department of Education.

• In November of 1987, ISEA hosts a live, televised debate on Iowa Public Television between the major Democratic candidates for U.S. President: Michael Dukakis, Jesse Jackson, Bruce Babbitt, Richard Gephardt, Al Gore, and Paul Simon.

• Thanks to hard bargaining and a major infusion of money, Iowa's average teacher salary climbs nine notches in 1988 to 30th in the nation.

• The 1989 Iowa Legislature rewrites the school finance law by eliminating "phantom students" but allowing for local instructional support levies. It also bans the use of corporal punishment in schools, and achieves the long-time ISEA goal of creating a Professional Standards Board. In April, Marshalltown is cited as the NEA's first Learning Lab dedicated to finding new ways of meeting student needs.

• New Department of Education rules on investigating charges of student abuse by school employees coupled with the legislative ban on corporal punishment prompt a wave of requests for ISEA legal assistance, beginning in 1989.

The '90s

• School reform is the topic of a first-ever ISEA-sponsored President's Conference for educators and administrators in 1990; the Legislature in that year approves major improvements in IPERS benefits.

• In September of 1990, ISEA sponsors the first in a series of conferences, featuring nationally acclaimed labor-management consultant Pat Dolan, in which teachers and administrators explore site-based decision making and other ways schools can restructure themselves to better meet student needs.

• In the fall of 1990, ISEA launches the first media campaign to spotlight the important role that educational support personnel play.

• Faced with skyrocketing health insurance premiums and threats against hard-earned insurance coverage, health care reform becomes a major topic of concern for bargaining teams and is the topic of a special summer leadership conference in 1991.

• In August of 1991, after more than a year of extensive information gathering, the ISEA releases *Time for a Change,* the nation's first report on the future of education from the classroom teacher's perspective. Also in that year, it produces a videotape called "The Class of 2001," which traces the societal and demographic trends that affect students and makes the case that schools must change to meet students' changing needs.

• In the fall of 1991, the ISEA is involved in some 400 active cases involving member rights and establishes a new Office for Advocacy Services to help make more efficient use of dues money earmarked for legal defense. In November, the New Iowa Schools Development Corporation is formed, making it the nation's first nonprofit organization dedicated to encouraging and supporting local school transformation efforts.

• The 1992 Iowa Legislature convenes against the backdrop of an ever-widening budget deficit and charges that education spending is to blame. Although an unprecedented ISEA "Keep the Promise" lobbying campaign and protest march help ward off more crippling budget cuts, education still suffers a loss of $40 million in promised funding and sees the 20-year old school finance formula scrapped in the marathon session.

Teaching Our Children?" • U.S. troops invaded Panama and arrested strongman Manuel Noriega • Braving tanks in Tiananmen Square, Chinese students demonstrated for democracy • The Berlin Wall came tumbling down

---

1990 - 1993

• Nelson Mandella won release from a 27-year imprisonment and received a hero's welcome in the U.S • Margaret Thatcher lost her iron grip on Britain's

conservative party and was replaced by John Major • Yellow ribbons in support of Desert Storm troops appeared everywhere • Televising of the Gulf War brought new dimensions to the news • The U.S. sent troops to starving Somalia to restore order and protect relief shipments • Americans heeded a call for change and entered "the Clinton era" • The U.S. and allies launched bombing raids on Iraq

• On March 10, 1992, the presidents of the three state universities set the stage for an education civil war by announcing that their colleges of education would no longer take part in the National Council for the Accreditation of Teacher Education (NCATE) process. The surprise announcement via news release comes with no prior discussions with other members of the education community including the ISEA and the Iowa Department of Education. NEA and ISEA have long supported NCATE approval as an important measure of professional standing.

• The state university presidents get in another round of fire when later, in March of 1992, they urge lawmakers, in an open letter appearing in the *Des Moines Register,* to take spending for K-12 schools off "automatic pilot."

• ISEA fights back when, on the eve of the 1993 Legislature, it calls for a reordering of state spending priorities and a shifting of funds from higher education and highways to local public schools. It cites data revealing that per-capita spending on public schools had plummeted in the 1980s from 11th to 34th in national rankings, while spending on higher education had increased from 12th to 7th and spending on highways had decreased only slightly from 9th to 12th.

• As educators and the Association prepare to meet the needs of the 21st century, they are assaulted by anti-public education forces on a number of fronts: Religious Right activists challenge school reform activity, a so-called taxpayers' rights group steps up its efforts to limit state and local spending—including public school funds—through an amendment to the state's constitution, and conservative legislators continue to try to erode public school funding and public employee rights. Building on the strong foundation built over the years, the ISEA joins forces with other education and community groups to fight back and preserve the state's proud heritage of excellence in education.

compiled by Lana Oppenheim

INDEX

Abels, Marcus, 154-55
Achieving Excellence in Our Schools, 125-26, 199
Adams, James M., 135
Adams, Marvin, 39, 82, 89-90, 117, 160-61
Alexander, Lamar, 133-34
Allegan County, Michigan, 175-77
Alton, George P., 69
American Association of University Professors, 33
American Civil Liberties Union, 107
American Federation of Teachers, 28-30, 33, 98, 168-69
Anderson, Lindy, 175
Anderson, Ted, 100
Anderson, William, 17-18, 29, 160-61, 168, 182, 185
"Apotheosis of the Rose," 151-52, 156
Armand Cosmetics, 140
Armstrong, Willie, 169
Arnold, Robert, 69
Avenson, Don, 77-78, 80

Bain, Helen, 158
Baldwin, Nick, 148
Barnum, Dennis L., 82, 187
Bauman, Wayne, 187
Begg, Wayne, 2, 14, 42-43, 69, 82, 85, 182, 185
Benton, Robert, 69
Berg, Kenneth P., 164-65
Bettendorf, Paul Norton Elementary School, 129
Bickelhaupt, Frances, 188
Bickelhaupt, Robert, 188
"Birth of Venus," 151-52, 156
Bishop's Cafeteria, 160
Bitterman, Dave, 188
Bittle, Edgar, 93-94, 101

Blake, Roger O., 14-15, 18-19, 43, 53, 85, 167-68, 180, 182, 185
Board of Educational Examiners, 123
Book of Memories, 144-45, 152
Borkenhagen, Phil, 99
Boyd, Byron "Ben," 140
Boyle, Neil J., 186
Branstad, Terry E., 75-80, 101, 115, 123, 133, 136
Brazzle, Dorothy, 160-61, 164
Brennan, IllaBelle, 189
Brooks, Archie, 154
Brooks, Helen, 189
"Brothers La Bochere," 140, 148
Brown, George, vii, 68-70, 92-94, 114
Brown, Helen, 14-15
Bryan, Ray, 52, 181, 185
Bryton Captial Managment, Inc., 155-56
Burchette, Ed, 145-46
Burlington Education Association, 32
Burlington Federation of Teachers, 30, 32

California Teachers Association, 159
Cameron, Don, 130
Canova, Barbara, 188
Caprata, Joyce, 190
"Cardinal Domenico da Rivarola," 140, 148
Carnegie Forum on Education and the Economy, 126
Carrigan, Ed, 170-71
Caviness, Freda, 82
Cedar Rapids Federation of Teachers, 30, 182
Central Michigan University, 169
Chaska, Minnesota, 130
"Children of Promise," 196
Christian Home Services, Inc., 164-66
Christies, 152, 156
Citizens for Public Rights, 92

Clark, Dick, 71
Code of Ethics, 9, 105, 107
Coffey, Tom, 87, 90-91
Colehour, Barbara, 188
Comer, Allison Lee, 172-74, 177
Comer, Justin Arthur, 174, 177-78
Comer, Sally O., vii, 169, 172-74, 177-78
Communique, x, 26, 54, 83, 98, 121, 129-30, 190
Conlin, Roxanne, 75
Conn, Blythe C., 97-98
Cook, Connie, 154
Cook, Lowell, 14
Cosner, Etta, 53, 182, 185
Council Bluffs Federation of Teachers, 30
Council Bluffs, Iowa, 30
Cowles, Gardner, 145
Creighton, Robert, 165, 183, 185, 195
Crow, Verl, 8-9, 181, 185, 187
Curtis, Neil, 89, 96-97, 180

Dancer, David A., 184
Davenport Federation of Teachers, 30
Davidson, T. E. "Ted," 90, 135, 137
Davies, J. Leonard, 59, 67
Deamer, Arthur, 2
Dean, Harry, 110
Decorah Education Association, 38
Denison, Iowa, 130
Des Moines Board of Education, 31
Des Moines City Council, 153-54, 156
Des Moines East High School, 132
Des Moines Education Association, 31-32, 84
Des Moines Federation of Teachers, 30-32
Des Moines Historic District Commission, 153
Des Moines International Airport, 163
Des Moines Plan and Zoning Commission, 153
Des Moines Register, 63-64, 147-148, 202
Dolan, W. P. "Pat," 131-33, 201
Dorrian, John "Pat," 154
Douma, Frank, 104
Drake University, 139, 141-42, 146
Duvall, George, x, 55, 71, 135, 183, 185

Eastman, Mary, 187
Eberly, John E., 98
Elder, Dave, 189

Fark, Lloyd D., 188
Federal Housing Administration, 148, 160-64
Fennville Board of Education, 173
Fennville Education Association, 169
Fennville High School, 170-71
Fennville, Michigan, 169-70, 172-73
Ferrone, Patrick F., 69
F.I.N.E. Schools Recognition Program, 136
Fischer, George, 13-14, 29, 44, 161, 193
Fisher, J. W., 188
Fitzgerald, Jerome, 93-94
Flagg, George, 154
Fleming, Mike, 44
Fleser, Daryl, 174
Flick, Bob, 14
Flynn, Peter, 190
Fossell, Judy, 189
Foster, Ruth, 167, 189
Fowler, Les, 90
Franken, Jolene, 187
Frazier, Orville, 92
Freeman, James, 69, 82, 86, 182, 185
Freeman, Kenneth M., 188
Futrell, Mary Hatwood, 126, 130

Galbraith, Ann, 168
Galbreth, W. Henry, 31
Galvin, Walter, vii, 33, 54-55, 112, 182, 185
Garnjobst, Virginia, 123
Gast, Elmer, 18, 27, 82-83, 85, 162-63, 182, 185-86
Gaylord, Paul, 87, 90
George, Nancy, 183, 185
Gettys, Joe, 53, 63, 66, 142, 181, 185, 187
Gilchrist, Robert J., 183, 185-87, 190
Gilderbloom, Elverta, 109-10
Glen Arbor, Michigan, xi
Godfrey, Charles, 164
Graham, Mary Jane, 159

Grasso, Dominic, 110
Grier, Perry H., 106
Griffin, Freida, vii, 110
Gritzner, Leland J., 36, 187
Gross, Douglas, 76-78
Grove, Richard Lee, 69
Grove, Wilbur "Bill," 189
Grubb, Joyce, 189
Gunderson, Don, 137

Hall, W. Earl, 188
Halliburton, Cal, 124, 187
Hamilton, Robert, 13
Hammond, Gerald, 119
Hansell, Edgar, 152-53
Hargrave, Dan, 186
Harmon, Henry G., 141
Harold, John, 3, 13, 17-18, 29-30, 32, 44, 80, 184
Harris, James, 33, 44, 85, 187, 195
Harrold, Doug, vii
Hart, Irving H., 1, 138
Heather Manor, xii, 158-66
Heathershaw, Jeanette, 163
Heathershaw, Lillian, 163
Heathershaw, Mae, 163
Helmick, Dorothy, 44, 167
Helstad, Merlin "Bud," 98
Heman, Sumner, 189
Henry, Maxine, 167, 189
Hildreth, Frank, 50, 142-43, 153, 181
Hill, D. F., 55
Hoglan, J. C., 57, 142
Holtoff, Ed, 177-78
Homes, Larry, 69
Hoogeveen, Robert D., 186
Horace Mann Home for the Aged, Inc., 159-65
Horace Mann Insurance Co., 7
Howard, Karen, vii
Hudnuts, 140
Hudson, Jack, 2, 182, 185
Hughes, H. Bryan, 155
Hunt, J. W., 188

Ingraham, J. R., 186
Internal Revenue Service, 149

Iowa Association of Classroom Teachers, 3, 11-15, 20, 22, 25, 29-30, 33, 50, 121, 167-68, 180, 193, 195
Iowa Association of Elementary School Principals, 3, 11, 24-25, 50, 136
Iowa Association of Manufacturers, 92
Iowa Association of School Administrators, 11, 24, 26, 92, 113-14, 136
Iowa Association of School Boards, 18, 27, 76, 82, 90, 92, 94, 97, 108, 113-14, 116, 123, 133, 135-36
Iowa Association of Secondary School Principals, 11, 24, 26, 50, 136
Iowa Business and Education Roundtable, 133
Iowa Department of Education, 76, 133
Iowa Department of Public Instruction, 11, 191
Iowa Farm Bureau, 58, 92
Iowa Federation of Teachers, 29-31, 33
Iowa Natural Heritage Foundation, 156
Iowa Retired Teachers Association, 159
Iowa Society for the Preservation of the Arts, 149
Iowa Taxpayers Association, 92
"I Would If I Could," 196

Janss, Peter, 117, 146
Jennings, Roy E., 58
John Birch Society, 109
Johnson, Eugene, 38-39
Jones, Raymond, 58
Jonson, Ken, 105-06
Jorgensen, Ric, 154-156
Jungmann, Doris, 188
Junkins, Lowell, 75-76

Karlson, Roy, 25, 121, 183, 185
Kennedy, John F., 67, 179
Kennedy, Robert F., 68
Keokuk Board of Education, 88-90
Keokuk Education Association, 87-91
Keokuk, Iowa, 18, 87-89, 91, 193, 195
Keokuk Public Schools, 87-88
Keokuk Trades and Labor Assembly, 89
King, Angie, vii, 127, 137, 183-84
"King of the Beggars," 143, 151-52

King's House, 140
King, Steve, 186
Klemme, Iowa, 107-08
Knott, Jim, 25, 121, 189
Kollmorgan, Marilyn, 188
Korean Conflict, 4
Kruse, Millie, 189
Kuhl, Edith, 50, 52
Kulas, Bette, 130

Lagomarcino, Virgil, 123
Lake Orion, Michigan, 169-70
Lamborn, Cliff, 94
Larson, Marvin, 43
Lawrence, Sir Thomas, 140
Learning Labs, 130-31
Leary, J. R., 89-91
Lee County, Iowa, 87
Leland, Robert, 89
Lemke, Ken, 136
Lepley, William, 133
Lestina, Dale, 89-90
Leuschner, Fred, 97
Lillard, D. R., 146
Lindsley, Clyde, 145
Linn County, Iowa, 80
Livermore, Ron, 76
Lodge, Duane, 82
Lottridge, Marlene, 186, 189
Loveless, Herschel C., 63-67
Lynn, Ralph, 188
Lyons, Lou, 188

MacDonald, Kenneth, 188
Maquoketa Education Association, 32-33
Maquoketa Federation of Teachers, 30, 32-33
Marshalltown Community School District, 130
Marshalltown, Iowa, 129-32
Martensdale, Iowa, 104-05
Martin, Charles F., 7, 12, 48, 57, 61, 108, 141, 143, 145, 160-61, 184, 189
Martinez, Dan, 124
Martin, Henry, 170-73
Martin, Sterling, 188

Mastery In Learning, 129
Mauer, Doris, 167, 189
Maxey, H. O., 186-87
McCarthy, Eugene J., 68
McCarthyism, 5
McClure, Robert, 129
McCracken, Helen, 14
McPherson, Mike, 154
Melcher, Ruth, 59
Memphis, Tennessee, 130
Mesicek, John, vii, 149, 186-87
Meskel, Virginia, 189
Michaels, Sheri, vii
Michigan, 169-70
Michigan Education Association, 169, 174, 178
Michigan Federation of Teachers, 174
Michigan Higher Education Assistance Authority, 178
Midland Schools, xi, 3, 13, 46, 57, 61, 141, 163, 192, 195
"Midland Schools of the Air," 191
Milestones, xi, 1, 138
Miller, Dick, 175-76
Miller, Jack 71
Missouri-NEA, 34
Missouri State Teachers Association, 34
Mitchell, Gary, 187
Mobile In-Service Training Labs, 121, 193-94
Monahan, William, 88
Mong, J. Larry, 96-98
Montezuma, Iowa, 69
Monticello, Iowa, 71
Morgan, Lana, vii
Mother Jones, 86
Muilenburg, Ronald, 186
Murray, John S., 188
Murray, William G., 63-67
Muscatine County Court House, 1
Muscatine, Iowa, 1
National Association of Secretaries of State Teachers Associations, 31
National Council for the Accreditation of Teacher Education, 202
National Defense Education Act, 4, 173
National Education Association, 1, 13, 29, 31-38, 40, 44, 68, 71, 84-85, 89-90,

105, 190, 125-26, 129-30, 132, 137, 168, 180, 194-96
National Labor Relations Act, 27, 84
National Labor Relations Board, 84
National Register of Historic Places, 148
"A Nation At Risk," 125-26, 198
"A Nation Prepared — Teachers for the 21st Century," 126
NEA Learning Lab, 130
Nelson, Linda, 190
Nestlerode, C. C., 55
Neu, Arthur, 71
Nevada State Education Association, 168
New Iowa Schools Development Corporation, 133-34, 201
New York, 30
Norland, Lowell, 93-94, 100
Nus, Fred, 9, 109-10
Nye, Frank, 188
Nyhan, Ray, 52-53, 69, 181, 185

Oakley, Brice, 93-94
Oetken, Phyllis, 189
Okino, Nelson, 99
Olin, Iowa, 194
Olsen, Leslie D., 186
Oppenheim, Lana, vii, 202
Oregon Education Association, 34
Ott, Gerry, vii, 91, 131-33
Ottumwa Education Association, 33
Ottumwa Federation of Teachers, 30

Parker, Addison, 152-53
Parks, Arvil C., 187
Partida, Eustolia, 188
Partridge, Patsy, 137
"Pedagogical Pete," 3
Penningroth, Charles, 188
Pennsylvania, 98
Pennsylvania Association of Elementary School Principals, 96
Pennsylvania Public Employees Relations Act, 98
Pennsylvania State Education Association, 97
Peters, Billie, 87, 90
Petersen, LeRoy H., 188

Peters, Jack W., 188
Pfile, Ken, 179, 186
Pickett, Louis L., 9
Pleasantville Board of Education, 109-10
Pleasantville Community Schools, 109-11
Polk County, Iowa, 119
President's Commission on Excellence in Education, 125
Price, Vesper, 160
Pritchard, C. William, vii, 85-86, 152-53, 155
Professional Staff Education Association, 86
Public Employment Relations Board, 33, 101
Pye, Charles F., 48

Quail, Sue, 189
Quester, 73

Ray, Robert D., 69, 71, 95, 99, 159
Reagan, Ronald, 197-98
Reece, Maynard, 191
Renfrow, Oscar, 109-10
Reida, Bernice, 187
Reida, Lydia, 167
Reinicke, Jan, 76
Rhinehart, Charles, 189
Rhinehart, Judy, 189
Rhodes, Eric, 31
Rick, Doreen, 190
Ride, Sally, 199
Ringland, Johnson and Crowley, 165
Robbins, Mable Iowa, 159
Robinson, William, 32, 82, 111, 147
Rogers, M. M., 15, 42-43, 162, 186
Rosenfeldt, Joe, 145
Ryan, Pam, 168

Salisbury Cathedral, 140
Salisbury, England, 140
Salisbury House, xii, 8, 53, 75, 102, 135, 139-157, 188, 191-92, 199
Salisbury House Preservation Committee, 148-50, 157
Salisbury House Preservation Fund, 147-48

Samuelson, Agnes, 141
Satory, Reynard M., 69, 182, 185
Sayre & Gribble, 119
Sayre, James, 153
Schauland, Evelyn, 14
Schlue, Frank, 189
Schmidt, Nancy, 154
Schmidt, Pamela, 189
Schnelle, Walter, 187
School Administrators of Iowa, 133, 135-37
Schrock, Al, 188
Schroeder, June, 189
Seeland, Jean, 190
Service Employees International Union, 183
Shearer, Fred, 187
Sherman, Bill, vii, 97, 150
Shipley, Patricia, 187
Shops Building, 141
Siekman, Beverly, 188
Sioux City Federation of Teachers, 30
Smith, James A., vii, 119
Smith, J. E., 29, 36, 187
South Carolina Education Association, 44
South Tama Public Schools, 130
Starie, John, 32
Stavely, Alline, 189
Staver, Richard G., 183, 185
Stella, Joseph, 140, 143, 151-52, 156
Stephens, Ray, 43
Stewart, Rachel, 124
Strong, Jane, 187
Student ISEA, xii
Student NEA, 184
Sullivan, Louis A., 69
Szymoniak, Elaine, 154

"Take Pride in Iowa Schools," 198
Tapscott, John, 71
Teacher Appreciation Fund, 144-45
Teamsters Union, 64
Texas State Teachers Association, 34
Thompson, Howard A., 97-98
Thompson, Oscar E., 181, 185
Tilp, Ken, xi, 56, 75, 77-78, 132, 137, 153, 155, 183, 186
Time for a Change, 126-28, 201

Tobin, Lynn, 91
Tollari, Joe, 190
Tracey-Engen, Liz, 189
"Tree of My Life," 140, 148, 151-52
Truesdell, Wayne, 92
Tryon, Gaylord, 136-37
Tupper, Phoebe, 56, 75, 123, 125-126, 136, 151, 183, 186
Tuttle, Otis, 188

Unger, William, 119
UniServ, ii, 38, 91, 121, 132, 182-84, 194-95
United Faculty, UNI, 33
Up The Down Staircase, 171
Urbana, Iowa, 106

Valley National Bank, 145
VanderWoude, Dick, 14, 22, 168
Van Dyke, Sir Anthony, 140
Van Hauen, Stanley, vii, 167
Van Steenhuyse, Helen, 135
Villotti, John, 190
Vint, John, vii, 37, 92-94, 101
Vollmer, Jamie, 132
Vrban, Anthony, 109-10

Wainwright, Joan, xi
Wakeman, Wally, 175
Walden, Clewis, 91
Walton, Donna G., 99
Walz, Grace, 169
Walz, Jim, 169
Wapello, Iowa, 106-07
Warren County Education Association, 97
Warren County, Pennsylvania, 96-98
Warrensburg, Pennsylvania, 97
Wayland Education Association, 174-75
Weber, Harold, 60-61, 181, 185
Weeks, Carl, 139-43, 145-46, 148, 152, 157, 188
Weeks, Edith, 139-40, 142-43, 148
Weeks, "Hud," 140, 148, 153
Wehrkamp, Glenn, 189
Wells, Kenneth P., 26, 32-33, 43-45, 48, 82, 147, 162-63, 182, 184-85
West Des Moines, Iowa, 104

Westerly, Rhode Island, 130
Wetherell, Harrison and Wagner, 161
White, Clair, 168
White, Janet, 144, 190
White, Maureen, 124
Whitfield, Allan, 141, 145
Whitson, Lois Mae, 189
Williams, Charles T., 189
Williams, Jeanette, 52
Wilson, Charles, 6
Wilson, Fern, 52

Wilson, Janet, vii
Wilson, Roy, 31
Wisconsin, 20
Wolkow, Beverly, 48, 184
Wood, Hugh, 188
Woodruff, L. L., 59, 181, 185
Wright, J. C., 58

Ylitalo, Gene, 87, 90
Yourd, John, 144